Good Care, Painful Choices

Good Care, Painful Choices

MEDICAL ETHICS FOR ORDINARY PEOPLE

THIRD EDITION

Richard J. Devine, C.M.

Paulist Press
New York/Mahwah, N.J.

Cover and book design by Lynn Else

Library of Congress Cataloging-in-Publication Data

Devine, Richard J.
    Good care, painful choices : medical ethics for ordinary people / Richard J. Devine.—3rd ed.
       p.   cm.
    Includes bibliographical references.
    ISBN 0-8091-4273-2 (alk. paper)
    1. Medical ethics. 2. Medical ethics—Religious aspects—Catholic Church.
I. Title.

R724.D485 2004
174.2—dc22

                                            2004005434

Published by Paulist Press
997 Macarthur Boulevard
Mahwah, New Jersey 07430

www.paulistpress.com

Printed and bound in the
United States of America

Contents

Introduction

Ethical decision making is an integral and essential dimension of being human. All human beings—at least those capable of deliberate choice—make moral decisions. Indeed only human beings are capable of this. All of us recognize in ourselves the ability to distinguish what we call a good choice from the opposite, the choice of what we know to be bad or evil. Sometimes our choices come easily; at other times they are truly dilemmas that challenge our ability to know and choose the good.

Moral dilemmas abound in life—in every person's experience. There is no part of our lives that is without its moral challenges. In the intimate relationships of family life, in our career and business lives, in our political and social endeavors, moral decisions that call forth insight and moral courage abound.

Health care—the delivery of medical treatment to cure illness or relieve pain and suffering—is no exception. Treatment decisions present us all—patients as well as health care professionals—with choices that challenge both our personal and our collective moral wisdom. The need to make moral choices in health care has been present, it would seem, since the days of the ancient Greeks. The commitment to values expressed in the Hippocratic oath—to cause no harm, to seek only to benefit the patient—is surely an expression of this.

If this has been true of every age, it is eminently true of the modern practice of medicine. The ability to cure illness, to relieve pain, to prolong life brings with it a train of questions that stagger the imagination. Deciding which is the moral choice has never been so complicated.

Within the Roman Catholic tradition, there is a long history of concern for making sound moral choices in connection with health care. The meaning and significance of human life—and hence of health—and the obligation to protect and promote it have their roots in the biblical tradition. As theology became structured and systematic in the Middle Ages, these and other questions were recognized as issues that formed part of the corpus of moral reflection. Naturally, as the practice of medicine and the delivery of health care became much more complex in the modern period, the numbers of questions to be considered and debated have multiplied enormously. It is no wonder that a "moral theology of health care" has taken shape in our time.

Medical ethics as a distinct field of moral reflection, therefore, is a relatively recent phenomenon. The historian of medical ethics could probably point to a number of events as recent as thirty years ago that marked the emergence of this new discipline—the triage decisions required in Seattle in response to the introduction of dialysis for end-stage renal failure, the emergence of authors who asked different and insightful questions about the moral consequences of medical decisions, the profound concern manifested for the welfare of human participants in medical research and experimentation. All of these and other events as well marked the birth of bioethics in this country.

However one sorts out the roots of this fast-growing field of ethical reflection, it is obvious from the literature and from the actual experience of health care professionals that the story of medicine will be henceforth changed. Medical decisions can never be simply clinical decisions again. The story of medicine will be forever linked to moral reflection on how "the good" can be achieved in the delivery of health care.

This volume is an example of that fact. It couldn't have been written fifty years ago. Today it is part of that ever-growing body of literature that offers moral reflection on the contemporary practice of medicine. It is intended to be a "popular" compendium of questions that have emerged in this new field. It is intended for the ordinary woman or man in the street—and so for the college student as a classroom text, for students and others addressing these questions in a structured way in discussion groups or workshops or seminars, for the interested citizen looking for basic information in this new field. It is intended for all those members of the general public who are interested in the ethical dimension of health care.

Additionally, this book is meant to address these ethical questions in the context of the understanding of the Christian faith community—specifically, as experienced within the Roman Catholic communion. But it is not—perhaps paradoxically—intended just for Roman

Introduction

Catholics! Because its focus is on values and since all genuine human values are rooted in our common humanness, it is hoped that this volume may offer valid moral insights to those outside the Roman Catholic Church.

This book is divided into five sections. Section One considers some basic understandings about morality and moral reflection. Chapter One addresses the person as the central human reality in questions about moral choice and moral action. Chapter Two focuses on the dynamic issue of moral decision making. Once a person believes a matter at hand calls for a choice, how can that person's choice be made morally sound? Chapter Three considers the human reality we know as conscience: the proximate norm for morally correct decisions.

Section Two begins our consideration of particular medical ethical questions—in this section, those that occur at the beginning of life. The first, abortion, clearly raises the question whether there will be any beginning of life at all. Chapter Five introduces the issues surrounding the treatment of handicapped newborns. It asks the questions, "Shall we apply the amazing techniques of neonatology to this infant? May we allow the child to die because of its handicapped status? Or must we strive to maintain its life despite its handicaps?" The third issue, in Chapter Six, concerns the creation of new life—bringing to bear the astounding accomplishments of artificial reproductive techniques to cure a couple's inability to bear a child through normal marital relations. Is this technique—called in vitro fertilization (IVF)—morally acceptable? Although IVF is the principal focus of the chapter, other ARTS—artificial reproductive technologies—are also briefly considered.

In each of these three chapters—and in those in the next two sections as well—each question is addressed from five points of view. First, what is the medical reality involved? All ethically correct decisions begin with good medical facts. Next, what does the law say about the question? Since there are legal consequences in most of these questions, it is important to know the legal ramifications of the issue. Third, how do the values and institutions of our society affect the way we think about the issue—that is, the socio-cultural dimension. Next, we review the formal teaching of the Roman Catholic Church on the question—if there is, in fact, an authoritative position taken by the church. Finally, we attempt a moral assessment of the question, seeking to identify the values involved and how they might be prioritized in order to lead to a choice of the greater good, the higher value.

Section Three looks at questions that relate to particular illnesses or medical anomalies. Thus, in Chapter Seven, we look at those illnesses or handicaps that are caused by defects in a person's genetic makeup, in the most fundamental "stuff" of life, the DNA. In the next chapter we address the astounding development of organ transplantation and the medical situations that necessitate such an extraordinary intervention on behalf of a patient. Finally, in Chapter Nine, we study the disease known as Acquired Immunodeficiency Syndrome (AIDS), surely the most devastating medical emergency to confront our contemporary society.

Section Four investigates questions related to the human condition when all medical resources are unable to stay the advance of disease and illness, moral dilemmas at the end of life. In Chapter Ten the question of death and dying offers the opportunity for a broad reflection on this final human challenge, how the dying person can deal in a moral fashion with this ultimate question. The next chapter raises the issue of euthanasia and physician-assisted suicide as one way of dealing with the fear of unrelenting pain and prolonged dying. Are these acceptable moral alternatives for the dying person? What of the decision to cease treatment in a terminal situation or even not to undertake treatment at all when it appears medically futile or excessively burdensome?

The final section addresses two questions that extend beyond any particular treatment decision or moral dilemma. The first, in Chapter Twelve, raises the question of informed consent—that critical interplay between physician and patient that allows the latter to exercise autonomy in making health care decisions. The final chapter moves beyond the realm of the individual and the moral dilemmas a person might face in matters of health care. In this case, the issue is the reform of health care. Obviously, not everyone has the possibility of responding to illness or threats to health by going to a doctor or to a hospital. This is true even in an advanced country such as the United States. What claim does a person have to receive medical treatment?

Introduction

Is health care a right? Or is it rather a privilege? For whom? For those who can afford it only? For everyone?

This, then, is the structural logic that ties together these thirteen chapters. At the end of each of these, a number of questions are posed to direct the reader to some of the more significant issues in the chapter or to challenge the reader to wrestle personally with the crucial questions that are raised throughout the text. Understandably, not everyone will agree with all the moral positions set forth. It is crucial, however, that all members of society have a basic appreciation of the issues that are involved in the ethical response to these medical questions. The way we resolve these questions will go a long way toward determining what kind of society we will bring forth in this third millennium. In a democratic society, these decisions belong not only to the politicians, nor to the physicians and the health care establishment. They do not belong only to the experts. They belong to all members of the society. The exchange of ideas and the debates must continue, but knowledge and reflection must come first.

PART ONE

Some Preliminary Questions

1 The Person: At the Center of Morality

WHO AM I?

Early in the play *Les Miserables*, the central character sings a powerful song, "Who Am I?" His name is Jean Valjean, but for nineteen years he has been imprisoned as #24601. At the time of his parole, he debates his identity with his captor, Police Inspector Javert. While Valjean insists on his proper name—"my name is Jean Valjean"—Javert refuses to call him anything but "24601." Finally, in his song "Who Am I?" Valjean identifies himself both by his proper name and by his prison ID number. "Who am I?" he sings—"I'm Jean Valjean...24601!"

"Who am I?" is a question everyone asks at one time or another. Jean Valjean is not the only one to ask it. Arriving at personal identity and self-awareness is, in fact, one of the central tasks of human development. It is a process that must take place before one is ready for the challenges of adulthood. And yet it is never fully achieved and done with, as Jean Valjean learned, for our self continues to grow and change, always becoming, even though in some way always the same. The same "I" who was the adolescent who mimicked adults in high school plays is the real-life adult who remembers the youth on the stage—much changed by life's experiences, of course, but unquestionably the same "I," the very same person.

It is the notion of "person" that we propose as our starting point in this foray into the world of medical ethics. "Person" is one of the "basic understandings" that are offered at the very beginning of this volume to provide a context for our investigation of questions such as abortion, euthanasia, and organ transplantation—all questions about persons. We will seek an adequate answer to "Who am I as a person?"

3

by combining insights drawn from our fundamental humanness (the anthropological answer), our being in the image of God (the theological answer), and our calling to be a disciple of Jesus Christ (the christological answer). It should be pointed out, parenthetically, that each answer is offered as true and valid, although incomplete. One who is not a Christian, then, but recognizes his creaturely relationship to God may very well feel comfortable with the first two parts of the answer without having to adopt the third.

THE ANTHROPOLOGICAL ANSWER

In the 1970s, medical ethicists recognized that the concept of person was central to their discussions, yet the term meant different things to different writers. And so the conversation quickly turned to determining what was the meaning of "person." What constituted a "person"? What distinguished a person from a not-a-person?[1] The discussion was not a purely philosophical exchange, to be sure. The abortion debate raised the question whether the fetus was a person or not.[2] A similar doubt was raised about the personhood of the elderly individual suffering from senile dementia. As people took sides, they began to list the "essential characteristics" of a person, in their view.[3] The debate is not over, nor is the discussion closed. What follows, then, is yet another effort to describe what we mean when we talk about a "human person."

Agent/Subject

Our first experience of persons is through actions. Persons are agents. They manifest themselves in "doing." We recognize them in and through the actions of which they are the source. As O'Connell points out:

> ...we never see "person" in its bare reality. What we see, what we experience in ourselves and in others is person-clothed-in-action. Or more precisely we experience actions that, we realize, do not stand by themselves, but rather reveal and manifest and express a person that lies beneath.[4]

4

The Person: At the Center of Morality

I see the young man riding the bike, the mother pushing her child on a swing in the park, the police officer directing traffic, and I conclude that a person exists who grounds each action, a person who is an agent. I do not directly experience the person, but I recognize the person in and through the actions performed by each human individual.

My experience tells me, of course, that the notion of person is not exhausted by my attribution of agency. If that mother comes to the park the next morning—and perhaps every morning—to push her little girl on the swing, I am able to recognize that other aspect of person—person-as-subject. What I discover is the continuing self, the responsible self, the deeper self—the subject. Actions—even agency—are transient. Eventually the swinging in the park ends and another activity, a new agency, succeeds it. But the person continues, identical, recognizable, responsible.

> To speak of the human person as a *subject* is to say that the person is in charge of his or her own life. That is, the person is a moral agent with a certain degree of autonomy and self-determination empowered to act according to his or her conscience, in freedom, and with knowledge.[5]

Neither person-as-agent nor person-as-subject exists separately, nor do we experience them apart from each other. My actions, whereby I respond to each day's demands and opportunities, are the very means whereby I constitute and define my "self." Thus agent and subject are intimately joined in my experience of myself and of all other persons. This in no way prevents us from understanding the difference, however.

Embodiment

This term expresses the corporeality, the materiality of every human person.[6] Human personhood requires enfleshment. The ancients defined the human being as "animal rationale"—a reasoning animal—to express this embodiment. Our bodies are not the vessels—much less the prisons—in which our spirits reside. We *are* our bodies. When we talk about stewardship of our bodies, it is not said as of

5

something we have or own. It is rather our responsibility for our very selves. When we talk about sociability, that is, to be in relationships, as an essential characteristic of the human person, we recognize that relationships are expressed through our bodies. When we speak of the human person as made in the image of God, we include our embodiment.

Our bodies, of course, place severe limits on us—spatial and temporal. And in the context of health care, it is our bodies that place such grave demands on us for their maintenance and repair. Our bodies, finally, at some point will no longer be capable of sustaining our lives, and it will be through them that we will experience our lives ending in death.

Knowing Personally

In order to function as human agents, persons can act only with knowledge. Because free and undetermined, persons must choose. Choice without knowledge would be blind and hence inherently not human. It is not claimed that the knowledge must be exhaustive or expert, but it must provide some modicum of awareness that allows the person to identify and recognize the object presented for choice.

The choices that concern us here, however, are moral choices, and hence the knowledge that is at stake is moral knowledge. What is moral knowledge? Is any knowledge about morality and the moral life sufficient to ground a moral choice? Certainly not. It is in this connection that those who discuss morality distinguish between speculative and evaluative knowledge.[7]

In a sense, moral knowledge can be either speculative or evaluative. The same facts, the same situation, the same principles, the same values can be known either speculatively or evaluatively. When a professor presents an abortion case to her class and speaks of the value of the fetus, she is communicating speculative moral knowledge. If, however, she is pregnant and is personally struck by the wonder of the new life stirring within her, her awareness of that value constitutes true evaluative knowledge. The priest in the pulpit preaching about the need to be faithful to one's word, to one's promises, offers a valuable moral insight, but both his knowledge and that of his congregation qualify as speculative moral knowledge. The personal awareness of the value of fidelity to a husband and wife in that congregation, however, an appreciation that springs as much from their hearts as from their heads, is genuine evaluative moral knowledge. And it is only evaluative moral knowledge that can be the basis of a moral choice, because moral decisions are choices about values that are personally *appreciated*—not known speculatively or theoretically, but personally appreciated and cherished.

In what ways, then, do speculative and evaluative moral knowledge differ? Speculative moral knowledge tends to be knowledge about facts and information. Because of this it is readily available to others. It can be easily taught and learned, proven and verified. In general, in the field of morals, it will be knowledge about moral life and moral values. Evaluative moral knowledge, on the other hand, is inherently personal, often intensely so. It is about the values contained in the concrete human situation—not known abstractly or theoretically, but personally grasped and appreciated as a value by a particular individual, felt and tasted as a value. Thus a child learns the value of truth telling from her mother not so much through repeated admonitions but from her experience of a truthful parent whom she loves.

It is only this kind of knowledge that can ground a moral choice since in such choices we personally embrace the value involved. Clearly such knowledge is difficult to express adequately and thus equally difficult to communicate. Hence the folk wisdom that virtue is caught, not taught. When our choices truly reflect a moral value that we personally appropriate, *that* is a moral choice, and moral growth truly ensues. Speculative moral knowledge, on the other hand, is like knowledge of the weather. It happens around us, all right, but nothing happens within us.

Choosing Freely

How free am I? How free need I be to make a moral choice? The issue of freedom has been a favorite topic in modern psychology. It seems quite clear that no one is totally or absolutely free. Our contemporary understanding of genetics makes that conclusion inescapable. In part, at least, our DNA, our biology, determines our options—in the sense of "places limits." Inherited color blindness takes away my freedom to appreciate a sunset as my normally sighted friends do.

7

Then my environment, my personal situation, also can place limits on my choices, on my freedom. If my family is barely surviving at the poverty level and my situation makes advanced education highly unlikely for me, I will not be free to be a doctor.

But limited choice does not mean unfree. As Richard Gula has pointed out:

> Our actions fall somewhere on the continuum between absolute freedom and absolute determinism. If this were not so, I suspect we would not have the experience of feeling unsettled or indecisive about our choices. Moreover, we would not have to deliberate about anything if we were completely free or completely determined.[8]

Moral theologians distinguish between two kinds of freedom: radical or core freedom and freedom of choice.[9] The former is much more critical for the moral life. It is the freedom that permits me to dispose of myself, to decide about my life in a most basic and fundamental way. It is the freedom of self-determination, radical and profound. It is the freedom that permits me to commit myself, my life, my person. Obviously, freedom at this level is not exercised frequently or lightly. Neither is it revoked or altered at whim, but then neither is it irrevocable or permanently fixed. It is, after all, freedom.[10]

Over against this radical freedom exists a second kind of freedom, freedom of choice.[11] This is the freedom that we exercise when we decide between alternatives, when we choose from among our options. It is our freedom as agents, our freedom *to do*. In a sense, it is a *limitation* of freedom, since the choice of one alternative then leaves us no longer free to choose the other possible options. The object of our choice may be inconsequential—to wear glasses or contact lenses—or it may be profoundly important—to seek a kidney transplant or to continue renal dialysis. It is the same freedom that makes them all possible.

One final observation. The distinction between radical freedom and freedom of choice does not mean that they are unrelated. As Gula observes:

> …our freedom to choose this or that—even within limits—is fundamentally a freedom to choose an identity, to become a cer-

8

tain sort of person.…[M]oral freedom is an act of self-determination, an act which, through all the pathways of particular choices, chooses who we want to be, persons either open or closed to the mystery of our life and of all life.[12]

Existing in Time

As already mentioned, it is our bodies that limit our persons locally and temporally. Because I have this body, I can exist only here or only there, but not both simultaneously. Because this body came into being at a particular moment of time, its existence is limited to that continuum of time that measures its life. Persons have histories because they have bodies.

The challenge of time, of course, is to accomplish life's purpose during the allotted space within which it is spent. *Past* burdens *present* with its choices, and thus limits the *future*. Existentially, of course, only the present is real. The past is real only as carried into the present; the future is real only as it exists in present possibilities. As Thomas Groome has so well written:

> I cannot separate what I have been from what I am, nor these from what I will become. I am who I am because of my past; my past is in my present. I will be who I will be because of my present and the past that is in it. My past, in fact, is not past at all— it is with me in my present. My future is not simply "not yet"—it is already finding form in and shaping my present. My past and future are for me only insofar as they are in my present.[13]

The Christian image of the pilgrim in time moving toward the kingdom aptly expresses this. We do not wander aimlessly, for earlier pilgrims have taught us the road. We, in our turn, will teach our successors through our stories, our myths, our ceremonies, and our customs. Thus the pilgrim people will journey toward the kingdom by creatively forming this future out of the rich heritage that is theirs.[14]

Because of its historical character, the human person is a dynamic reality rather than a static one. Personhood is never fixed and unchangeable. Personal history implies change, growth. The moral possibilities are different at different stages of development. The moral challenge is to seize each present opportunity to affirm and embrace genuine moral values in our concrete choices. The journey can never be repeated; the pilgrim can never retrace his steps as the road plays out.

And just as moral persons inexorably change, so too do the cultures that provide the environment in which the moral life is lived. This confronts both the individual person and the community in which culture takes shape with the necessity of continually reflecting on changing values and moral possibilities. Maguire says this well:

> Reason has its work cut out for it in every area of moral experience. Among its critical tasks: to find and compare ethically meaningful empirical data; to search for the unasked questions; to test the regnant authorities before which minds may be playing dead; to cope with the inevitable partiality of our knowledge; to jog the lazy memory; to fight the allure of too facile consensus; to break the stranglehold of habituation; to check our myths and other filters; to solve the conflicts between and among principles; and to tend to the reformulation and correction of principles in view of new experience.[15]

In Relationships—Belonging Together

In recent years it has become fashionable to talk of the "global village." The image seeks to convey the notion that the world has shrunk to the size of a cozy village. Through contemporary advances in technology—particularly communications—the remotest parts of the world can now watch *The Six O'Clock News* or tune in to MTV. As a result, peoples' interconnectedness has increased enormously. Corporations have become transnational; national economies have become interdependent, as we move inexorably toward a worldwide culture. T-shirts reading "Harvard University" can be spotted in Rome, or in Cairo, or in Manila—not just in Harvard Square. Our human relationships, our connectedness, our interdependence are inescapable.

And yet this contemporary phenomenon of culture only points to what is profoundly human, what is characteristic of every human person—to be in relationships. It is through relationships that we come into being, and it is through relationships that we move forward toward full human growth and development. Without relationships we cannot "become." To be totally devoid of relationships, to be completely shut off, to be totally isolated runs contrary to human need and health—it is to frustrate the fundamental truth of being human.

This fact needs to be appreciated when we reflect on our present reality—on our society and on our culture. Whatever breaks down relationships, whatever threatens the bonds of our interconnectedness, will likely be inimical to human moral growth and development. If in vitro fertilization, for example, proposes donor gametes, third party participation in reproduction, and multiple sets of "parents," it is hard to see how family structures and interpersonal bonds will not be weakened. If the American fixation on almost absolute autonomy in health care decisions threatens our sense of communal responsibility for health care policies and priorities, it will surely be inimical to our sense of the common good in the delivery of health care. It will certainly lessen our appreciation of our communal responsibility for one another.

Unique and Unrepeatable

One of the sources that promote our interpersonal relationships is our likeness to one another. We possess a common humanity and it provides the glue that binds us together. We find ourselves bound together in a common history, facing a common destiny, threatened by the same dangers, enjoying the same delights. We are comfortable with one another, at home with our common humanity. But equally important in cementing our common bonds is the fact that no two of us are exactly the same. This is what makes us interesting, intriguing, challenging. Our biology makes us different; our genetic inheritance constantly churns up different traits and characteristics that enrich each and all. Even in the case of identical twins, when nature as it were stutters, so many differences in nurture and experience occur that no one would ever mistake the siblings for clones. This then is our dowry from life—our unrepeatable uniqueness.

Maguire finds an analogy for this truth in the human process of knowing.

> We will look for no perfect sameness in the knowing experience
> if we relinquish the simplisms of a mirror image of knowledge.

11

A mirror inertly and indiscriminately reflects the physical object before it. In the conscious awareness that we call knowledge, a vital and multi-dimensional process of attunement, interpretation, filtering, accenting, and imagining is going on. The process reflects the complex uniqueness of the knower *(actio sequitur esse)*. This is true to an extent in knowledge of *things;* it is especially true in the knowledge of *values.*[16]

And since moral choices are bound inseparably to evaluative knowledge, the uniqueness of our valuing of moral goods makes moral generalizations always approximate and tentative. This is not to question the validity or the value of those goods that our common wisdom has judged promotive of human growth. It simply is a caution that permits us to affirm the uniqueness of the individual and the uniqueness of the situation in arriving at moral choices.

THE THEOLOGICAL ANSWER

The previous reflections are based on a rational analysis of the human person. As such, they may recommend themselves to people of every faith and to those of no faith. They require acceptance of no particular dogmatic position, no required doctrinal understandings whatever. They are, hopefully, conclusions drawn from an objective observation of the human situation, of the human experience—keeping in mind, of course, the particularity and subjectivity of all "objective" knowledge.

What follows next, however, is a different kind of answer to the question with which we began—"Who am I?" Because it is a *theological* answer to the question, it is an answer that is based on divine faith, and such faith is not part of our fundamental human nature. The human person is *capax fidei*—capable of believing—but belief is not a native human endowment. It is a gift, pure and simple. Of course it is important to have the capacity to receive the gift. After all, what sense would the gift of a mirror make to one who is blind? To be capable of believing, then, is of critical importance, but it is not the gift of faith.

Faith, then, allows us to act beyond our natural abilities, to function outside our natural capacity. Because it is a gift, it is not surprising that it leads us first of all to know the giver; it leads us to knowledge of the giver, to acceptance of the giver, to belief in the giver. The giver we call God, whom we recognize as good—as *the Good*, the source of all else that is good. Human goodness, then, is a reflection of God's goodness, as moral goodness is a participation in the divine goodness.

Human beings can learn much about God and God's goodness, of course, in God's self-revelation in the Bible. It is here that they discover how to speak about God—to say, for instance, that God is love. It is also learned in the Bible that God is the reason for being moral. Human beings are called to choose genuine moral value—to live the moral life—from their very nature, but God is the source of that nature. God is the source of the moral life for the believer.

Made in God's Image

What else does the Bible explain about the nature of the human person? How does it help us answer our question, "Who am I?" In its very first pages, the Bible offers a fundamental insight about human beings—and about God—in the creation story. After describing how God drew all things—the earth and the sky, the sun, moon and stars, living creatures—out of primal nothingness, the author of Genesis writes:[17]

> God said, "Let us make man in our own image, in the likeness of ourselves, and let them be masters of the fish of the sea, the birds of heaven, the cattle, all the wild beasts and all the reptiles that crawl upon the earth. God created man in the image of himself. In the image of God he created him, male and female he created them.

This poetic description of the human person appears as a leit-motif throughout the biblical texts. The psalmist writes, for instance:[18]

> You have made [man] little less than a god.
> You have crowned him with glory and splendor,
> made him lord over the work of your hands,
> set all things under his feet.

The image is repeated at the beginning of the Book of Wisdom, where the author notes that "God did make man imperishable; he

13

made him in the image of his own nature." St. Paul repeats this conviction when he writes to the Corinthians that "a man is in the image of God and reflects God's glory." Finally, we find that James uses the same expression in his epistle when he writes, "We use [the tongue] to bless the Lord and Father, but we also use it to curse men who are made in God's image."[19]

What insights about human nature does this image offer the believer? It says, first of all, that women and men, because made in God's image, have a dignity and a value independent of anything they would ever accomplish or achieve. Their dignity is a given; their value is a gift. Even more, they are endowed with a sacredness, a radical goodness, that shares the goodness of God. After all, they are in God's image! There's a family likeness!

Knowing this, the believer recognizes a fundamental relationship with the creator in such a way that it is constitutive of what it means to be human. Believers can make no sense of themselves unless their lives begin with and are founded on their relationship to God. This is the radical self-understanding that faith brings. God calls the human person into being, graces each individual with life, and calls for a loving response from the free and responsible creature. From God's side, the relationship is permanent, fixed, unbreakable. God will always be faithful in that offer of love. Even when the believer stumbles and denies the relationship, God never turns away. The divine love is everlasting.

God's image is never lost—even in the sinner. It encompasses the totality of the human reality—body and soul—which, of course, has significant moral implications for questions of health and health care. As the basis for mutual respect and reciprocal care, the sacredness conferred by the divine image establishes a fundamental point of view in medical ethical questions such as abortion and euthanasia.

The reality of the Godhead—for the believer who acknowledges a trinity of relationships in the divine being—also offers a model for human relationships. Just as perfect love and self-giving ground the relationships of Father, Son, and Spirit, so these should characterize the relationships of women and men with God and with one another. And because the image of God is so radically imprinted in human nature, to the degree that the human creature achieves fullness of growth and development, to the same degree the image of the creator will be enhanced. Even more amazing, the biblical record reveals that whatever love, whatever caring, human beings offer one another, God accepts as done to him![20] As Gula writes so well:

> This theological vision of the person helps us to see that our fundamental relationship to God gets expressed in and through the ways we use our gifts and enhance the giftedness of others. To be the image of God is an imperative calling us to live out of the fullness of the gifts we have received by moving out of ourselves and into the world of our relationships. To withdraw into ourselves, to hoard our gifts, and to cut off the dynamic of receiving and giving love by refusing to gift another is to abort our gifts and to mock God. It is sin, simply put. It denies the sort of self-giving which being the image of God demands, and it blocks the movement toward living fully in communion with God and others.[21]

THE CHRISTOLOGICAL ANSWER

The biblical self-revelation of God tells us yet more. The New Testament of the Christian faith community announces that God reveals and manifests the divine love supremely and definitively in the person of Jesus Christ. The believer who is a Christian, therefore, has another basis for self-understanding, for answering the question "Who am I?" If the believer is called into being out of love and created in the image of God, infinitely more is Jesus the expression of God's love, even as the Son is the image of the Father. And it is he whom the Christian follows.

> Belief in Jesus means that one belongs to and follows "the Way." The disciple of Jesus responds by a way of life. The changed relationship of the disciple of Jesus to God involves a changed relationship with others—fellow believers in the community, friends, enemies, the poor. The Catholic understanding of the evangelical command to love God and neighbor as oneself has always insisted on bringing together the proper love of God, neighbor, and self. All agree that love of God is intimately connected with love of neighbor, but the Catholic theological tradition has

insisted on a proper love of self that can and should be integrated with love of God and neighbor.[22]

What does following Jesus call the Christian to? What are the demands of discipleship? Charles Curran identifies the characteristics of the relationship between disciple and master.[23] First of all, the call to discipleship is a *gift*. Just as a fundamental acknowledgment of God as creator is itself the fruit of God's gift of faith, so one's ability to recognize and respond to Jesus' call to follow him is gift and grace. They are the prior condition and the necessary source of faith in Jesus. Until God calls and gifts the disciple, there can be no discipleship. What Jesus said to his first disciples is true of all Christians—"You did not choose me; no, I chose you."[24] Secondly, discipleship is a call to *relationship,* to friendship, to love.

> This is my commandment: love one another as I have loved you....By this love you have for one another, everyone will know that you are my disciples.[25]

Faith in Jesus binds the believer to the Lord, the disciple to the master—and to the Father who sent him. It is a bond that will endure if only the disciple remains faithful. Human threats, force, violence—none of these will be able to separate the faithful follower from the master. On the other hand, lack of faith and trust in the Lord will lead to the dissolution of the bonds of love. The gift is free on God's part; the response of the disciple must also be free.

The disciple enters into a relationship not only with Jesus and the Father. Discipleship brings *membership in community*. One who would follow Christ necessarily enters into relationship with all those who would follow the Lord. This *ecclesia,* which we now call church, looms large in the biblical record. Mutual care and concern, communal ownership of goods, communal worship of their risen Lord—all these were the experience of the apostolic community.

> These [converts] remained faithful to the teaching of the apostles, to the brotherhood, to the breaking of bread and to the prayers....The faithful all lived together and owned everything in common; they sold their goods and possessions and shared out the proceeds among themselves, according to what each one needed. They went as a body to the temple every day, but met in

their houses for the breaking of bread; they shared their food gladly and generously; they praised God and were looked up to by everyone.[26]

Their experience they rooted in the preaching of Jesus—he had called them "branches" and he was the vine. They were the living stones from which was built up the temple of the Lord.[27] Thus Christian discipleship from the very beginning was never understood as a call to follow Jesus in isolation, but rather it was a vocation to fellowship and service.

> Discipleship calls for fundamental change in our relationship with others—the poor, the needy, the enemy. The great love commandment in the Synoptic Gospels has intrinsically and inevitably bound together the love of God and the love of neighbor. As John reminds us, we cannot love the God we do not see if we do not love the neighbor whom we do see. Discipleship by its very nature involves not only the relationship to God but also relationships within the community of disciples and relationships with all God's people.[28]

What else does discipleship demand? Jesus had said to the rich young man who wished to follow him, "Go and sell what you own and give the money to the poor…then come, follow me."[29] It was the same message he had proposed in the parable of "the pearl of great price."[30] The merchant in the parable sold all that he had in order to purchase this pearl. So too, the parable implies, must his disciples be prepared to *renounce everything* to follow Jesus. This radical commitment was necessary in order that the follower might make Jesus the center of his life, giving meaning and value to all else that life might hold. When asked what was the great commandment of the law,[31] Jesus had replied, "You must love the Lord your God with all your heart, with all your soul, and with all your mind." It was a perfect description of what he expected of those who would follow him.

To achieve this radical commitment, the disciple would need to undergo a *profound conversion*. This change of heart was explicit in the preaching of Jesus,[32] as it had been in the message of John the Baptist before him. This was the point of the parable of the vinedresser responsible for pruning away the dead branches from the vine. In similar fashion the disciple must prune away all those distractions, those sinful attractions, those worldly allurements that might draw the follower away from his Lord, that might risk the loss of the pearl of great price. The early Christian community described this process of conversion as a dying to the sinful self and rising to a new life, even as Jesus had died and had risen.

Conversion, to be sure, cannot be a single act, a once-and-for-all renunciation. For the disciple, it must be a process—indeed a lifelong undertaking. Human imperfection and sinfulness are not easily rooted out. Growth is always limited by one's present possibilities. Conversion can move forward only "from grace to grace," since it is in the final analysis God's gift that will make the disciple's self-gift both total and radical.

CHANGING HUMAN NATURE

Even while recognizing that human nature has a sacred character made "in the image and likeness of God," a new question—philosophical and theological—arises as bio-technology develops the capacity to "tinker" with this gift of nature. Most commentators, it would seem, see no problem in utilizing this technology—genetic engineering, for example—to correct genetic anomalies in an individual's DNA. [See Chapter 7 for a full discussion of this subject.] But once such a dramatic intervention becomes possible in order to cure, there will surely be the temptation to employ the same technology to "enhance," to improve, an individual's traits and characteristics. Would such an intervention be morally acceptable? Leon Kass asks the question this way:

> What if anything can we say to justify our disquiet over the individual uses of performance-enhancing genetic engineering or mood-brightening drugs? For even the safe, equally available, non-coerced and non-faddish uses of these technologies for "self-improvement" raise ethical questions, questions that are at the heart of the matter: the disquiet must have something to do with the essence of the activity itself, the use of technological means to intervene in the human body and mind not to ameliorate disease but to change and (arguably) improve their normal workings. Why, if at all, are we bothered by the voluntary self-

administration of agents that would change our bodies and alter our minds?

What is disquieting about our attempts to improve upon human nature, or even our own particular instance of it?...If there is a case to be made against these activities—for individuals—we sense that it may have something to do with what is natural, or what is humanly dignified, or with the attitude that is properly respectful of what is naturally and dignifiedly human.[33]

One response to this conundrum is the too-facile dismissal of the whole enterprise as "playing God." Whether this critique implies a prideful assumption of powers proper to the Deity or rejects the use of such powers without the guidance of God-like wisdom,[34] it is a negative response to non-therapeutic interventions. But "playing God" is more a slogan than a reasoned intellectual position. Granted that human nature is surely a gift, why would that fact alone preclude any non-therapeutic intervention? Must the gift be accepted as is? Kass thinks not.

Only if there is a human givenness, or a given humanness, that is also good and worth respecting, either as we find it or as it could be perfected without ceasing to be itself, does the "given" serve as a *positive* guide for choosing what to alter and what to leave alone. Only if there is something precious in the given—beyond the mere fact of its giftedness—does what is given serve as a source of restraint against efforts that would degrade it. When it comes to human biotechnological engineering, only if there is something inherently good or dignified about, say, natural procreation, human finitude, the human life cycle (with its rhythm of rise and fall), and human erotic longing and striving: only if there is something inherently good or dignified about the ways in which we engage the world as spectators and appreciators, as teachers and learners, leaders and followers, agents and makers, lovers and friends, parents and children, and as seekers of our own special excellence and flourishing in whatever arena to which we are called—only then can we begin to see why those aspects of our nature need to be defended.[35]

This, then, is the debate that is moving onto center stage. Which "enhancements" will we allow? Which reject? Certainly not all! And what will be our criterion for choosing? The debate deserves our profound reflection and thoughtful participation.[36]

CONCLUSION

These, then, are the answers to the question "Who am I?" Not of course separated and disjoined as they appear in this analysis, but all at once—a totality, a wholeness, a synthesis. This is what a moral person is. This is where morality begins. Next we must turn to the person in action, making moral choices, arriving at moral decisions.

STUDY QUESTIONS

1. What is the relationship between being and doing in the human person?
2. What kinds of knowledge can be distinguished in human knowing? What sort of knowledge is necessary for a true moral choice?
3. Besides knowledge, what else is essential for a human choice to be truly moral?
4. How is the human person made "in the image and likeness of God"? What are the consequences of this?
5. What demands does authentic discipleship make on one who would follow Jesus?

NOTES

1. I wish to acknowledge my debt to Richard Gula (and to Louis Janssens before him) for this most useful analysis of human personhood: *Reason Informed by Faith.* Mahwah, NJ: Paulist Press, 1989, 66–72.

2. Richard McCormick rejects the argument that the personality of the fetus is a crucial issue in arguing the morality of abortion. Cf. *Notes on Moral Theology: 1965 Through 1980.* Washington, DC: University Press, 1981, 444–47.

3. "The Concepts of Health and Disease," in *Philosophy and Medicine*, Stuart F. Spicker and H. Tristram Engelhardt, eds. Boston: Reidel, 1975; Joseph Fletcher, *Humanhood: Essays in Biomedical Ethics.* Buffalo: Prometheus, 1979; cited in Benedict Ashley and Kevin O'Rourke, *Health Care Ethics.* St. Louis: Catholic Health Association, 1982, 5.

4. Timothy E. O'Connell, *Principles for a Catholic Morality*. San Francisco: Harper and Row, 1990, 66.

5. Cf. note 1, 68.

6. Cf. James F. Keenan, S.J., "Christian Perspectives on the Human Body," *Theological Studies* 55:2 (June 1994): 330–46.

7. Although the terminology may differ, authors take great pains to explain this distinction as critical for understanding truly moral choices. Cf. O'Connell, note 4, 58–63; Gula, note 1, 83–87. Daniel Maguire talks of "affective appreciation" in *The Moral Choice*. Minneapolis: Winston Press, 1979, 263ff.

8. Cf. note 1, 76.

9. Cf. note 4, 53–58; note 1, 75–83.

10. The concept of radical freedom is closely related to the theory of fundamental option and fundamental stance. For a discussion of these concepts, cf. note 4, 72–74; note 1, 78–81.

11. Also called categorical freedom, whereas radical freedom is termed transcendental freedom. Cf. note 4, 70.

12. Cf. note 1, 82–83.

13. *Christian Religious Education*. New York: Harper and Row, 1980, 13.

14. Ibid.

15. Cf. Maguire, note 7, 263.

16. Ibid., 334.

17. Gn 1:26–27. All scriptural citations are taken from the Jerusalem Bible. London: Darton, Longman and Todd, 1966.

18. Ps 8:5–6.

19. Wis 2:23; 1 Cor 11:7; Jas 3:9.

20. The author recognizes that the limitations of the language have customarily resulted in describing God through the use of masculine pronouns and adjectives. It needs to be acknowledged that God is neither masculine nor feminine, neither male nor female. If masculine language is used in this text, it is simply because no satisfactory linguistic alternative is at hand.

21. Cf. note 1, 66.

22. Charles E. Curran, *Directions in Fundamental Moral Theology*. Notre Dame: University of Notre Dame Press, 1985, 75.

23. Ibid., 70–71.

24. Jn 15:16.

25. Jn 15:12; 13:35.

26. Acts 2:42–47.

27. Jn 15:5; 1 Pt 2:5.

28. Cf. note 22, 70–71.

29. Mt 19:21–22.

30. Mt 13:45–46.

31. Mt 23:37–38.

32. Mk 1:15.

33. Leon R. Kass, "Ageless Bodies, Happy Souls," *The New Atlantis* 1 (Spring 2003): 17.

34. Ibid., 18.

35. Ibid., 20.

36. Cf. Dan Callahan, "Too Much of a Good Thing: How Splendid Technologies Can Go Wrong," *Hastings Center Report* (March–April 2003): 19–22; Mark Frankel, "Inheritable Genetic Modifications and a Brave New World," *Hastings Center Report* (March–April 2003): 31–36. For a reflection on the potential conflict between human nature and artificial intelligence, cf. Charles T. Rubin, "Artificial Intelligence and Human Nature," *The New Atlantis* 1 (Spring 2003): 88–100.

2 Moral Decision Making: Morality in Action

MORALITY

As the Introduction pointed out, this investigation of the moral theology of health care begins with some basic understandings of morality and the moral life. The moral life, of course, is the life of a human person, and so Chapter One took that as the starting point. "Who am I? What is a human person?"—these were the questions it sought to answer. As it turned out, the answer was complex because the human person can be described from various viewpoints. For this reason, "person" was described first anthropologically, then theologically as made in the image of God and, finally, christologically as a follower of Jesus.

As the first chapter pointed out, persons are known through their actions. This, then, raises the question of decision making—how does someone make a moral choice? A few general ideas about morality will set the context, and then the question of making a correct moral decision will be studied. It would be a mistake, of course, to reduce the whole of the moral life to the question of decision making. It is, nevertheless, a crucial issue, particularly in view of the many decisions occasioned by the delivery of health care.

Is Morality Real? A Reflection on Experience

Suppose we begin with our own experience. If I asked you to give me an example of a moral action from your personal experience, what would you answer? Or an immoral one, for that matter! If I asked you to describe something that someone did to you that you felt was immoral, could you think of an example? Think of some of the situations described in the newspapers or on TV—the person with AIDS who deliberately spreads the virus to as many sexual partners as possible, the individual who set fire to the social club in the Bronx in which eighty-seven persons died, the young couple who mugged and robbed elderly women to support their drug habits. Would you be able to judge whether these actions were moral or immoral?

Take examples closer to home—suppose her boyfriend gave your sister a ring, and then you learned he had stolen it? How would you judge his making a gift of the ring? Would it be morally correct for your sister to keep it? Suppose your little brother's tonsillectomy was botched because the surgeon was drunk? Moral? Immoral? What if your neighbor lies about you in court under oath? Would you be able to judge whether this was moral or immoral? Could you tell that these were different kinds of wrong actions from actions like driving the wrong way up a one-way street, or putting the stamp in the lower right-hand corner of the envelope, or not following the directions on the detergent bottle? I suspect you would!

It seems that we have a common-sense conviction that some actions are morally right and others morally wrong. We may not agree about which is which in every case—but we all understand the question. Then too there are some actions that hardly anyone would defend as moral. Is there anyone who would justify rape or child abuse as moral? As good? Would anyone defend the judge who lets a criminal go free in return for a bribe? Or the killing of a homosexual simply because he was gay? Clearly we approve of some behaviors—the mother who cares for her sick child and puts herself at risk—and disapprove of others. We praise some and blame others. Some we reward and others we punish. We go further. We praise the person who does the action as "a wonderful human being." Or we describe another person as "an animal" or, more graphically, "a skunk."

What does all of this mean? It suggests that we are saying something real about human behavior. Not everyone agrees about this, of course. Some maintain that morality is simply a matter of social agreement or convention. Sometime or other, they say, people recognized that life would run smoother if people all lived by some agreed-on norms—if they told the truth, for example, and respected each other's property. These became the "rules of the game," they argue. Now there is no denying that there are some rules like that. Traffic regulations are a good example. But there is an enormous difference between making an illegal turn and rape. And it is not simply a difference in the seriousness of the action. We recognize that they are really different kinds of wrong actions.

Moral Actions, Moral Persons

The reality of the moral dimension in human behavior becomes more obvious, it seems, when we reflect on its implications for the way we think about people. When you describe someone as a liar or a thief or a murderer, you are saying much different things than when you describe the person as left-handed or good-looking or humorous. The difference is much more central too. It says something much more radical and crucial about the person. It is obvious which goes more to the heart of a person's character, of a person's humanity—to say he is a painter or that he is honest, to say she sews well or that she lies, to say that he is thin or that he is cruel.

"Moral" and "immoral," then, are really different in our experience. They say something about human reality. When we tell our children "Good people don't steal," we are not afraid that some other mother somewhere is saying "Good people steal." We do not have to stop and ask ourselves, "Now which is right: stealing or not stealing?"—as we might have to ask ourselves, "Should I turn it clockwise or counter-clockwise?" We never say "Stealing…not stealing! It's all the same. Take your pick. Just be consistent." We have a common-sense conviction that it does matter because these are really different, and *one is consistent with being a good human being and one is not.* We reward the person for returning our wallet and we punish the person who steals our wallet, and it is not simply because people have agreed to do it that way. Rather it is because we believe that there is something radically fitting for the human person in the one case and inappropriate in the other. We believe that the moral and the immoral are truly different and that the difference is rooted in human reality—indeed, in our very humanness.

Implications

What, then, are our conclusions from all this? Here are some important insights. First, *human behavior, human actions, have a moral dimension* provided the act is done deliberately, that is, with knowledge and with freedom. This moral quality is real, rooted in human nature, and right/wrong, moral/immoral, good/evil are really different from each other. Actions have a quality of "oughtness," enabling us to say that "a human person (I, you) should do this, should not do that."

Second, *all human behavior has a moral dimension.* In fact "moral" means "human" in the "ought" or normative sense—that is, what human beings ought to do, not what they are observed to do (the descriptive sense). So we can say, "It is human to lie" (the descriptive sense), meaning that human beings do it; we can also say, "It is not human to lie" (normative), meaning human beings should not do it. When we say that rape is inhuman, we are speaking normatively— human beings should not do it; it is immoral. "Any person who abuses a child acts like an animal and is not a human being," then, is a normative statement; human beings should not do it.

Next, *only human actions have a moral dimension*—even though we say "bad dog" when our pet defies house-training or "bad polly" when the parrot swears at our mother-in-law! We really do not believe the animal has made an immoral choice!

Finally, human behavior has a moral dimension, *whether it is the action of an individual or of a group.* So when the board of trustees raises tuition, when a gang robs a bank, when business partners in a pharmacy agree to cheat customers—all of these individuals share the moral responsibility of the group decision or action. All participate in the moral goodness or badness of the action, provided they were involved in the decision.

SUBJECTIVE AND OBJECTIVE MORALITY

Most people understand morality as that dimension of human behavior that flows from our capacity to distinguish genuine moral values and to choose them. This is the realm of conscience, of subjective morality. Conscience is our human awareness of value and of our human responsibility to choose it. We recognize in ourselves the human capacity for free decision making, for autonomous choice, and our accountability for what we choose. Even more, we sense ourselves called in the concrete situations of our lives to distinguish what is truly of moral worth and then, finally, to choose what we believe to be the good.

All of this implies that we know there is a real world outside of ourselves, something that is not simply of our own making. It exists outside of us, at times despite us. We do not call it into being and we cannot wish it away. We live in it, work in it, make our choices in it. Part of this is the world of value. All of us recognize that there are many things in life that we cherish and treasure—all kinds of things. It may be something as simple as a favorite dessert or it may embody a quality of excellence—a perfectly pitched baseball game, for example. Some things, we recognize, enrich human existence—not simply in a passing sense but permanently. Even though we may not like the opera, we may sense that life would be poorer without *Don Giovanni*. Modern art may not attract me personally, but I can appreciate that paintings by Cézanne or van Gogh have a special contribution to make as a human expression of what is beautiful in the world.

There is still another world of value that all of us recognize. It is the world of ethical or moral value. All of us acknowledge that kindness is one of these values. We recognize that telling the truth has an importance of its own, even if it may be inconvenient for me in a concrete situation. In this realm of moral value we include human goods such as compassion, honesty, fairness, and courage. We can realize these values outside of us in the concrete situations that we encounter. We acknowledge their importance for us personally and for human existence in general, and we appreciate them in other human beings and in ourselves when we encounter them.

This is the world of objective morality, the world of moral values. They are there to be discovered and chosen. Their existence does not depend on our communal agreement to them; rather, we have to seek them out. We recognize them as qualities of human behavior that all moral agents should want to realize if they wish to be fully human. We know that we are saying something real about the person we describe in moral terms—a generous man, a thief, a compassionate woman. To repeat the point again, it is something more important than being described as a teacher, or good-looking, or left-handed. It says something more central, more radical, more crucial about a person's humanity, about being a human being, to say that a person is cruel than to say he is thin. It goes much more to the very heart of a person's humanity to say that he is honest than to describe him as a painter, to say that she lies than to say that she sews poorly.

It is critically important to know the difference between subjective and objective morality, to recognize that both aspects of morality are real and are important. Many people confuse the two. They say that even though some actions are moral and others immoral, what makes them right/wrong is what the person thinks at the time. Morality, for them, is what you think is right or wrong; it depends on a person's conscience, on an individual's judgment. Again, in one sense that is true. That is the realm of conscience—of subjective morality. It is critically important, surely. As a result, if I sincerely try to discover what is the right thing to do and then do what I believe to be morally right, I make a morally correct decision. I follow my conscience. That is the subjective side of morality where conscience is the norm—where my knowledge and my freedom are essential to the morality of my action.

On the other hand, I need to recognize that I may have made a mistake in judging something good to be bad (or vice versa). I may have mistaken a value for a disvalue. They really are not the same. They exist outside of me, and the challenge to me in life is to discern which is which, to choose what is really good and to reject what is really bad. That is the world of objective morality. The human task is to discover what is really good in the concrete situation and to choose it, to determine which is the higher good, the life of the fetus or the reputation of the unwed mother—or which is the lesser evil, a self-induced death to be free from pain or respect for my stewardship of life while enduring the pain of terminal illness—and then to decide. It is not logical to say that both are higher goods or that they are both lesser evils. One has to be a higher value, a greater good; one has to involve less disvalue than the other—and not just in our minds but in the real, concrete world outside of us, the world that is not of our making. Our task, our human responsibility, is to discover which is which and then to choose. It is at this point that objective morality and subjective morality come together.

Think of it another way. For the sake of understanding the difference, begin with the conviction that God exists. When God looks at the same human situation that confronts us, God knows which is the greater value, the higher good. God knows which we should choose. That is objective morality, the objectively right or wrong. It is not just opinion, not just someone's personal view. God knows which value is higher, which good should be chosen, which choice is more in harmony with the way God made us. It is beyond opinion, beyond argument or debate. It is fact. That is objective morality.

All this does not take away our obligation to try to discover the higher value. It does not deny the possibility that we may end up with different views. That is how objective morality differs from subjective morality. In the former case, one value is objectively really higher than the other—and God knows which it is. But our ability to reason to that higher value, to discover which is really higher than the other, sometimes encounters obstacles and we come up with the wrong answer. Fortunately, if we try in good faith to discover the higher value and fail, God judges us by what we believed to be right. God does not judge us to have acted immorally, but we are in error.

TO SUM UP THIS INTRODUCTION TO MORALITY

Our experience convinces us that we are truly free; we are not compelled to choose to do this rather than that—either by anything within ourselves or outside of us. Because free, we are confronted with choices, with the need to decide freely to seek this good or that good, this value or that value. Some choices have minimal importance because the good/value is not particularly significant, not personally a value we cherish—what to wear today, what to eat for breakfast, which route to take to school. But others have the ring of importance for us—the request of a friend for help, a tearful plea to be forgiven from someone who hurt us, the earnest appeal from someone we love to be honest about the level of commitment in our relationship. These decisions are important because they have the ring of "should" about them. They go to the heart of what it means to be a "good person." Even though in each case we realize we are free—to help or refuse to help, to forgive or not, to be truthful or to deceive—we know in our heart (conscience) that we are confronted with a choice of values that make women and men different from the rest of creation because they deal with being "good" persons, authentic human beings, genuinely faithful to our human nature. These values exist outside of us, and the challenge for us is to make the right choice, to choose what is truly good. We don't make telling the truth good; rather we choose the good when we choose to tell the truth.

But an equally true and real part of our experience is the realization that I have the faculty/capacity for judging what is truly good, authentically human. We call this faculty "conscience," and this leads us into the world of subjective morality. It is not always obvious what is true human value or the most appropriate human thing to do. Different people tell us different things. Sometimes two values collide; they represent conflicting choices. We can't have both or all; we must choose between them. In these instances we simply have to do our best to judge what is genuine human good or the greater good—or the lesser evil. We have to follow our conscience. We can listen to what other people say, to what our faith teaches us, but ultimately we must decide in the solitariness of our conscience—what is truly good, where the disvalue lies. If we make our best effort to judge this honestly and decide sincerely, then we should have no concern about following our conscience. We can do no more! But we must always remember that we can make a mistake—our conscience can err in its judgment. What we thought was good or evil was in reality the opposite. This we know from experience. Our choice was not really the greater good or the lesser evil. We need to remember that conscience does not create value or what is good. It discovers and chooses it.

METHOD IN MORAL DECISION MAKING

Although we will argue for a method in moral decision making, we will not insist that one is needed in *all* our moral decisions. It is our common-sense conviction that often—even usually—we do not need one. When someone asks us a question, we do not have to stop and ask ourselves, "Shall I tell the truth or lie?" Every time you take a test, you do not have to stop and ask, "Shall I cheat or be honest?" If I work the check-out counter in a supermarket, I do not agonize over making change—"Shall I give the customer correct change?" Much of our behavior—even though always moral or immoral if it is deliberate—is guided by habit. We have a "standing intention" to be honest, to speak truthfully, to act kindly and thoughtfully, to fulfill our responsibilities. These are our "life values"; they are the values we choose to live by.

Habits are, of course, the way human beings deal with their freedom. This is true not simply in our moral life, but in every dimension of human decision making. We develop physical habits that allow us to perform complicated actions without having to think deeply about them—whether it is driving our car or driving a golf ball. So too we develop intellectual habits, the ways in which our minds learn new information or develop new mental skills. For this reason different people have different learning styles and different ways of remembering things. Moral habits are similar. Choosing the good would be just as oppressive as deciding which route to take to school if we had to agonize over our choices; freedom would be a burden—hence the human tendency to develop habits. In the area of moral choice, we call these habits "virtues" when they are good habits; the opposite we call "vices." They reflect each person's value system, that is, the complex scheme of moral values that we have elected to live by. Virtuous habits do not interfere with or lessen freedom; they rather enhance it by making it easier for us to choose what is truly good. Similarly vices, bad habits, do not take away freedom but they incline us to choose what is evil. Hence, to return to the point made above, virtues facilitate our moral choices and thus our moral life.

Even though this may be true about our ordinary, routine moral decisions, there are times—we know this from experience—when our common sense urges us to proceed carefully and thoughtfully. When the object of our decision is extremely important or serious (e.g., in cases when the termination of life support is being considered), or when the circumstances of the situation are especially complicated and confusing (as in the case of a decision regarding a newborn with disabilities), or when we simply never had any experience like it before, then caution and care are called for. This is precisely when method is most needed. Habit will not work here because we have never had the opportunity to develop habits for such situations. Method is the answer.

A Two-Step Method

In his book *The Moral Choice,* Daniel Maguire proposes a two-step method to work through serious or complicated moral decisions.[1] The first step he calls the *expository* phase, in which one strives to clarify or explain the reality of the situation. He suggests that this be done by asking what he calls "the reality-revealing questions": *What? Who? Why? How? When? Where?* He maintains that one must then also weigh the consequences of the decision or action. These questions seek to lay out for examination the full human reality in all of its significant circumstances. Thus he places himself in that line of moralists who maintain with St. Thomas Aquinas that the good or evil of human actions is found not only in the act itself or in the intention, but also "in the circumstances." Why is it so essential to understand fully the reality of the situation? Because that is where we will find the values that are involved! As was pointed out earlier, morality is objective because moral values exist outside the individual who is called to choose the good. By identifying all of the significant circumstances, one seeks assurance that all the values that are involved have been recognized.

The second step is what Maguire calls the *evaluational* stage. Once all of the values have been identified (through the expository process), the one making the decision must prioritize these values. In other words, the individual asks, "Which is the higher value? The greater disvalue? Which value is greater? Which is the greater good in view of all the circumstances? Are there alternative choices? Which one would allow me to preserve the greatest amount of good—not in some mechanical, utilitarian sense, but which choice will promote authentic human living, will enhance genuine human values?"

Expository Phase: The Reality-Revealing Questions

"What" is the first, the foundational question, in one's effort to know the reality involved in a moral choice. It may or may not be the most important issue involved in deciding on the morally correct choice, but it is always the first. "What" reveals the nature of the action in question—terminating a pregnancy prematurely, discontinuing life support, saying what I know not to be true. It is fairly obvious that one has to know "what is" before knowing "what ought." It should also be pointed out that it is important for the nature or the "whatness" of the action to be named in a morally neutral way. Since there can be no judgment yet about the moral rightness or wrongness of the action being contemplated (there are still six more questions to ask!), we must not name the "what" in a way that prejudices that judgment. Thus abortion is called "a premature termination of pregnancy"

rather than "murder." Similarly, "lying" would prejudice the final moral analysis, and so the action should be described as "saying what we know not to be true." "Taking someone else's property" names the action better than "stealing"—better, that is, for this stage of the process. Ultimately, "stealing" may be the final moral judgment, but it would be premature at this point. Some "whats" are more morally significant than others; that is, they alert our moral consciousness to the moral seriousness of the action. Thus, allowing an infant to die and whistling obviously have different moral weight. Last of all, as already suggested, knowing the "what" does not give us a final moral verdict. We need to know as much about the circumstances as we can, but we will never be on target in our moral evaluation unless we know the "what" as clearly as possible.

"Who" is the second central question. After all, morality is all about the "who"—in the sense of the one who is the agent, the subject who acts. Morality is not simply the way we describe the "ought" dimension of actions; more importantly and more centrally, it is first of all the way we describe persons who act. Only secondly are actions morally good or morally bad. Maguire points out that the moral dimension of the person is one of the principal ways in which a human being becomes. Personal life, he says, is a process—a "personing" process. Through our moral decisions we grow into that individual who we can be—the virtuous, honest, upright, trusting person or the liar, cheat, and fraud who also lies within our potentialities. It is important to remember that persons are unique and individual, since we come into being only through our interaction with other persons. Since this must always be unique and unrepeatable, persons too are individual, the product of their social interaction. There is a great temptation to generalize—even to universalize—about human persons, and so we need to exercise great care when we try to express general moral principles about persons.

There can, of course, be many "whos" in any human action. The "who" that concerns us here, however, is the agent of the action, the one who decides and acts. Because of the uniqueness of persons, it should come as no surprise that the "who" is very central to the moral evaluation of human actions. Thus the same action (the same "what") can be moral for one "who" and immoral for another. Sexual intercourse ("what") can be perfectly moral when the "who" is a woman's

33

husband and quite morally objectionable when the "who" is her father or her lover.

"*Why*" calls attention to another circumstance. It identifies the motive, the purpose, the intention that the agent has in mind. Another term that is sometimes used is "end." We have all heard the expression "The end never justifies the means." The end is the "why." This old saying would have us realize that even if the end or motive that I have in mind is good, the means I use to achieve that end must also be good. The good end never makes up for the evil means used. If I want to give you a diamond ring for your birthday, no one could object. If I steal it from Macy's, no one would try to justify this. Not all examples are so obviously flawed, however. It was argued historically, to cite one example, that it was justifiable to drop atomic bombs on the noncombatant populations of Hiroshima and Nagasaki in order to reduce dramatically the numbers of American casualties in the Pacific theater during World War II. The end justified the means. It is a tempting argument—but one that needs to be firmly rejected. As we shall see, moral goodness is only assured when *all* of the circumstances are good, not simply the "end." "Why" is very important, then—the single most important circumstance that we consider when we analyze human decisions. It is easy to see why this is so when we recognize that "why" always leads us to the *value* that is the focus of the agent's decision. I decide to act because I find this value, this good, as the basis for my choice, my decision to act. My gift of $200 can be in recognition of your birthday, or a bribe, or the price of having sex with you. In each case, it is the "why" that is centrally important to the moral analysis. Psychologists tell us, of course, that our "whys" are often confused and complicated—multiple even. This does not take away from the central importance of motive to the morality of our actions, however.

"*How*" is another question that needs to be asked in arriving at a moral assessment. Less important than "why," "how" describes the means or the method used to achieve our end. Very often it has little bearing on the morality of our action—what difference does it make whether the murder was committed by using a gun or a knife?—but it is not always so. For instance, it *does* make a difference if the $200 I give you as a birthday gift comes from my savings or from a bank withdrawal made with someone else's bank card! Similarly it makes a great difference whether the surgeon who is removing your swollen tonsils uses an approved surgical procedure or takes some risky short-cuts. "How," then, identifies the means used by the subject or agent to accomplish his purpose or end. Sometimes, we know, means get turned into ends. A job normally is the means a person uses to fulfill himself and to survive financially. Sometimes, however, the job consumes the workaholic's life and actually becomes his purpose in life. Food, to use another example, is supposed to provide for our health and well-being and ultimately contribute to our happiness—and so it is a means. The habitual overeater, however, turns food into the goal of life and thus sacrifices health and probably happiness too.[2] When we consider "how" as one of the reality-revealing questions, however, we are looking at the means by which the agent achieves his purpose.

"Where" and *"when"* are the two final reality-revealing questions and can be examined together. Quite simply, they designate place and time. Normally they have little impact on any analysis of the moral quality of our actions or decisions. True, they describe two of the circumstances of any concrete action, which always occurs within a particular time and place, but usually they are not morally significant. Sometimes, however, an action may be morally correct and defensible on the level of "what," "who," "why," and "how," but it becomes ethically inappropriate or unbefitting persons because of time and place considerations. Thus for a pregnant mother to go horseback riding at the end of the third trimester (when) would be morally objectionable, just as it would be for her to smoke throughout her pregnancy. Similarly, for a married couple to engage in sexual intercourse is unobjectionable—unless it occurs on the "E" train (where)! The death squad in El Salvador who killed Archbishop Romero committed a murder; the fact that they did this as he celebrated Mass in the cathedral gave the crime an additional malice. Under normal circumstances, however, "where" and "when" are not particularly important factors in moral decision making, even though any moral evaluation of an action needs to attend to them to be certain of this.

The final issue to which we must attend is what we call *"consequences."* In general, the term describes the "effects" of our actions. Because the "effects" or "consequences" that we *intend* to achieve by our action have already been examined when we considered the question "why," "consequences" for us will designate the effects which were *not intended.* It is not difficult to imagine such effects, whether immediate or future. If I torch an abandoned building in my neighborhood to drive out the drug sellers who are using it, then this effect is my motive and answers the question "why." If there happen to be some homeless people sleeping in the building who are killed in the blaze, this effect was not my intention and hence it is a "consequence." If I am prosecuted by the law and sent to prison, these too are "consequences" beyond my intention! Are we, then, morally responsible for all "consequences"? Not for *all*, certainly, but only for those we foresee or *should* foresee. Thus if I rob a bank, the money that I take is my motive, my "why" for robbing the bank. But if I rob it at gunpoint, I should foresee that there may be resistance that will lead me to use the gun, and someone may get killed. The death is not my intention and hence it is a "consequence," but I should have foreseen it and so I am responsible for it. To use another example, the purpose of the atom-bombing of Hiroshima and Nagasaki was to bring the war in the Pacific to a quick end, with a consequent reduction of American military casualties. The fact that several hundred thousand Japanese civilians would be killed may not have been the intention of those who ordered the bombing, but they surely foresaw it. It was an obvious consequence of their decision and they had to bear moral responsibility for it. To whatever degree, therefore, that consequences are foreseeable or knowable, we are responsible for them, even if we do not directly intend them.

These, then, are the reality-revealing questions that enable us to come to know the circumstances that determine or define the situation which presents itself for our decision. Should we terminate a pregnancy, keep an aged parent at home or in a nursing-care facility, or take a full-time job and place the children in child care? These questions never reveal the entire reality in any exhaustive way, but it is the best we can do. By examining all of these circumstances, we can come to know the competing values that present themselves for our decision—and this concludes the expository phase of our two-step method.

Evaluational Phase: Choosing the Good

Basically there are just two more things to be done before we make our decision. First of all we need to prioritize the values that are at stake. There may be few or there may be many, but we need to ask ourselves how we would rank them—saving the life of the fetus or preserving the reputation of the unwed mother, bringing in a second full-time salary or being in the home to raise the children, committing our own resources to the care of our aged, dependent father or entrusting his care to a nursing home. These examples are oversimplified, of course, and real-life scenarios may involve many more values, but the process should be clear. We need to take the values we have identified through the expository phase of our method and try to determine, as objectively as possible, which represents a higher value, a greater good. Obviously, since this will always be a personal assessment, the answer to the question will be a subjective one; ideally this is where the objective and the subjective aspects of morality come together.

A second consideration, before we decide, involves the question of alternatives. Is adoption a viable alternative to the abortion? Would a part-time job be sufficient to meet our financial needs? Would a home-care health assistant enable us to keep our father at home? The consideration of alternatives can be important because there may be some creative possibility that allows us to preserve/achieve more values than the either/or choice (fetus/reputation, full-time salary/home with children, home care/nursing facility). If there are no alternatives, of course, the choice is simplified—without ever being simple!

That is all that is left, of course—to choose. Having weighed alternatives, after honestly assessing the competing values, the morally good choice is what is most humanly valuable, what is most appropriate, befitting for a human person. What is truly the good or the greater good? This will always be a subjective assessment made in the forum of conscience, but the closer the subjective choice corresponds with what is objectively the higher value, the better the moral choice.

STUDY QUESTIONS

1. The text cites personal experience as one of the bases for concluding that we have a human capacity to make moral judgments. What do you understand by "personal experience"? Does your personal experience lead you to the same conclusion that we have this capacity? Explain.
2. The point is made that it is not only our actions that are moral or immoral; our persons are also moral or immoral. Do you agree? Explain.

3. Which human actions have a moral dimension? Explain.
4. What is (are) the most important difference(s) between subjective and objective morality?
5. It has been asserted that our human goal and challenge is to choose the good; and if we must choose between goods, then the higher good. Explain.
6. Why is a method necessary or useful in making a moral decision? Is one always needed? When is it needed? Not needed? Why?
7. Give a general overview of the method for moral decision making described in this chapter.
8. What is the objective of the expository phase? Why is it important? Of the evaluational phase? Why is it important?
9. Which is more important—the expository or the evaluational phase? Explain.

NOTES

1. *The Moral Choice*. Minneapolis: Winston Press, 1979, 128–88.
2. Ibid., 136.

3 Conscience: The Moral Guide

INTRODUCTION

In its simplest expression, the Christian belief is that God is involved in an ongoing personal love relationship with his human creatures, both as a community and as distinct individuals. God teaches us who he is and what he does through a self-revelation of himself to his people. God also calls us to grow in our personal relationship with him, a relationship of loving. This growth occurs through our doing good, thereby nourishing our love relationship, and through our avoiding evil, thus eliminating obstacles to that same relationship.

In order to do this, each of us needs to understand what is truly good and loving and hence to be done, and what is truly evil and hence to be avoided. For this purpose, God places within us the capacity to grow in our ability to understand what is good and what is evil. We call that capacity "conscience."

Nearly everyone is familiar with the term "conscience," even though not everyone has a truly adequate understanding of its meaning. When someone asks you if "your conscience bothers you" regarding something you did, you surely grasp the meaning of the question. When a friend urges you to "follow your conscience" regarding some planned action, the advice is clear enough. But what exactly is this "conscience" they are talking about?

Many contemporary references to conscience are confusing, providing people with inadequate or even erroneous notions of what conscience really is. One example is the radio advertisement about the need for adequate business insurance—it presents the voice of a businessman in dialogue with a second voice that identifies itself as his conscience. The conscience then challenges the businessman through "bottom-line" questions that promote the insurance company sponsoring the ad: "Do you really have enough insurance? Suppose your partner died? Suppose…? Suppose…? Remember, we're partners; I go wherever you go." This understanding of conscience, of course, is not intended to be a technical description of what conscience really is; even so, it is very misleading on a number of counts, as the pages that follow will try to show.

In the first question posed above, the friend asks, "Does your conscience bother you?" (about an action already placed). This describes conscience as functioning after the fact, a kind of retrospective conscience.[1] The second statement—"Follow your conscience"—understands conscience as functioning before the event, in a proactive way, guiding our decision regarding a particular behavior we are considering. Conscience is actually serving the same function in each case—assessing the morally good or evil quality of our behavior. Of course, our response to the assessment after the fact leaves us with options very different from the evaluation that precedes the action.

THE EVOLVING UNDERSTANDING OF CONSCIENCE

Scripture is a logical place to begin this effort to understand the meaning of conscience in the life of the Christian. It is in the Bible, after all, that we have a record of God's dialogue with his people, and so it can offer us some insight into what God wishes us to understand on this subject. At the same time, the Bible offers us a valuable insight into how our ancestors in faith understood conscience, and that gives us a helpful starting point for our own understanding.

The *Hebrew Scriptures* will disappoint us if we expect to find a Jewish use of the term "conscience." The word simply does not exist in biblical Hebrew. The concept, however, is clearly there, and it is expressed by using the word "heart." The psalmist urges, for example, "If today you hear his voice, harden not your heart." In the story of Job, we hear him defend his actions with the words "My heart does not reproach me." Finally, the prophet Ezekiel announces:

> The Lord Yahweh says this: I will gather you together from the peoples, I will bring you all back from the countries where you have been scattered and I will give you the land of Israel.…I will

give them a single heart and I will put a new spirit in them; I will remove the heart of stone from their bodies and give them a heart of flesh instead, so that they will keep my laws and respect my observances and put them into practice. Then they shall be my people and I will be their God.[2]

Heart, then, in texts such as these, expressed for the ancient Jews the reality we call conscience.

It is in the Christian scriptures, the *New Testament*, that we first find an explicit biblical reference to the term "conscience" (in Greek, *syneidesis*). Of course, the metaphorical term "heart" is still employed to express this concept, which is not surprising since the earliest Christian literature grew organically out of the ancient Jewish tradition. And so Jesus complains, "This people honors me with their lips, but their heart *(kardia)* is far from me." Again, in his first epistle, John writes:

This is our way of knowing we are committed to the truth and are at peace before him, no matter what our consciences *(kardia)* may charge us with; for God is greater than our hearts *(kardia)* and all is known to him. Beloved, if our consciences *(kardia)* have nothing to charge us with, we can be sure that God is with us.[3]

It is Paul, however, who is the chief New Testament author to deal with conscience. He drew his teaching, understandably, from the philosophical systems and literature of his time. In his letters and in the record of his ministry found in the Acts of the Apostles, therefore, we receive a rich introduction to the role of conscience in the life of the Christian. Thus, for example, it is conscience which:

— guides the Christian in making moral choices and gives an inner awareness of moral quality.
— judges from within the person, accusing an individual of acts unbefitting a Christian.
— assists us from within to avoid behaviors that would merit God's disapproval.
— provides a powerful source of moral direction.[4]

These earliest Christian insights about conscience provided by Paul were treasured by the first Christian communities and thus became part of their fundamental understanding of the moral life.

In the centuries that followed, Paul's words were commented on and explained by the church *fathers*, the leaders of these early Christian communities, often their bishops. However, their interest was largely homiletic and pastoral rather than theological. It is not surprising, therefore, that Paul's initial teaching about conscience did not receive much additional development during the period of the fathers.

This had to wait for the *Medieval Period* when theological speculation came into its own at the newly established universities that sprang up in European cities such as Paris, Oxford, and Bologna. The nature and characteristics of conscience figured importantly in the discussions and debates of the masters and their scholars throughout this period (twelfth through fourteenth centuries). Some theologians argued that conscience was a faculty of the soul, while others insisted rather that it was a good habit that enabled the faculty to perform its functions well. They debated whether it was related to the human reason or to the will.[5] These and a hundred other questions were debated as different theologians tested one another's understanding of the issues.

One of these questions—"What could/should an individual do when unable to decide if a given act was morally good or evil?" (doubtful conscience)—became a focal point for debate in moral theology within the church for almost three hundred years (sixteenth through eighteenth centuries). This is reflected in the writings of those theologians writing manuals of moral theology for the training of priests in seminaries, the *Manualists*.[6] While the history of this long struggle to clarify the nature and function of conscience might be of considerable importance for the development of theology, it did little to enrich the concept of conscience. As a result of the debate, conscience came to be viewed apart from the whole person, the agent of the action. Equally harmful was the tendency to understand conscience as completely rationalistic, that it was an activity of reason alone and operated in a purely deductive way (Evil must be avoided. This action is evil. Therefore…) as if the human mind approached moral judgments by means of syllogisms.

Very briefly, these were the understandings regarding conscience within the Roman Catholic tradition as the church entered the second half of the twentieth century. As in so many other areas of Catholic belief and practice, it was *Vatican Council II* that brought together the best elements of the long theological tradition within the church and initiated a new era of speculation and understanding on the subject of conscience. In two council documents, in particular, these elements were highlighted. In the pastoral constitution, The Church in the Modern World, the bishops who gathered at the council taught:

> In the depths of his conscience, man detects a law which he does not impose upon himself, but which holds him to obedience. Always summoning him to love good and avoid evil, the voice of conscience can when necessary speak to his heart more specifically; do this, shun that. For man has in his heart a law written by God. To obey it is the very dignity of man; according to it he will be judged. Conscience is the most secret core and sanctuary of a man. There he is alone with God, whose voice echoes in his depths.[7]

At the council, in their Declaration on Religious Freedom, the bishops also turned their attention to the question of the inviolability of conscience. Thus they wrote:

> On his part, man perceives and acknowledges the imperatives of the divine law through the mediation of conscience. In all his activity a man is bound to follow his conscience faithfully, in order that he may come to God, for whom he was created. It follows that he is not to be forced to act in a manner contrary to his conscience. Nor, on the other hand, is he to be restrained from acting in accordance with his conscience, especially in matters religious.[8]

THE CONTEMPORARY TEACHING

Taking these conciliar statements as our starting points, then, what insights can we offer that will enrich our understanding of the nature of conscience and its role in the life of the Christian—of any human person, for that matter?

1. The debate in the Middle Ages was whether the action of conscience was a function of the intellect (the practical reason) as it recognized moral value/disvalue or one of the will, choosing the good. After Vatican Council II contemporary theology suggests a more holistic understanding—conscience arises out of the whole person. It is, simply put, "me coming to a decision."[9] Just like all my other decisions, my

43

moral choices bring together in a synthesis the insights provided by my mind, attractions arising in my will, the nonrational contributions of my emotions, the impulse of the heart that "knows not reason," and stimuli from memories of past experiences. Obviously, my choices—moral or otherwise—are complex, not simple. In any case, they are hardly the conclusion arising from completing a syllogism![10]

2. Conscience operates in the human person on different levels.[11] In its most radical sense, conscience is that basic capability, the raw capacity, within the human person that draws that individual to the good and away from evil. St. Thomas Aquinas calls conscience in this sense *synderesis*, a grasping of the first moral principles—to do good and avoid evil. It flows from our very human nature, allowing us to distinguish good and evil in such a way that we may seek the former and avoid the latter.

But such a vague, generalized conviction is hardly enough to enable us to deal with concrete, everyday moral choices, and so, at a more immediate level, conscience functions as moral reasoning (St. Paul's *syneidesis*). In other words, the person seeks to identify some proximate, concrete action as morally sound or morally reprehensible. It is a discernment process that engages the whole person, who wrestles with this immediate, practical question: "Is this course of action good, something I would want to do, or is it evil and so to be rejected?" It is a searching by an individual for moral clarity in a totally human, wholly personal way—prior to the choice. It seeks moral truth in a concrete situation by drawing moral wisdom from whatever sources are available—personal experience, the advice of family and friends, the teaching of the church, the counsel of an advisor or spiritual guide. Its objective is to arrive at that personally "evaluative knowledge" spoken of in a previous chapter.[12]

Eventually clarity arrives and the person concludes: "It is the morally good thing to do; I want/choose to do it." All of the uncertainties—ideally at least—are resolved and the individual ends at the conviction: "I will do this because it is the right thing for me to do now." This, too, is conscience, in its most immediate and practical choosing of a morally good action. It is a choosing that reflects the kind of person I am. It affirms my recognition of genuine value in the action that I have been contemplating. It is at this point that conscience becomes my personal guide to right action. As Vatican

Council II said, it is the law "which holds [me] to obedience." I must follow its direction—I have no other guide. It is then that I am morally bound to follow its directive. It is at this point that the maxim applies: Let your conscience be your guide. Of course, it will be a secure guide only if the necessary analysis and reflection took place during the moral reasoning process that preceded my decision.

This analysis may seem more complicated than our experience of conscience would lead us to believe, but this threefold distinction of conscience—generalized conviction, moral reasoning, choice of the good—needs to be carefully understood if one would really understand the way conscience functions in the moral life. The practical consequences that flow from this are many.

3. Our understanding of conscience is necessarily influenced by our notion of morality. If the latter is basically conceived as deontological—that is, morality is ultimately the human response to law and the fulfillment of obligation—then the role of conscience is reduced to conforming actions to laws.[13] If morality is seen as my loving response to a God who calls me to choose the good, then conscience leads to personal responsibility and mature moral choices.

MORAL CHOICE AND MORAL CHARACTER

1. What we do as a result of the action of conscience is critically important in revealing who we are—to those around us as well as to ourselves. My actions express the real me! As Jesus pointed out, "Make a tree sound and its fruit will be sound; make a tree rotten and its fruit will be rotten. For the tree can be told by its fruit."[14] Our actions reveal our character. A caring parent reveals that fact in caring acts. He or she is caring by acting in a caring way. A schoolboy who pushes his classmates around is recognized as a bully. Not just *acts like* a bully—*is* a bully. The CEO who tells lies is recognized as a dishonest person—has a dishonest character.

2. Equally important is the fact that my actions in turn constitute me as a moral agent. In all of creation as we know it, this is peculiar to human persons. It is our dignity and our destiny to be cocreators of our moral selves, to make ourselves who we really are. As Maguire has written:

To grow as a person is to be more of a person. It is growth in essence. (Growth can also be reversed and personal life can become less personal and human than it was.)

...With moral decisions we flesh out our possibilities and carve the shape of our personhood. Moral decisions make us frauds, villains, and ruthless exploiters, or saints, prophets, and heroes, or a little bit of each. In the exercise of responsible freedom, we become a certain kind of person.[15]

3. It has been a constant conviction within the Roman Catholic tradition that the final decision/choosing of conscience (the third sense of conscience in #2 above) is the proximate norm for action. It is then that conscience truly becomes our guide. The decision might be erroneous—the moral reasoning activity that preceded it is always subject to this possibility—but right or wrong, the individual must follow conscience. There is no other guide. Equally important, this must be respected by others, especially by those in authority, those with power—by public officials, for example, and by church authorities. The radical freedom from which our choices flow must be respected. On the other hand, the possibility of error should lead the individual to use all available means to guard against this, recognizing the danger of prejudice, bias, ignorance of the facts, self-interest, and personal sinfulness.

4. While the functioning of conscience is supremely personal and individual, the formation of conscience—which is a continual process, even lifelong—occurs within community. In fact, many different communities vie with each other to play a significant role in the development of their members' consciences. For the Christian, the church as the people of God has a paramount role to play in this process. In this connection Curran writes:

> The Church as the mediator and sign of the Gospel strives to have its own people become signs of that Gospel to others. From an ethical perspective, the Church is a great help in the formation of conscience precisely because it can overcome the two basic dangers of finitude and sinfulness which always threaten the individual. Because of our finitude we are limited historically, spatially, and temporally. The Church as a universal community existing in different cultures, in different times, and in different places is thus able to help overcome the limitations of finitude.

The Church as the community of Gospel and grace also tries to overcome human sinfulness and egoism. Although the Church remains a sinful Church still in need of continual redemption, the believer sees in the Church the presence of redeeming grace and a power to overcome sin and its ramifications.[16]

One of the providential instruments available for the moral instruction of believers within the Roman Catholic communion is the *magisterium*. This term has been used almost exclusively in modern times to refer to the church's authoritative teaching office. Thus it includes the teaching office of the pope and of the bishops, and of those Vatican congregations through which the pope exercises his worldwide administration of the Roman Catholic Church. Moral instruction can take different forms—letters or encyclicals, instructions, decrees, declarations—and these teachings can have different degrees of authority and weight. In every case, however, the magisterial teaching is the only "official" teaching of the church and enjoys a special place in the moral formation of the believer's conscience. This is due to the conviction held by Catholics that the mandate given by Jesus to his apostles—"Go, make disciples and teach all nations"[17]—has been passed down historically within the church to the hierarchy in every age. The pope and bishops, therefore, teach "in the name of Christ."[18]

5. The ability to act according to one's own conscience is the sign of a morally mature person. We recognize that the path to this goal begins in childhood, when our decisions and actions are formed under the influence of external authority. At the beginning, then, we act the way we are told or as we see others act in order to be considered one of the group. Gradually we develop the capacity to figure things out for ourselves; we learn to make up our own minds about what we should do and what we should avoid. We act no longer because that is what someone in authority tells us to do, even though it may very well be the same thing. We have arrived at moral maturity when we are able to judge and decide our actions based on the values that we hold dear, the things which give meaning to our lives. This is what some call "being authentic"; we are able and willing to employ our freedom to give our lives meaning and direction.[19]

6. Moral education has as a goal to prepare individuals to make mature moral decisions as adults. For Christians this means equipping them to make their own moral choices in the light of their Christian

calling. For one thing, then, moral education needs to assist persons to acquire the skills needed for the practice of sound moral reasoning. This includes the ability to identify those factors in each concrete situation that are morally relevant, to develop a sensitivity to the values that are embedded in the concrete situation, and to develop the capacity to weigh and prioritize the goods that invite one's choice. While recognizing that the final choice is never based on purely cognitive evidence, the Catholic tradition has always placed great emphasis on the role of reason in making responsible moral decisions.

MORAL CHOICE AND MORAL AGENT

It would be a mistake, however, to identify the moral life with individual moral choices or even with the sum of one's moral choices. In the final analysis, the moral life is more a question of *who* we are than of *what* we do. It is the person, the subject and source of moral actions, that is the central reality of moral living. This realization has led many commentators to stress the importance of moral character in addressing people's needs in moral education. After all, it is from a person's moral core—the "heart," to return to the biblical metaphor—that actions flow. As already pointed out, our actions both reveal the kind of moral persons we are and at the same time confirm and solidify or modify and change that moral personality, that moral self.

How can we understand this concept of "moral character"? When we try to assess other people's character, what do we look at? Not just at their actions, their choices; we look too at their attitudes, their expectations about life, their habitual ways of dealing with people, with crises, with joys, and with disappointments. What gives life real meaning for them? How do they see the world, as friendly or as hostile? How do they react to new situations, as challenging or as threatening? These and a hundred questions like them enable us to penetrate the superficial aspects of a person and get to know the "real" person that lies at the core. If, then, moral education is to be truly adequate, it must deal with the question of character—it must help the individual answer the question "What kind of person do I want to be?"

48

MORAL CHOICE AND MORAL VISION

If our moral choices flow naturally from the kind of person we are, from our moral character, another very important determinant of these choices is the way we see. We can only choose what we see and in the precise way we see it. Our *vision*, then, plays a central role in our moral life. It follows, logically, that one of the crucial tasks of moral education is to help an individual to see—to see what life is all about, what gives it meaning, what constitutes genuine human value.

Learning to see, of course, comes naturally, without our even seeking it. Initially we learn to see the world with our parents' eyes, especially our mothers'. From them we learn to see the world as hospitable or hostile, other people as friendly or threatening. We see our lives as an opportunity to explore or as a refuge from the unknown.

Vision is always learned in community—the community of the family first, but soon many communities compete to teach us their view of life, their vision. The school, the street, the church, the marketplace, the "wide screen," and the "small screen"—all are sources of vision, and from these often-contradictory points of view each adult must fashion a personal vision. Unfortunately, many of these competing visions are truly inimical to the Christian vision, and the images they employ are often subtle, powerful, and continuous. It would be foolish to suppose that they do not influence the way we see. The Christian faith community seeks to offer its members an authentic vision of life. Through moral education this community seeks to assist the individual Christian in this challenging task: how to see the world and how to see life, one's own life—its meaning, challenges, and opportunities—one's destiny. Since character and vision give direction to the moral life, then the importance of this task of moral education cannot be overestimated.

STUDY QUESTIONS

1. How is "conscience" related to objective morality? To subjective morality?
2. The term "conscience" can mean a number of different things. Explain.
3. Trace the "theological history" of the term "conscience."
4. Summarize the most important points in our contemporary understanding of "conscience" among Roman Catholic theologians.

5. What is the relationship between moral choice and moral character? Which comes first? Explain.
6. What is the significance of conscience formation?
7. How can conscience be both supremely personal and necessarily communitarian?

NOTES

1. In the theological tradition the technical term is "consequent conscience"; it refers to the activity of conscience regarding an action that has already occurred. On the other hand, it is called an "antecedent conscience" when it assesses behavior that has not yet taken place. It is this aspect of conscience that will be the focus of most of our attention in this chapter.

2. Ps 95:7; Jb 27:6; Ez 11:17, 19–21a.

3. Mt 15:8; 1 Jn 3:19–21.

4. Rom 2:15; Heb 10:22; Acts 24:16; 1 Tm 1:19f.

5. St. Thomas Aquinas, for example, taught that *synderesis* was a habit perfecting the practical reason and enabling one to know first, self-evident principles of practical moral reasoning. This habit was the source of our natural inclination to the good, according to Thomas. Conscience *(syneidesis)*, on the other hand, was the act of the practical reason, enabling the subject to move from knowledge to act. (I, q.79, a.12, 13).

6. For a more detailed description of this period, cf. Charles A. Curran, *Directions in Fundamental Moral Theology.* Notre Dame: University of Notre Dame Press, 1985, 217–25.

7. *Gaudium et Spes* (The Church in the Modern World), n. 16 in *The Documents of Vatican II,* Walter M. Abbott, S.J., ed. New York: Herder and Herder, 1966.

8. *Dignitatis Humanae* (Religious Freedom), n. 3; cf. note 7.

9. Richard M. Gula, *Reason Informed by Faith.* Mahwah, N.J.: Paulist Press, 1989, 131.

10. In a similar vein, Curran observes, "The recognition of the importance of the affective aspects and feelings in the formation of conscience have important practical ramifications. Much can be learned from all branches of psychology. Appeal must be made not only to the intellect but to the imagination and the affectivity of the person. In this connection one can mention an element that unfortunately has been lost in recent Catholic life—emphasis on the lives of the saints. The saints furnished inspiration and supplied heroes for many younger Catholics in the past. These stories in their own way fired the imagination, triggered the feelings and inflamed the hearts of those

who strove to follow in the footsteps of the saints. With the passing of this emphasis on the lives of the saints, Catholic life has lost an important element in conscience formation." Cf. note 6, 236–37.

11. See Timothy E. O'Connell, *Principles for a Catholic Morality*. New York: Harper, 1990, 110, for a very helpful explanation distinguishing the three different functions of conscience—generalized conviction, moral reasoning, and choice of the good.

12. Ibid., 12–13.

13. Cf. note 6, 227.

14. Mt 12:33.

15. Daniel Maguire, *The Moral Choice*. Minneapolis: Winston, 1979, 146–47.

16. Cf. note 6, 248–49.

17. Mt 28:19–20.

18. Vatican Council II, *Lumen Gentium,* n. 25. Cf. note 7.

19. Thus conscience needs to be carefully distinguished from the Freudian concept of superego. Very briefly, the latter is the accumulation of an individual's experience of imposed rules and standards, of commands and prohibitions that were part of the person's experience as a child growing up. They are all the things people in authority told us that "good boys/good girls always do" or "never do." They are the rules we observed growing up in order to maintain the love and approval of those who could give or withdraw these. When these dictates of childhood continue to control an adult's behaviors, however, that individual has failed to achieve moral maturity. When the norm for our actions tends to be authority toward which we feel the obligation of obedience, it is the superego at work. On the other hand, when we choose to act because of the values involved, then a mature moral conscience is directing our choices. If we act out of the desire for approval or out of fear of losing love, moral maturity has yet to be achieved, whereas if we act out of love for others or because our acts reflect the kind of person we want to be, it is moral conscience at work. For a fuller discussion of this point, cf. Gula, note 9, 123–30.

PART TWO

Questions at the Beginning of Life

Part Two concerns questions at the beginning of life. This section will consider three issues—abortion, the treatment of newborns with disabilities, and the use of advanced reproductive technologies. There is no necessary reason to begin here—other than, perhaps, that it is the beginning. The questions are not the same nor are the principles or values involved identical. In the case of abortion, what is asked is whether this new life should continue. Is it ever morally acceptable to terminate a pregnancy deliberately? If yes, then under what circumstances? If no, then how do we respond to some very difficult human situations?

Newborns with disabilities present a different set of issues. The pregnancy is at an end. The child has been born, but under circumstances suggesting either that survival is at risk or that the child's level of functioning—and eventually the adult's as well—will always be limited. Some would call it "defective," but that already indicates an interpretation of the facts based on expectations of "normalcy." It leaves little room for that range of functionality that allows "normalcy" to be measured in the first place.

The introduction of in vitro fertilization and other technological aids to fertilization and reproduction raises a wholly different set of questions. It asks, for example, whether there are limits to the means that a couple can morally employ to ensure offspring. This question, in turn, raises the much more fundamental question of who has a "right" to parenthood. Can anyone—morally, of course—have a child? Is there a right to have a child? If "yes," what is its source? Who has such a right—any couple, married or unmarried? A single person? Is any means morally acceptable?

These, then, are the issues that raise so many questions and result in such passionate debates "at the beginning of life."

4 Abortion

INTRODUCTION

Abortion divides our society as relatively few issues have done in our history as a nation. The public debate on the question continues to be vociferous, at times violent, even though the Supreme Court might appear to have resolved the issue in 1973.

One reason why this question refuses to be resolved is the fact that for many on both sides of the debate, abortion involves moral values. Thus many proponents of abortion insist that a woman's freedom to determine her own reproductive activity is a question of justice, a moral issue surely. Similarly, many who condemn abortion insist that the destruction of the fetus is indeed the destruction of innocent human life and therefore homicide—even murder.

Another reason the debate has proven to be so intractable is the failure of many on both sides to hear the others' arguments. Thus for many pro-abortionists the only issue is the mother's freedom, while for many anti-abortionists the sole value is the life of the fetus. It is difficult to imagine how the controversy can be resolved so long as this single-focus understanding of the question dominates the debate.

Abortion is not the first issue that has divided American society because of the different moral judgments held by diverse segments of the population. The United States is, after all, a pluralistic society, and its history of debate on moral questions is nothing new. The country was born because many believed that their rights as citizens ("taxation without representation") were being violated. Again, in the middle of the next century, the nation was torn asunder on the question of slavery, which for many on both sides of the struggle was clearly a moral issue. A hundred years later, racial discrimination in this country and the war in Vietnam were issues that produced protests, marches, and public debate because they were perceived by many to be profoundly moral questions.

As the issue of abortion continues to divide us, we can expect the debate to continue to erupt in a public way as challenges are offered to current legal understandings of the question. Before that aspect of the matter is addressed, however, it is first necessary to understand clearly what is meant by the term "abortion" and what medical procedures are currently available to procure one.

THE MEDICAL-SCIENTIFIC DIMENSION

Nature

Abortion is the deliberate and voluntary termination of pregnancy prematurely and the expulsion of the fetus from the womb. Usually the fetus is not viable but, as will be seen, that is not always the case. Sometimes, despite the intent to destroy, the fetus, or abortus, is delivered alive, giving rise to "wrongful pregnancy" suits. Because it is described as "deliberate and voluntary," the term "abortion" does not include the spontaneous, premature termination of pregnancy that is known as a miscarriage, even though this is sometimes termed a "spontaneous abortion."

Surgical Methods

At the present time there are two principal surgical methods of procuring an abortion during the first three months of pregnancy, that is, during the first trimester. The first is known as *dilatation and curettage* (D&C) and utilizes a procedure that is also used at times to treat certain female uterine problems. The physician first stretches the mouth of the womb (dilatation) and then introduces a sharp, curved spoon-shaped instrument (curette) into the uterus. With this, the physician cuts the embryo away from the site of implantation and scrapes the inside walls of the uterus. This material is then withdrawn from the womb.

Abortion

Safer than D&C, and hence more commonly used now for first-trimester abortions, is the *suction method* (vacuum aspiration). A suction tube is inserted into the womb and the embryo is pulled away from the wall of the uterus and withdrawn from the womb. Whichever method is used, the embryo is dismembered in the process.

After the twelfth week of gestation, a physician will ordinarily choose to terminate pregnancy by *dilatation and evacuation* (D&E). Although the details of this may vary from one practitioner to another, there are essentially two steps. First, the cervix must be widened and enlarged (dilatation) to facilitate the evacuation of the uterus. Depending on the stage of gestation, a variety of surgical instruments is used to remove the fetus.

The surgeon then inserts an instrument resembling a pair of pliers with teeth. With this tool the abortionist takes hold of fetal tissue within the womb. By twisting the instrument he or she separates that fetal part from the fetus and withdraws it from the uterus. This procedure is repeated until the womb is emptied of the fetus and the placenta. A curette may then be used to clear the uterine wall. A final pass of the suction instrument allows the surgeon to be confident that the uterus is entirely emptied. Obviously the longer the gestation, the more complex the evacuation of the uterus. After fourteen weeks, the fetus must be dismembered and the skull crushed to allow passage through the cervix. Great care must be taken to assure the total evacuation of the uterus.

An alternative procedure for abortions after the first trimester—although no longer in frequent use in this country—is *salt poisoning*. After withdrawing some of the amniotic fluid surrounding the fetus, the physician injects a strong saline solution through the abdominal and uterine walls into the amniotic sac. This strongly corrosive liquid burns the skin of the fetus, giving it the bright red glow that explains why it is sometimes called the "candy apple baby." The fetus also ingests the liquid, goes into convulsions, and usually dies "in utero." Normally, labor begins within twenty-four hours and the fetus is delivered dead, although not always.

Finally, a surgeon may choose to terminate the late pregnancy through a procedure called dilatation and extraction (D&X), the so-called "partial-birth abortion (PBA)." This requires that the physician arrange a breech delivery through the use of forceps. Next, the legs, arms, and torso are withdrawn from the woman's body. While the head still remains in the birth canal, the surgeon punctures the back of the skull with scissors, which are then fully opened. Into this opening a suction curette is inserted and the contents of the skull are emptied, allowing the physician to crush the skull and complete the delivery.[1]

Proponents of this procedure insist that it is necessary to protect the health or life of the mother. Authoritative medical experts such as the AMA and the former surgeon general C. Everett Koop deny this categorically and insist that the procedure is not medically indicated. Indeed, it has now been reported that a majority of partial-birth abortions are elective therapies that involve a healthy mother and a normal fetus. Again in support of the procedure, some sources have argued that it hardly ever takes place ("perhaps five hundred cases annually in this country") and so any opposition to it is clearly an overreaction. Investigation has subsequently established, however, that in New Jersey alone fifteen hundred such procedures occur every year. Clearly, national figures would be considerably higher.

Nonsurgical Methods

Not unexpectedly medical science continues to search for surer and safer methods to procure an abortion as early in the pregnancy as possible. Since 1988 an abortion pill called mifepristone (RU486) has been available to women in a number of European countries. Under the name of mifeprex, it is now available in this country as well and provides a nonsurgical, early-abortion option for American women. Essentially, its action blocks a hormone (progesterone) necessary to support an ongoing pregnancy. Subsequently, the physician administers a prostaglandin, misoprostol, which initiates uterine contractions and, if all goes well, the abortus is then eliminated from the womb, ending the pregnancy.

The individual seeking the abortion must report to her physician within the first seven weeks of pregnancy. On this occasion she is given three tablets of mifeprex, the antiprogesterone which prevents the fertilized egg from developing further. Two days later, the woman must return to the physician to receive two tablets of misoprostol, the drug that induces contractions of the uterus, causing the embryo to be expelled from the woman's body.

To guard against adverse side effects, the woman typically remains for several hours in her doctor's office. She will begin to experience symptoms similar to those occasioned by a miscarriage—cramping and bleeding. The actual abortion may occur during this time. Other side effects may include nausea and vomiting. If the abortion does not occur at this time, the woman returns home and awaits the abortion there.

In either event, the woman is required to return to her physician for a physical examination to determine that the abortion has occurred and to check for any complications. In those cases in which the pill fails to cause the abortion, a surgical removal of the fetus is required. Some conditions, such as cardiac or adrenal disorders, are counter-indicators for the use of this pill.

Proponents of the pill argue that its availability has made abortions more accessible and more private, hence free from interference by anti-abortion activists. Although not entirely free from risk, it avoids the inherent risks of surgery. One disadvantage is that it takes longer to accomplish than a surgical abortion—sometimes as long as ten days before all side effects have subsided. Some medical authorities have expressed serious reservations about the pill since not all patients "will follow up appropriately."

Nonsurgical abortions early in pregnancy have also become available through the use of the drug methotrexate. Officially approved by the FDA as a treatment for certain cancers, arthritis, and other diseases, some abortion providers have begun to use the drug "off-label" to terminate pregnancy. An injection of methotrexate kills the embryo, and a second drug, misoprostol, is administered a week later to cause uterine contractions and evacuate the uterus. This two-step process is thus similar to the procedure for RU486 described above. Quite understandably, while these new nonsurgical procedures will undoubtedly reduce the number of later abortions, it may also reduce public sensitivity to the destruction of fetal life.[2]

Incidence

In the final decade of the twentieth century, there was in excess of one million abortions every year. The numbers (1.4 million) peaked in 1990 and by 1995 had dropped 15 percent (1.2 million), according to the Centers for Disease Control. The ratio of abortions to live births and the rate of abortions per one thousand women also dropped to their lowest levels since 1975.

This trend has continued to the final year of the century and beyond. In 1999, almost 862,000 legal induced abortions were reported to the CDC, reflecting a drop of 2.5 percent over the preceding year. The ratio of legal induced abortions to live births (256/1000) was again the lowest since 1975. The abortion rate for women aged fifteen to forty-four was unchanged from the two preceding years (17/1000). Also unchanged was the higher number of abortions obtained by white women, unmarried women, and women under twenty-five years of age. Almost three-fifths of the reported abortions occurred during the first eight weeks of gestation. Not quite 90 percent were performed during the first trimester.[3] Whether such trends will continue is unclear. Of the million plus abortions annually, no more than 7 percent are due to some threat—either physical or psychological—to the mother's life or health; less than 1 percent involve pregnancies resulting from rape or incest. The vast majority—92 percent—are elected for social, economic, or personal reasons.[4] Suction and D&C accounted for 98 percent of all abortions.

What additional information is available to help us understand the current practice of abortion in this country? Andrew Greeley summarizes some of the data drawn from the National Longitudinal Study of Youth, conducted annually at Ohio State University since 1979:

> By 1988 almost one out of four American women born between 1958 and 1965 had had an abortion. The average age at which abortion occurred was 18.6 years after two years of sexual activity. Nine out of ten of the women were unmarried at the time of their abortion. Half of the abortions occurred among women who were 18 years old or less—presumably high school students. A third of the abortions took place among those who were 17 and younger and a quarter 16 and younger. Three-quarters of them occurred before the woman's 21st birthday.
>
> One out of six women in these age cohorts who described themselves as Catholic in 1979 had had an abortion by 1988. The Catholic rate of 17 percent is lower than the 23 percent rate of other Americans, and the difference is statistically significant.

Religious background does make a difference in whether a
woman has an abortion or not.[5]

Greeley points out, interestingly, that abortion does not correlate
with social class or with an individual's intelligence. Neither does it correlate with age or the experience of sex education. What does make a
difference? Only two factors, race and religion. Thus African American
women are "only three-quarters as likely as whites to report an abortion." In addition, religious affiliation clearly makes a difference. In the
1983 survey, 35 percent of the young Catholic women reported that
they had not yet become sexually active ("were still virgins"; hence,
abortion would not be a decision) in contrast to 27 percent of Protestant
Americans. Religious devotion, as measured by regular church atten-
dance, also is a significant factor: "Of those who attend church regularly,
only about 10 percent have had an abortion, regardless of religion."[6]

Abortion for "Fetal Indications"

Before leaving this consideration of the medical/scientific information related to abortion, some words should be added regarding fetal
testing. One of the grounds that lead to a termination of pregnancy is
an awareness of some genetic defect affecting the fetus. Several later
chapters will treat this question at much greater length; for now, suffice
it to say that an array of testing mechanisms has been developed by
medical science to determine if in fact the fetus is suffering from some
physical defect. The most commonly used are the following:

1. Blood testing is a simple process for detecting some fetal
problems. Analysis of a blood sample permits identification of such
anomalies as sickle-cell anemia, for example.

2. Ultrasound is another way of identifying fetal defects. In this
process, a sonogram is produced by passing sound waves through the
pregnant woman's body. The differing body densities allow the waves
to pass through at different speeds. The sonogram then permits the
detection of such physical conditions as anencephaly or spina bifida.

3. In addition, amniocentesis is an effective means of detecting
genetic disorders in a fetus. The amnion is the membrane forming a
sac around the embryo. Through this procedure, a needle is used to

penetrate this sac and to withdraw fluid and sloughed-off cells. These are then grown in a culture and examined for genetic anomalies.

Although not all the physiological causes of genetic defects can be detected or identified, science has been increasingly successful in diagnosing the presence of genetic flaws. Amniocentesis, however, cannot be employed before the second trimester (fourteen to sixteen weeks), and it may take an additional two to six weeks for the culture to grow sufficiently for an analysis. As a result, the procedure can reveal genetic difficulties only fairly late in pregnancy.

4. Finally, chorion-villi testing has been developed to remedy some of the deficiencies of amniocentesis. The chorion is also a membrane, external to and enclosing the amnion and the embryo. Villi are small fingerlike processes of the chorion. The procedure requires first that a catheter be inserted into the uterus; then guided by ultrasound, this device removes a small amount of chorionic-villi tissue. This sample is then analyzed to detect genetic flaws. Although the chorion-villi sample is not part of the fetus, it does contain fetal tissue. CV sampling is done within the eighth to twelfth week of gestation (usually during the ninth to tenth week) and preliminary results are available in a day or two; final analysis takes fourteen days. Since it is not necessary to wait for second-trimester fetal development to use this procedure and since there is no need to grow a culture, the genetic diagnosis is available much earlier in pregnancy.

Both amniocentesis and chorion-villi testing do carry some risk for the pregnancy, however. In 2000 the risk of miscarriage for amniocentesis was judged to be .5 percent or less. Chorionic-villi sampling carried a somewhat greater (1 percent) chance that the pregnancy would be lost. CV sampling can detect genetic abnormalities, including chromosomal, metabolic, and blood-borne conditions. It does not reveal neural tube defects such as spina bifida or anencephaly. A blood serum test in the sixteenth week can compensate for that.

Preimplantation Genetic Diagnosis

Is there no way, then, to escape the trauma of pregnancy where a possible genetic defect takes away the joy of carrying a new life? No way for a couple to avoid the risk of amniocentesis and the subsequent termination of pregnancy when evidence of a genetic disease is discovered in the fetus? Yes, there is. It is called Preimplantation Genetic Diagnosis (PGD).

This procedure begins with a cycle of in vitro fertilization, since it is necessary to screen the zygotes before they are inserted into the woman's uterus prior to implantation. A couple will choose this option, typically, when one or both of them has been genetically screened and discovered to be a carrier or affected by a late-onset genetic disease (e.g., Huntington's disease). As each zygote produced through IVF reaches the 8-cell stage (blastocyst), each cell is separated and screened for one or more genetic anomalies. Those found to contain the flawed gene are then destroyed, while those that are free from any abnormality are implanted into the woman's womb.

PGD was first used successfully in 1989, and by 1997 thirty such babies had been born worldwide. At the present time, testing is available for approximately thirty X-linked or single-gene disorders as well as for chromosomal anomalies, such as Down syndrome. Without denying the medical and financial advantages of this means of eliminating potentially diseased individuals, some critics are asking if this is not the start down the "slippery slope." Will we also, they ask, eliminate embryos with a predisposition for cardiac disease or cancer? Will the procedure be used for gender selection, perhaps, or to eliminate an unacceptable sexual orientation?[7]

While a full discussion of both IVF and genetic screening must wait until subsequent chapters, PGD was introduced here because the destruction of the defective zygotes is morally equivalent to the elimination of the unborn conceptus through any other method of abortion. But whatever medical procedure is used and whatever its concrete outcome, another dimension of abortion that must be appreciated is its legal character.

THE LEGAL DIMENSION

Criminalization of Abortion

The criminalization of abortion in this country has a long history. Although Connecticut adopted the first criminal anti-abortion statute in 1821, it was not until the middle of the last century that anti-abortion legislation became generalized.[8] Typically these statutes permitted abortion only when the mother's life was in danger. Gradually, however, the grounds for allowing pregnancy to be terminated prematurely were expanded. For example, therapeutic abortion was allowed in some jurisdictions whenever the physical or mental health of the mother was gravely threatened. By the time the Supreme Court issued its historical decision in 1973, fourteen states had accepted this view.

Abortion to terminate pregnancy resulting from rape or incest and abortion for fetal indications are two other situations that some jurisdictions came to accept. Some states, in fact, decriminalized abortion altogether until viability was reached—but not Texas, however, and it was the Texas abortion statute that was at issue in the *Roe* v. *Wade* decision.

Roe v. *Wade*

In January 1973, by a vote of seven to two, the Supreme Court ruled that the Texas statute, and by extension many other similar laws in other jurisdictions, was in violation of the United States Constitution and its Bill of Rights. The Court judged that the law in question was violative of the mother's right to privacy, which it found to be included among those guaranteed by—although not explicitly named in—the Bill of Rights. This decision established the *national public policy* regarding abortion.

In its statement of its decision, the Court set out the following conditions, which it made binding and applicable to all state abortion statutes:

1. *First Trimester*—A physician may freely perform an abortion requested by a woman for any reason. Any attempt by the state to limit this right of the patient and doctor will be unconstitutional.
2. *After the First Trimester*—A woman has the same right to an abortion as in the first trimester. A state may make only such regulations as are reasonably related "to maternal health." Thus, for example, it may require that an abortion be performed only in a clinic or on an inpatient basis in a hospital, or it may specify the type of physician who can perform the operation.

3. *After Viability*—The state may prohibit abortions once the fetus is deemed capable of "meaningful life outside of the womb" [i.e., viability], except "where it is necessary…for the preservation of the life or health of the mother." On the other hand, the state may allow abortions as freely after viability as before that stage of development.

It is important to note that the question of viability is a medical issue, that is, it is up to medical science to determine when "meaningful life outside the womb" is possible. The point in pregnancy when this moment is reached has been advancing as scientific progress is made.

After Roe v. *Wade*

As various states sought to incorporate the Supreme Court's conditions into their abortion statutes in the years following *Roe-Wade,* a series of decisions followed in the lower courts, as well as in the Supreme Court, that helped clarify and develop the implications of that first historic decision.

Thus in 1976, the Supreme Court issued its judgment in *Planned Parenthood of Central Missouri* v. *Danforth.* This decision invalidated a Missouri statute giving the father of the fetus a veto power in first-trimester abortions. Similarly, it ruled out the requirement that the parents of minor females must also give consent in all first-trimester abortions that were not life-threatening for the mother. Thus the Court ruled out the right of any third party to participate in the abortion decision.

Another crucial decision was reached a year later (1977) in *Beal* v. *Doe.* The high court ruled that those states that participate in the federal Medicaid program were not required to provide funding for nontherapeutic abortions under the Social Security Act. In other words, though there was a constitutional right to an abortion, there was no right guaranteeing funding for such an intervention.

The provision in *Roe* v. *Wade* that will continue to attract great interest, however, is that which recognizes an important state interest in the potential life of the fetus. In the view of the Court this interest can become compelling when the fetus becomes viable, and thus a state can proscribe abortion altogether after viability, except "when the life or health of the mother is at risk." At the present time, advances in medical technology are pushing viability earlier and earlier into a woman's pregnancy, making neonatal survival possible at twenty-four weeks and earlier. At the same time, prenatal screening for genetic indications offers more and more bases for late second-trimester abortions. The trimesters, it would seem, are on a collision course, and no one can say how this conflict will eventually be decided.[9] The legal questions are numerous, as has been noted:

> If a duty to care for viable fetuses does exist, what are its dimensions? How much care must a fetus receive? Who will pay for it? Who is to provide informed consent to the fetus's medical care? What claims may the fetus make against its parents? Against others?[10]

Thornburgh

On June 11, 1986, the Supreme Court addressed some of these issues in *Thornburgh* v. *American College of Obstetricians and Gynecologists.* The Pennsylvania Abortion Control Act, which was the object of the Court's review, was found to be unconstitutional in a number of its provisions. By a five-to-four vote the Court rejected the requirements:

1. That a woman contemplating abortion be given information regarding such matters as possible risks of the abortion, the probable age of the fetus, and the fact that medical assistance may be available to her should she continue the pregnancy.
2. That a report be filed on each abortion indicating the performing and referring physicians; the woman's age, race, marital status, and number of prior pregnancies; the date of her last menstrual period; the probable gestational age of the conceptus; and a number of other items of information.
3. That in a post-viability abortion a second physician be present and the technique be used that provides "the best opportunity for the unborn child to be aborted alive."

These provisions relating to informed consent, state regulation of the medical profession, and the state's interest in viable fetal life were reviewed by the Court and were judged unconstitutional because they appeared to "intimidate women into continuing pregnancies" and would have a chilling effect on "the exercise of constitutional rights," in the view of Justice Blackmun, who wrote the majority opinion.[11]

Webster

On July 3, 1989, Chief Justice Rehnquist delivered the first of the five opinions that formed the Supreme Court's response to the case of *Webster* v. *Reproductive Health Services*. At issue was the statute signed into law in the state of Missouri but in large measure rejected by both district and appeals courts. In its preamble, the law declared that human life begins at conception. It then banned abortions at public hospitals except when a mother's life is at stake and prohibited use of public funds in abortion counseling. The case provided an opportunity for the first Bush administration to petition the court to overturn *Roe* v. *Wade*.

The *Webster* decision of the Court:

1. Bypassed the question of the principle embraced in the preamble as untimely since it was a purely "abstract proposition" at the time of the decision.
2. Upheld "the act's restrictions on the use of public employees and facilities for the performance or assistance of nontherapeutic abortions."
3. Ruled that the denial of public funding for abortion counseling was not at issue since the appellees withdrew their objection.
4. Sustained the constitutionality of viability-testing provisions of the act, which were "designed to ensure that abortions are not performed where the fetus is viable—an end which all concede is legitimate."
5. Rejected the petition that *Roe* v. *Wade* be overturned since the Missouri statute was judged not to afford an occasion for reopening that decision. Not all of the justices agreed on this point, however.[12]

Casey [60 U.S. 4795 (1992)]

On June 29, 1992, the Court published a major decision in its evolving treatment of the question of abortion, *Planned Parenthood of Southeastern Pennsylvania* v. *Casey*. This time it was once again the Pennsylvania Abortion Control Act of 1982, but now as amended in 1988 and 1989. Again the first Bush administration petitioned the Court to overturn *Roe* v. *Wade* (the fifth time in a decade that an administration had submitted such a request, as the Court itself noted). Speaking for the majority, Justices O'Connor, Kennedy, and Souter delivered the opinion which:

1. Ruled that a woman's constitutional liberty to have some freedom to terminate her pregnancy is not so "unlimited, however, that from the outset the state cannot show its concern for the life of the unborn." Thus *Casey* departed from *Roe's* limiting of a state's interest to post-viability pregnancies.
2. Refused to overrule its 1973 *Roe* v. *Wade* decision (5–4).
3. Affirmed a state's right to "enact abortion regulations that do not pose an 'undue burden'" on a woman seeking an abortion. An "undue burden" was defined by the court as one that intends or causes a substantial obstacle for a woman seeking to terminate her pregnancy.
4. Upheld provisions in the act requiring that a woman give informed consent when seeking an abortion and be provided with state-determined information at least twenty-four hours prior to the abortion. This information may reflect a state's preference for childbirth over abortion; thus in a distinct departure from *Roe*, *Casey* did not require the state to be neutral prior to viability. It does require, however, that a woman visit the clinic or hospital twice.
5. Accepted the provision that an unemancipated minor have the informed consent of one parent to the abortion, unless a "judicial bypass" is obtained.
6. Upheld "reporting and record-keeping requirements for facilities providing abortion."
7. Rejected the requirement that "a wife notify her husband of her abortion intent."[13]

Thus in the minds of some, *Casey* departs significantly from both the spirit and the substance of *Roe*. Further, in this view it makes abortion more difficult for many women—particularly those who are young, poor, rural, or women of color. Finally, these critics insist that this decision will reduce the number of facilities and of physicians available to perform abortions.[14]

The *Casey* decision is significant for several reasons beyond the approval of these ancillary aspects of the abortion issue. First of all, the Court reaffirmed *Roe* v. *Wade* at a time when many legal observers were predicting its demise. Additionally, the Court clearly affirmed its authority to define

> fundamental unenumerated liberty rights through "reasoned judgment" in interpreting the liberty clause of the Fourteenth Amendment. Recognizing that basic rights of "liberty"—the joint opinion never mentions "privacy"—are not confined to those rights mentioned in the Bill of Rights nor those specifically recognized by past traditions, it drew upon past cases recognizing rights to bodily integrity and "a person's most basic decisions about family and parenthood." If past decisions protect personal decisions "relating to marriage, procreation, contraception, family relationships, childbearing and education," then a woman must also have a basic right to terminate pregnancy, because it is a central aspect of that protected sphere of decision making. Because nothing had occurred since Roe to cast doubt on the validity of these underlying precedents, the principle of *stare decisis* and respect for the Court's legitimacy required adherence to the basic right recognized in Roe.[15]

Further, the Court reaffirmed that the state had "an important and legitimate interest in potential life," which could outweigh the mother's right to terminate pregnancy after viability—roughly at the twenty-fourth week of pregnancy. Prior to viability, priority had to be granted to the mother, who had the right to "define [her] own concept of existence, of meaning of the universe, and of the mystery of human life." Finally, the Court rejected the trimester framework established by *Roe* for evaluating abortion restrictions. Instead it judged that state regulations that are "thoughtful and informed" were acceptable at any point during pregnancy provided they do not inflict an "undue burden" or interpose a "substantial obstacle" to a woman's access to abortion.[16]

Stenberg v. *Carhart* (99–830) 530 U.S. 914 (2000)

So what has happened since the *Casey* decision in 1992? Interestingly, proponents of the pro-life position have developed a new strategy. One important finding of the *Casey* opinion of the Court was that state legislatures could enact statutes that would restrict abortion so long as these imposed no "undue burden" on the woman's decision. The Congress, not the states, was the first to take advantage of the opening provided by *Casey* and so in 1996 by a large majority passed the first nationwide ban on partial-birth abortion. President Clinton promptly vetoed the bill. The House of Representatives voted to override the president's veto, but the necessary votes were lacking in the Senate and so the act was prevented from becoming law. The following year, the Congress—both the House and the Senate—approved a slightly revised version of the same bill. The White House repeated its rejection of the Congress's action, and once again (1998) the veto was overridden by the House but sustained in the Senate. A third attempt by the Congress to ban PBA occurred in 1999–2000 when it reenacted the 1997 statute. This time, however, the congressional session ended and so the bill died without the need of a presidential veto.

It has fallen to state legislatures, therefore, to challenge the appropriateness of this abortion procedure. By late 1997, seventeen states had passed such legislation, while eight of these had been blocked by lower court decisions. The Ohio statute was the first to reach the appellate level and was subsequently struck down by the Sixth Circuit Court of Appeals. This decision was allowed to stand by the Supreme Court in March 1998, without the Court's ruling on the merits of the issue.

While in almost every case, statutes originating at the state level died either at the local or the appellate level, one finally reached the Supreme Court. A prohibition of PBA arising from the Nebraska legislature was accepted by the Court for its review, the first substantive challenge to abortion to reach the Court since *Casey*. On June 28, 2000, the Supreme Court issued its decision (*Stenberg* v. *Carhart*). By a 5-4 vote the Court rejected the Nebraska ban on PBA, because in the view of the Court the statutory language might be interpreted to also prohibit the D&E procedure and because the statute contained no health exception but only considered a risk to the life of the mother. The Nebraska statute was declared unconstitutional. Based on the opinion of the Court delivered by Justice Stephen Breyer, it would appear that the *amicus curiae* brief of the American College of Obstetricians and Gynecologists weighed heavily in the Court's conclusion that "D & X may be safer than available alternatives."

The failure to provide a health exception raised a sticky issue. Pro-life supporters have traditionally resisted the inclusion of such an exception since in their view the broad and often flimsy interpretations of "health" issued since *Roe* v. *Wade* would eviscerate any statute restricting abortion. Equally adamant in favor of the exception are the pro-choice partisans who insist that the lack of a health exception will render any statute unconstitutional, based on *Casey*. Undoubtedly, the last word has not yet been spoken.

THE SOCIOCULTURAL DIMENSION

All of our decisions are made in the context of the society and the culture in which we live. This would include our family, our circle of friends, the business community in which we earn our living, our church, our neighborhood, the media—the list could be extended on and on but the point is too obvious already. All of our choices are complicated, that is, made complex, because of the multiple influences that are part of our daily experience. Our choice of moral values is no exception. These must somehow fit into the total matrix of values that we have embraced and that constitute our personal value system. Sometimes the value involved in a particular moral choice is supported by other values that are part of our system; at other times they must compete with one another. For example, a young woman may have great respect and appreciation for life—her own, her family's, her friends'—but when the life of her fetus threatens to interrupt her college education or her career, then she may very well decide that the life of the fetus is less important to her (a lesser value) than completing her college degree.

In any event, social institutions surely influence our appreciation of values. Take, for example, the influence of the law on our attitudes about abortion. It is sometimes argued that the influence of the Court on public attitudes and behavior is inconsequential; thus it is maintained that the current mores of the American people are what determine the court's position in matters moral or ethical. Without denying that such an influence does in fact exist, this in no way excludes the impact of the philosophy underlying the Court's decisions on public morals and behavior. For over two decades the courts have been telling the American people that the decision to engage in sexual activity is a private matter, a fundamental right of each individual, to be exercised apart from any governmental interference or intrusion. So too is the decision to reproduce and the decision to carry a child so conceived to term. The message has not gone unheard, surely. It seems impossible to suppose that such a message has had no influence on America's sexual mores. While the Court does not deserve all of the credit or the blame for the general relaxation of sexual restraint in this country, it seems naive to say it has had no effect at all.

What sociocultural influences, then, what societal values or attitudes play a significant role in the question of abortion? While a full discussion of these cannot be presented here, some understanding of their impact may be helpful.[17]

Human Sexuality: What does the contemporary scene say to us about sexual activity and its accompanying pleasure? Does one have any responsibility for the consequences? Is there evidence that we have trivialized sexual expression? What effect has the separation of sexual activity from a permanent, covenanted relationship had on the issue of childbearing? The answers to these questions have greatly influenced our outlook on abortion.

While in the view of many the prevalence of abortion is a renunciation of sexual responsibility, it is not suggested that contemporary American society is without any vision of sexual responsibility. In this context, Lisa Sowle Cahill has commented:

> Cultural standards of sexual responsibility include consent, communication, respect, honesty, well-deliberated choice about conception and birth, and health (including optimal sexual function and the avoidance of sexually transmitted diseases). There is also in evidence a desire, if not a moral demand, to find personal meaning and fulfillment in committed long-term sexual relationships. These are all values and provide at least the basis for a sexual discipline that assumes sexual equality. But the values neglected in this ethic are parenthood and real permanency, both of which call for realism, flexibility, sacrifice and hard work, as well as a talent for knowing when to compromise.[18]

Privacy: At the present time, many Americans are convinced that no one other than the individual himself/herself has any legitimate interest in the exercise of sexuality or in any life that may be conceived from this activity; it is an utterly private affair. In this context, the decision to reproduce or to terminate pregnancy is solely the mother's. Clearly this fairly general conviction plays a significant part in the abortion debate.

Interventionist Mentality: In its simplest form, this view suggests that whatever is possible for technology to do is good. Apply this philosophy to human problems and the response is to eliminate them. Rather than modify the environment or urge compassion, society often prefers to eliminate or at least hide human "failures" such as children with physical or developmental disabilities or the senile elderly. Hence, if the unborn fetus causes problems, eliminate it, since the technology is readily available.

Utilitarian Outlook: This philosophy proposes that results are what count; what works is good. Apply this to the way society looks on human beings and a highly functional concept of the human person results, with a great loss of the sense of the inherent value or dignity of the individual. Concretely, the influence of such a view can be traced in such different areas as medical experimentation, military strategy, government budget cutting, and reproductive technology. Hence, if the pregnancy at this time "doesn't work," is not useful, then terminate it.

Influence of the Media: The more frequently one is exposed to suffering and deprivation in the media (and not in concrete experience), the more likely one is to end up getting used to it, thus blunting moral attitudes and sensitivities. For example, it becomes harder to get upset about a single abortion when we read that a million are being performed each year.

Society's attitudes, therefore, are influenced by these and other factors. What do Americans think about abortion at the present time? Thirty years have passed since 1973's *Roe v. Wade.* What has changed? First of all, consider the number of abortions recorded. In 1968, 18,000 legal abortions were reported. In 1973, the number rose to almost 745,000. By 1993, that figure had almost doubled to 1,495,000. Over the final decade of the twentieth century, the numbers began to decline each year, so that in 2000, 1,313,000 were reported.

What are the opinions of Americans with respect to abortion? In their May 2003 survey, Gallup pollsters reported that two-thirds of Americans believed that abortion was morally wrong, which reflected a significant shift from survey results two years earlier when 45 percent of Americans agreed with that view. Despite this conviction, however, almost 60 percent believe that the abortion decision should be left up to the woman and her doctor. Yet even here this view breaks down so that only slightly more than one-quarter of survey respondents believe abortion should be legal in all circumstances. In 2001 a Gallup poll reported in the *New York Times*[19] indicated that the number of Americans who considered themselves pro-life rose from 33 to 43 percent during the previous five years. At the same time, the pro-choice adherents declined from 56 to 48 percent.

A *USA Today*/CNN/Gallup poll suggests that most Americans take a pro-life position even though they do not always describe themselves as pro-life. Of those polled, 16 percent position themselves at one end of the spectrum endorsing a legal ban on all abortions, while 55 percent would limit the legality of abortion to extreme situations such as rape or incest, or to save the life of the mother. This translates into 71 percent of all Americans rejecting the vast majority (97 percent) of all abortions performed in the U.S.[20]

American ambivalence toward abortion clearly reflects itself in these conflicting data, showing that American society greatly values both the sanctity of life and women's individual autonomy in arriving at a reproductive decision. While a pro-life viewpoint seems to be gaining ground, there is no doubt that the two sides guarantee a lively debate for the foreseeable future.

THE TEACHING OF THE ROMAN CATHOLIC CHURCH

Introduction

Even though the documents cited below are recent expressions of the magisterium (i.e., the teaching authority) of the Roman Catholic Church on the matter of abortion, this teaching is rooted in the church's earliest and consistent evaluation of human life. This grew organically from the church's roots in its Jewish origins. Within Judaism all human life was regarded as God-given, even fetal life. It was the creator who called each individual to a personal relationship

74

from the womb. All stand as equals before their creator, therefore, the unborn as well as all others, even though formal membership in the people of Yahweh remained to be enacted ceremonially after birth through circumcision. Thus the Jews, and the Christians who followed them, rejected the pagan practice of abortion and infanticide as irreligious (i.e., a direct insult to God), rather than simply inhumane. Life was sacred, because it was a gift of God.

This rejection of abortion by the Christian faith community was expressed in the church from the time of the fathers of the apostolic period—for example, in the *Didache,* an early book of church discipline—and consistently thereafter. The language would change as the scientific understanding of human reproduction evolved, but the basic Christian conviction would never falter:

> The value of human life…was seen in God's special and costing love for each individual—for fetal life, infant life, senescent life, disabled life, captive life, enslaved life, yes, and most of all, unwanted life. These evaluations can be and have been shared by others than Christians, of course. But Christians have particular warrants for resisting any cultural callousing of them.[21]

Pope Pius XII—1951 Address to Midwives

> Innocent human life, in whatsoever condition it is found, is withdrawn, from the very first moment of its existence, from any direct deliberate attack. This is a fundamental right of the human person, which is of general value in the Christian conception of life; hence as valid for the life still hidden within the womb of the mother, as for the life already born and developing outside of her; as much opposed to direct abortion as to the direct killing of the child before, during or after its birth. Whatever foundation there may be for the distinction between these various phases of the development of life that is born or still unborn, in profane or ecclesiastical law, and as regards certain civil and penal consequences, all these cases involve a grave and unlawful attack upon the inviolability of human life.[22]

Vatican II—1965—The Church in the Modern World
(Gaudium et Spes)

> For God, the Lord of life, has conferred on men the surpassing
> ministry of safeguarding life—a ministry which must be fulfilled
> in a manner which is worthy of man. Therefore from the
> moment of its conception life must be guarded with the utmost
> care, while abortion and infanticide are unspeakable crimes.[23]

Pope Paul VI—1968—Of Human Life *(Humanae Vitae)*

> Therefore we base our words on the first principles of a human
> and Christian doctrine when we are obliged once more to declare
> that...above all, direct abortion, even for therapeutic reasons, [is]
> to be absolutely excluded as lawful means of controlling the birth
> of children.[24]

Declaration on Procured Abortion—Congregation for the Doctrine of the Faith *(Quaestio de Abortu)*—November 18, 1974

> 11. The first right of the human person is his life. He has other
> goods and some are more precious, but this one is fundamental—
> the condition of all the others. It does not belong to society, nor
> does it belong to public authority in any form to recognize this
> right for some and not for others: all discrimination is evil,
> whether it be founded on race, sex, color or religion. It is not
> recognition by another that constitutes this right. This right is
> antecedent to its recognition; it demands recognition and it is
> strictly unjust to refuse it.
>
> 12. The right to life is no less to be respected in the small
> infant just born than in the mature person. In reality, respect for
> human life is called for from the time that the process of gener-
> ation begins. From the time that the ovum is fertilized, a life is
> begun which is neither that of the father nor of the mother; it is
> rather the life of a new human being with his own growth. It
> would never be made human if it were not human already.

13. This has always been clear, and discussions about the moment of animation have no bearing on it....[25]

Some Reflections on the Teaching

The abortion debate raises several issues that need to be clarified early on. The issue cannot be resolved by appealing to the notion of person and affirming or denying personhood of the fetus. "Person" is a philosophical or legal concept that one tends to define according to one's purposes. It is not possible scientifically to verify or to disprove whether the fetus is or is not a person, that is, when the moment of humanization has occurred. Rather, the fundamental issue is *how one evaluates fetal life*, what value one places on nascent, human life—for the fetus is surely living and certainly human.[26] Then, secondly, one must somehow balance that value with the competing rights of the mother.

As the debate has evolved since *Roe* v. *Wade*, the Catholic Church's argument has gradually moved away from an outlook that was based primarily on God's "ownership" of the human person and the question of the time of ensoulment. Even though many believe that the Catholic Church insists that the human soul is present from the first moment of conception, the fact is that it does not. It is an open question and theologians continue to discuss and debate the matter. In place of these issues, however, contemporary emphasis has been placed on the human character of the fetal life as established by the empirical life sciences. Thus it is asserted:

1. Genotypically, biological science affirms that the fetus is a human being since the fetus possesses the essential quality of human life; that from conception the zygote has a unique genetic code established in its DNA structure which is both determinative and complete. Additionally, there is no scientific basis that the fetus passes through subhuman stages before qualifying as human.
2. Phenotypically, also, the fetus is a human being since it is not part of the mother but distinct with "separate circulations, neither contiguous nor continuous."
3. Thus fetal life is surely "life belonging to the human species"; left to itself, although dependent on the mother, it "can only become a live human being or a dead fetus." Its individuality is evident in its

77

"functional independence, genetic self-determination and biological continuity from the moment of conception."[27]

Obviously, not all parties in the abortion debate assess the value of fetal life in the same way. Clearly, there are those who insist that it is merely maternal tissue, able to be excised just as an infected appendix or any other dysfunctional or unwanted part of the mother's body. At the opposite end of the spectrum are those who maintain that nascent life must be carefully guarded in all situations, with few or no exceptions. In this view it is an almost absolute value. In between are those who recognize the fetus as human life with a clear claim to protection. That claim, however, can be superseded by many other values that relate to the mother, to the fetus, or to the family.

The Classical Christian Teaching

In summarizing what he believed to be the "classical Christian teaching," prominent Jesuit ethicist Richard McCormick set forth the following basic principles:

1. Human life as a basic gift and good, the foundation for the enjoyment of all other goods, may be taken only when doing so is the only life-saving and life-serving alternative, or only when doing so is, all things considered (not just numbers), the lesser evil.
2. By "human life" I mean human life from fertilization or at least from the time at or after which it is settled whether there will be one or two distinct human beings. It is known from embryology that twinning and recombination can occur only during the first two weeks after fertilization.
3. For an act to be life-saving and life-serving, to be the lesser evil (all things considered) there must be at stake human life or its moral equivalent, a good or value comparable to life itself.[28]

Moral Evaluation

1. Moral choices are choices about moral values. Where values are in conflict, the individual is called upon to choose the greater good, the higher value. The traditional Christian insight has been that the life of the fetus is an "almost absolute value." To choose

another value—the avoidance of embarrassment, a career, even the elimination of a severely defective fetus—would be to fail to choose the higher good. The only exception, in McCormick's view, would be when the competing value would be another "human life [the mother's] or its moral equivalent." To analyze the situation another way, this dilemma is a classic example of having to choose between two evils. When one must decide between two courses of action and both alternatives are disvalues or "evils," it is morally correct to choose the lesser evil.

2. Although McCormick believed that his summary, while not identical with the official Catholic view, was faithful to the historical conviction of the Christian faith community, it should be said that it offers an outlook that recommends itself to members of other faiths and to those of no particular faith. One of the basic difficulties for those who accept abortion is to limit the sanctity of human life to extrauterine life. Many arguments put forward in support of abortion would seem equally applicable as a justification for infanticide, for instance. The viewpoint described above, therefore, should not be viewed as a singularly Catholic or even Christian outlook.

3. In order to sort out the abortion question reasonably, it is essential to distinguish two separate—although related—issues. One is the matter of free choice. Is a woman free to interrupt pregnancy already in progress and terminate the life of the fetus? At any time and for any reason? If the answer is "yes," can any external authority—the state specifically—override this right because of its recognized, legitimate interest in preserving human life, or even potential life? These are the questions addressed by the Supreme Court in its decisions stretching over more than three decades. Basically its present answer has been that a woman's fundamental right to abort is guaranteed by the Fourteenth Amendment to the Constitution. In the view of the Court, this right is not absolute, however, and may be legitimately restricted by a state, whether before or after viability, when it exercises its legitimate interest in protecting human life or at any time when its regulations are neither unduly burdensome nor impose a serious obstacle ("undue burden") to a woman's access to abortion. The woman has the legal right to choose, but in the words of the *Casey* decision, that right is not absolute.

Good Care, Painful Choices

The second matter is the issue of the moral character of the woman's free choice. Even though she may be legally free to choose abortion, a woman's free choice is not necessarily a moral choice. Morality is much more complicated a question than simply being free to act, for it introduces the matter of values. It is important to point out that the woman's freedom to choose is never the value that leads her to elect to terminate her pregnancy. Hence, in the concrete situation, it is never the right to choose versus the life of the fetus. No woman ever chooses to have an abortion simply because she has the legal right to choose. She always elects termination of pregnancy for the value reflected in her motive—her career, her education, her unwillingness to marry the baby's father, her economic situation. That's the value that must be weighed against the value of the fetus.

Does the woman, then, choose the abortion for some trivial—insignificant—ephemeral value? For a value clearly less than the value of the fetus? Then her choice cannot—at least objectively speaking—be moral, even though free. A free choice does not of itself guarantee a moral choice. Is her choice of abortion in view of some value at least as weighty as the life of the fetus—her own life, for example? Then, at least in the view of some theologians, her free choice may also be a moral choice. Once her decision is directed to a value less than life itself, however, her action can no longer be judged objectively moral.

4. To see the pro-life/pro-choice debate as a conflict between two mutually exclusive positions is a serious misreading of the issues involved. It is unfortunately an error that tempts both sides in this controversy. It is an error because the value of a human life and the value of freedom of choice must not be pitted against each other in an either/or fashion. Thus we must not lose sight of the fact that a woman's freedom to embrace childbearing, to assume parenthood, is without doubt a value of great importance—to women, obviously, but to society at large as well. Unfortunately it is not a reality for many women today—not only in third-world cultures and in underdeveloped societies, but also in the highly developed, industrialized West. Often women simply are not free when it comes to choosing pregnancy and childbearing—and this clearly is an injustice.

Abortion

As Lisa Sowle Cahill has commented:

> Abortion is not an issue only of killing, but also of women's equality. Women's ability to act as full moral persons is contingent on their ability to refuse the consequences of male sexual domination (and violence)....The abortion rights platform is envisioned by its defenders, not as primarily about the approval of killing, but about women's self-determination.[29]

Certainly women's status in contemporary American society is not one of equality with men. According to the Children's Defense Fund, every day in America more than 3,500 children are born to unmarried mothers and 60 percent of these are born into poverty—a sign that women may not be so fully in charge of their reproductive choices.[30]

5. Having said all this, however, it is clear that many problems remain in the way we sort out the abortion question. The particularly difficult question of pregnancy resulting from rape or incest is especially nagging—how to weigh the proportion between the life of the fetus and freedom from a pregnancy resulting from such an act of physical and psychological violence.

6. Another problem arises in the matter of abortion laws and the public funding of abortion. What attitude may/must a Catholic legislator or political figure have toward these issues? If public funding for abortion is denied, the argument goes, it will be the poor who must bear the children they do not want. If funding is assured, then those who believe abortion is murder must support it through their taxes. These are all questions that will continue to press us as a people for some solution. The experience of public figures such as Mario Cuomo and Geraldine Ferraro indicates that the American public—and not simply the members of the Catholic hierarchy—are intensely interested in their responses to these dilemmas. As has been observed in almost every presidential election since the time of Richard Nixon, the right of the president to nominate justices to the United States Supreme Court will be tested by the Senate based on the nominee's position on *Roe* v. *Wade*.[31]

STUDY QUESTIONS

1. Explain the meaning of abortion (as understood in this chapter). How does it differ from a miscarriage?
2. What are the principal methods of effecting an abortion at the present time in the United States? What factors determine the use of one method rather than another?
3. What is the present national public policy in this country regarding abortion? Explain its historical origins.
4. Trace the legal history of abortion between 1973 and 1992.
5. It will be difficult to achieve a national consensus regarding abortion until we reach a more general agreement about certain societal values. Explain.
6. This chapter maintains that a woman's reproductive freedom, although of great worth and importance, is not the central ethical issue in the abortion debate. Explain why this is asserted and what is the central ethical issue.
7. Explain Richard McCormick's "classical Christian teaching" that deals with the abortion question.
8. What scientific arguments can be advanced in support of the human character of fetal life?

NOTES

1. A partial breech delivery is not considered a "birth" according to the common law, where it is the passage of the head that is essential. *Partial birth abortion laws*—see members.aol.com.

2. Lisa Sowle Cahill, "Abortion Pill," *Hastings Center Report,* October/November 1987, 5–8. Cf. also *Bioethics Reporter,* vol. 1, 1985, 515.

3. Centers for Disease Control. *Morbidity and Mortality Weekly Report,* vol. 51. November 29, 2002, SS-9. Also see www.cdc.gov.

4. Rachel Benson Gold, *Abortion and Women's Health.* New York and Washington: The Alan Guttmacher Institute, 1990, 11.

5. "The Abortion Debate and the Catholic Subculture," *America,* July 4, 1992, 13.

6. Ibid., 14.

7. Edgar Dahl, "Ethical Issues in New Uses of Preimplantation Genetic Diagnosis," *Human Reproduction* 18, 7 (2003): 1368–69. See www.genetics-and-society.org/resources/items/20030601_humrepro-dahl.html.

8. Walter Wadlington, Jon R. Waltz, and Roger B. Dworkin, *Law and Medicine.* Mineola: The Foundation Press, 1980, 707.

9. Ibid., 747.

10. Ibid., 750. Cf. also Thomas M. Shannon and Allan B. Wolter, "Reflections on the Moral Status of the Pre-Embryo," *Theological Studies,* December 1990, 603–26.

11. *Origins* 16:6, June 26, 1986.

12. *Origins* 19:9, July 13, 1989.

13. *Origins* 22:8, July 9, 1992.

14. At the present time, approximately twenty-two states have enacted parental consent legislation in the case of abortions sought by minor females. The Congress is currently considering legislation that would make it a federal offense to assist a minor female to cross state lines to avoid seeking parental consent. Cf. also Janet Benshoof, *"Planned Parenthood* v. *Casey,"* *JAMA* 269:17 (May 5, 1993): 2249–57. For changes in the availability of abortion, cf. "Abortion: the untold story" in *U.S. News & World Report,* December 7, 1998, which maintains that "despite the violence and the rhetoric, women who choose still have access."

15. John A. Robertson. "*Casey* and the Resuscitation of *Roe* v. *Wade,*" *Hastings Center Report,* September/October 1992, 25.

16. Cf. also June O'Connor. "The Summer of Our Discontent," *Hastings Center Report,* September/October 1992, 28–29.

17. For a fuller discussion, cf. Richard A. McCormick, S.J., "Abortion: A Changing Morality and Policy?" *Health Progress,* February 1979. Found in Thomas Shannon, ed., *Bioethics.* Mahwah, N.J.: Paulist Press, 1981, 25–43.

18. "Abortion, Sex and Gender: The Church's Public Voice," *America,* May 22, 1993, 10.

19. *New York Times,* January 21, 2001.

20. See www.abortioninfo.net/facts/people1.shtml.

21. Cf. note 17, 34.

22. Pius XII, "Address to Midwives," 1951.

23. *Gaudium et Spes,* in *The Documents of Vatican II,* Walter M. Abbott, S.J., ed. New York: Herder and Herder, 1966, n. 51, 256.

24. *Humanae Vitae,* in *Vatican Council II: More Post-Conciliar Documents,* vol. 2, Austin Flannery, O.P., ed. Northport: Costello Publishing Co., 1982, n. 14, 404.

25. Sacred Congregation for the Doctrine of the Faith, *Declaration on Procured Abortion,* in *Vatican Council II: More Post-Conciliar Documents,* vol. 2, Austin Flannery, O.P., ed. Northport: Costello Publishing Co., nn. 11–13, 445. This same condemnation has been renewed in his 1995 encyclical, *Evangelium Vitae,* by Pope John Paul II with the words, "I declare that direct abortion, that is, abortion willed as an end or as a means, always constitutes a grave moral disorder, since it is the deliberate killing of an innocent human being" (n. 62). *Origins,* April 6, 1995, 711.

26. It should be noted that the Congregation for the Doctrine of the Faith in its 1987 *Instruction on Human Life (Donum Vitae)* accepts these same views regarding the status of the embryo. At the same time, it acknowledges that the church has taken no definitive stand on the question of human ensoulment.

27. Hans Lotstra, *Abortion: The Catholic Debate in America.* New York: Irvington Publishers, 1985, 48–50.

28. Cf. note 17, 31–32.

29. Cf. note 18, 8.

30. Children's Defense Fund; see www.childrensdefense.org.

31. Additional moral questions, not considered in this chapter, that arise in connection with the matter of abortion include the moral status of the conceptus (cf. notes 9 and 17), fetal tissue transplantation (cf. Chapter Seven), and embryo reduction (cf. Chapter Six).

5 Newborns with Disabilities

THE MEDICAL SCIENTIFIC DIMENSION

The Question

It is only fairly recently that this question has come to perplex the nation at large and become one of the most controversial ethical dilemmas being debated in health care. The question—to save or to let die—is not entirely new, but the advent of sophisticated, high-tech medicine in neonatology has made it possible to assist many newborns to survive who would surely have died only a short time ago. Thus the new question is whether the effort to save should be continued or undertaken at all. Add to this the wide publicity given to several cases over the past three decades, and it is not difficult to understand why the fate of neonates with disabilities is so broadly debated—not only by health care providers and experts in bioethics, but also by legislators and by legal practitioners as well.

Since the early 1980s, between three and four million live births have been occurring annually in the United States. Of these, many thousands have been afflicted by one or more genetic anomalies. (Genetic anomalies are inherited from parents; congenital anomalies occur during pregnancy). For example, nearly 4500 babies were born in 1995 with heart malformations, 1600 babies were afflicted with Down syndrome, and 1000 were born with spina bifida.[1] In addition, over 400,000 are babies with low birth-weights (2500 g.–5.5 lbs. or less), because of prematurity or other causes. An additional number suffer from very low birth-weights (1500 g.–3.3 lbs. or less). Low-birth-weight infants are forty times more likely to die within the first month of life than normal-weight babies, and five times more likely to die later in their first year of life than normal-weight babies.

Low-birth-weight infants—whether premature or simply small for gestational age—account for more than 65 percent of the twenty-three thousand neonatal deaths in this country annually. More than 400,000 newborns are admitted into intensive neonatal care each year at an annual cost of 12 billion dollars. Where the average cost of delivering a healthy baby is $1200 nationally, the average cost for delivering a low-birth-weight baby is $50,000. First year medical care for a low-birth-weight baby is $15,000 but this rises to $32,000 for a very low-birth-weight newborn.[2]

Etiology

The causes of infant disabilities are many. Some are traceable to genetic anomalies inherited from one or both parents. Following the classical Mendelian laws, these genetic flaws in the parent(s) are transmitted to some or all of their offspring.

In addition to anomalies caused by defective genes, the environment and parental lifestyle can also give rise to health problems in newborns. Substance abuse—of drugs, alcohol, or tobacco—is a major contributing factor. In addition, exposure to radioactive material or to hazardous chemical waste places newborns at serious risk.

Detection

In response to the occurrence of these disabilities in newborns, medical science has developed a number of tests to detect their presence during fetal development.[3] Positive test results, of course, raise the question of continuing the pregnancy—thus facing the parents with an abortion decision. Many anomalies go undetected, however, and even when a genetic defect is detected, in many cases the parents choose to continue the pregnancy. Some newborns, therefore, come into the world burdened with physical and mental disabilities. Since contemporary neonatal medicine can sustain their lives in many cases, the question that arises is whether or not these neonates should be so supported.

THE LEGAL DIMENSION

The treatment dilemma for newborns with disabilities, as has been noted earlier, has come to public attention only relatively recently. Prior to that, it is assumed that the physician often used his own judgment regarding the medical appropriateness of aggressive treatment. Sometimes the parents were involved; often they were not. In any case, it seems to have been viewed as a strictly private matter. Not so any longer.

1970s

In 1973, at the Johns Hopkins Hospital in Baltimore, a Down syndrome baby was born with an intestinal atresia (the absence of a normal body opening). The hospital staff requested parental permission to correct the blockage and thus allow the infant to be fed. After some discussion of the question with their religious advisor, the parents refused permission for the surgery on the grounds that having a developmentally challenged sibling would be unfair to the other children in the family. The infant died seven days later due to lack of nutrition and hydration. The case received broad attention in the press, however, and a number of commentators criticized the decision as unethical.

Also in 1973, the Duff-Campbell study[4] reported that at the Yale–New Haven Hospital, in 299 consecutive deaths in the special care nursery, forty-three had been due to the intentional withholding of treatment. The following year, a special Senate subcommittee began to hold hearings on ethical issues in medicine, including the care of the newborn.

1980s

During the 1980s several other cases captured public attention and contributed to the development of national policy in this matter. In Danville, Illinois, Siamese twins were born—joined at the waist, sharing three legs. The obstetrician and the physician-father agreed to a not-to-treat decision, and a "Do not feed" notice was displayed in

87

the nursery. Nurses complained, however, and an anonymous call to the Children's and Family Services Department led that agency to take custody of the children. They were treated in a Chicago hospital, while the doctor and the father were charged with conspiracy to commit murder. The case was eventually dismissed for lack of evidence since it could not be established who signed the "Do not feed" order. The children survived separation surgery and eventually they were returned to their parents.

In 1982, in Bloomington, Indiana, "Baby Doe" was born, a Down syndrome child with esophageal fistula. A "no treatment" decision was reached, but this was challenged in the court. The parental decision was upheld in the trial court and in the appeals court. On April 16, Baby Doe died before the U.S. Supreme Court could review the decision.

The Reagan Initiative

The following month President Reagan instructed the Secretary of the Department of Health and Human Services to notify hospitals of potential loss of public funds if nutrition or medical/surgical treatment were withheld from newborns with disabilities. He appealed to Sec. 504 of the Rehabilitation Act of 1973 for authority for his administrative decree. In March of 1983 the Secretary of Health and Human Services proposed formal regulations specifying that a public poster be displayed in every hospital that would provide information on the question. It would indicate that denial of treatment to such infants was illegal and invite use of a Hospital Information Hotline. It gave HHS authority to protect infants so reported. It was, moreover, to be effective immediately and required no thirty-day comment period before being implemented.

A coalition of interested groups (e.g., American Academy of Pediatrics, National Association of Children's Hospitals) brought suit against the regulations in federal court. On April 14, 1983, Judge Gesell determined that the regulations were procedurally illegal. In addition he took exception especially to the "potentially disruptive hotline." Undaunted, HHS then revised its regulations and published new Proposed Rules on July 5, 1983, and this time invited comment. Although the rules retained the public notice provision and the hotline, they admitted that there would be no obligation to treat an infant if there were no medical benefit.

On December 30, 1983, HHS promulgated a set of Final Rules and announced that they would take effect on February 13, 1984. The following month, a coalition opposed to the Rules—including the American Medical Association and the American Hospital Association—filed suit in Federal District Court for the Southern District of New York. The court declared the regulations invalid and enjoined their enforcement. On appeal, the Court of Appeals affirmed the decision of the District Court. Finally on June 9, 1986, the United States Supreme Court in a plurality opinion affirmed the opinion of the Court of Appeals.

While this controversy over whether legislation to protect those with disabilities could be used to save newborns was going on, the President's Commission for the Study of Ethical Problems in Medicine and Biomedical and Behavioral Research issued a report in 1983, *Deciding to Forego Life-Sustaining Treatment.*[5] It insisted that there was need for a review of hospital policies, especially of the moral difference between discontinuing and withholding treatment. In the case of newborns with disabilities, it urged that the standard must be "so severe that continued existence would not be a net benefit to the infant."[6] If medical treatment were to be discontinued, it urged that humane and comfort treatment always be provided. It also recommended that public supportive services be offered to all in need.

The Congressional Response

Subsequently on October 9, 1984, Congress passed the amendments to the Child Abuse Prevention and Treatment Law that specified that the denial of medical treatment when medically indicated would be considered child abuse. Medical treatment was understood to include nutrition, hydration, and medicine. The legislation acknowledged, however, that treatments which merely prolonged dying—for the irreversibly comatose, for example—were not obligatory; neither were those that would be ineffective in ameliorating or correcting life-threatening diseases. It also included as nonobligatory therapies that were futile or virtually futile to assure survival.[7] This legislation provides the basis for this country's national public policy with respect to infants born with disabilities.

On December 10, 1984, interim guidelines implementing HHS regulations were issued. The guidelines urged that an Intensive Care Review Committee in each hospital function as the internal review body in the treatment of newborns with disabilities. This legislation notwithstanding, whose values shall be determinative in treatment decisions for newborns—the parents' or the caregivers'—continued to be debated and discussed.

In 1986, the United States Supreme Court interpreted the "Baby Doe Regs" in *Bowen* v. the *American Hospital Association* (476 U.S. 610, 106 S. Ct. 2101 [1986]), following a legal challenge to their implementation. The decision of the Court reinstated the right of parents to make health care decisions for their newborn children. Among the issues settled by *Bowen* were the following:

1. "State law vests decisional responsibility in the parents in the first instance, subject to review in exceptional cases by the State."
2. Parental jurisdiction is thus determinative in health care decisions regarding infants born prematurely or with disabilities, not the federal or state authorities.
3. Without parental consent, any treatment of newborn infants is "actionable."

Following *Bowen* some state courts have since interpreted their responsibility in protecting the rights of the newborn patients.

Although without the force of law, the American Medical Association weighed in on this question in the early 1990s. In its Code of Medical Ethics, the Association declared:

> The primary consideration for decisions regarding life-sustaining treatment for seriously ill newborns should be what is best for the newborn. Factors that should be weighed are: (1) the chance that therapy will succeed, (2) the risks involved with treatment and non-treatment, (3) the degree to which the therapy, if successful, will extend life, (4) the pain and discomfort associated with the therapy, and (5) the anticipated quality of life for the newborn with and without treatment.

Furthermore, the AMA determined, full information must be provided parents of these newborns "so that parents can make informed decisions for their children about life-sustaining treatment."[8]

THE SOCIOCULTURAL DIMENSION

Contemporary American society embraces a number of values that have considerable influence on the way its citizens view the question of infants born with disabilities. For instance:

Interventionism—"If you can fix it, fix it!" is one attitude that applies to this health care dilemma. If the medical technology is available to deal with a particular physical problem, use it—regardless of the condition of the infant after treatment.

Vitalism—Another point of view says life is a supreme value, an absolute good. It must be preserved no matter how minimal the level of life, according to this outlook.

Success—"Be number one!" "You can do anything you set your mind to." "Anything worth doing is worth doing well." These and a thousand other slogans reflect the American dream of succeeding in whatever we do in life. If you have a baby, it has to be the best, the most beautiful, the healthiest, the brightest. A baby with disabilities is a failure in this worldview. An infant with a genetic defect is "nature's mistake," not meant to be.

Pleasure/Pain—A strong current of hedonism runs through American life. For many, pleasure is *the* goal in life; pain is countercultural. The "good life," then, means living life to the full—physically, emotionally, even spiritually. We cannot imagine how we could endure being deprived of the freedom, the enjoyment, the thrill of living. Many choose not to go on, not to have their lives sustained when misfortune deprives them of these values. Based on their personal experience, then, many people judge that anyone would be better dead than disabled, better dead than in unremitting pain. Because they would rather die than be crippled, or be sustained by dialysis, or suffer mental illness, they conclude that everyone else would too. They judge that a life deprived of the pleasures they have enjoyed, a life burdened with pain and hobbled with disabilities, is of no real value. As a result they elect to spare the newborn the pain and the burden and they refuse it treatment and the chance to live.

Be all that you can be—The previous paragraph does not describe all Americans, of course. There are many within the general population who hold vastly different views about disabilities. Those who take part in "Special Olympics," for instance, and the parents of children with disabilities who band together to support each other—these individuals find genuine human meaning and value in achieving one's full potential, even though it falls far below the statistical norm or average.

Egalitarianism—American culture affirms that all Americans are equal. If this is so, then individuals with disabilities deserve to share equally in the possibilities that this country offers; they ought to have an equal chance to live whatever "good life" is possible for them. Children with disabilities, specifically the newborn suffering from one or more conditions, are no exception. To discriminate against those with disabilities, in this view, violates the egalitarian view rooted in the American tradition.

ROMAN CATHOLIC CHURCH TEACHING

There is no major teaching or document of the church that refers specifically to the dilemma of the medical care of newborns with disabilities. The church's general teaching on the question of termination of treatment applies here, however, and the principles that are enunciated in its documents on that question are helpful in dealing with this question. The concrete circumstances that arise in the case of neonates, however, are sufficiently different to require additional reflection. No automatic application of principles is possible here, any more than it is in any other concrete instance of a moral problem.

Principles on the Treatment of Newborns with Disabilities

While no Vatican statements have addressed the question of newborns with disabilities, the Catholic bishops of the United States have offered some guidelines on this matter. On July 25, 1985, the

Pro-Life Committee of the National Council of Catholic Bishops—in collaboration with the American Jewish Congress—issued a set of principles that it proposed for the American scene.[9] Thus:

1. Human life is sacred. Every newborn has the right to basic care: nurture, sustenance, and relief from pain. When parents cannot or will not provide this, the government should step in to provide this.
2. Medical intervention is not obligatory when it would be clearly futile or merely prolong dying.
3. Disabilities in themselves do not justify the denial of treatment when that treatment offers hope of benefit and it is not excessively onerous.
4. When medical experts disagree about the alternate methods of treatment, it falls to parents to choose what seems in the child's best interest.
5. Government ought not intervene unless it is evident that one of the preceding principles is about to be violated.
6. It is government's responsibility to support continuing treatment and care of children with disabilities so that undue financial considerations not prejudice the parents' decision.

THE MORAL DIMENSION

Basic Considerations

As mentioned in the previous section, one approach to this dilemma is to reduce the issues to the same calculus that arises in the consideration of withholding or withdrawing treatment; that is, do the health care choices in this particular case amount to ordinary or to extraordinary means?[10] As will be explained more fully in a later chapter, ordinary means are those that bring the patient more benefit than burden; thus there is a reasonable proportionality between the two, and such means are morally obligatory. Extraordinary means, on the other hand, cause the patient more burden than benefit; hence there can be no reasonable obligation to make use of them. There are some important additional observations to make, however.

Contemporary medicine has shifted the question from "Is this treatment too dangerous, too difficult?" "Will it only prolong dying?" to "Even though we can save this infant, *should* we? *Must* we?" This shift has tended to change the argument, traditionally expressed in terms of means to be used (ordinary/extraordinary), to quality-of-life debates.

Many people reject this quality-of-life analysis outright (as irrelevant at best; immoral at worst) out of fear that it reflects unfavorably on the value of life itself or on the respect and care due the disabled, the aged, the weakest members of society.[11] It should be clear, however, that the ordinary/extraordinary formulation always involves quality-of-life considerations since it is these circumstances (pain, cost, oppressively burdensome conditions, separation from loved ones) that make the therapy extraordinary. Thus the terms ordinary/extraordinary are labels that cloak quality-of-life considerations.

It should also be noted that the Christian tradition has sought a midground between medical vitalism (preserve life at any cost) and medical pessimism (eliminate life that is too burdensome, unproductive, useless, frustrating) by defending the values of life, health, and responsibility in stewardship.

In this connection, it should be remembered that Pius XII (1957) explained that extraordinary means were not obligatory, since to demand more than ordinary means would be burdensome and would make the attainment of the higher, more important good too difficult.[12] What is this higher good? The Judeo-Christian answer is love of God and love of neighbor, that is, the love given and received in interpersonal relationships. The Christian insight, moreover, says that the love of God is expressed in and through the love of neighbor and constitutes the meaning and substance of life. Thus when the struggle for survival, when focusing everything (time, attention, energy, resources) on self, destroys the possibility of relationships or one's ability to enter into them, these means for the struggle become extraordinary because they jeopardize or distort the very meaning of life and make mere physical life the ultimate value, an absolute good.

Concrete Criteria

Richard McCormick and John Paris[13] have developed the following set of criteria for cases involving newborns with disabilities:

1. "Life-saving interventions ought not be omitted for institutional or managerial reasons."[14]

2. "Life-sustaining interventions may not be omitted simply because the baby is [developmentally challenged]."
3. "Life-sustaining interventions may be omitted or withdrawn when there is excessive hardship on the patient, especially when this combines with a poor prognosis (e.g., repeated cardiac surgery, low-prognosis transplant)."
4. "Life-sustaining interventions may be omitted or withdrawn at a point when it becomes clear that expected life will be relatively brief and only with artificial nutrition."
5. "Life-sustaining interventions may be omitted or withdrawn if the infant's potential for human relationships is simply nonexistent or would be utterly submerged and undeveloped in the mere struggle to survive."

It must be pointed out, however, that other Christians—particularly some Roman Catholic theologians—would argue against such a single-minded focus on cognitive potential. Rather, they would argue, one must assess each treatment option for possible benefit to the neonate—some even arguing that sheer physical survival could be a net gain. McCormick and Paris would counter that this approach reduces the newborn to his or her treatable disease, to the disregard of the infant's total well-being. Given the complexity of the issues involved, no one should be surprised at this broad divergence of opinion among medical ethicists struggling to sort out this question.

Some Final Reflections

It is important to note that the decision to treat or not to treat is not simply a private matter. To provide life-saving treatment to the incompetent or disabled is a matter of gravest public concern.[15] Neither is it simply a medical matter; it is not exclusively a scientific judgment. Rather it is a value judgment about the origin, destiny, and meaning of human life and death. Similarly, the right to decide is not exclusively a parental prerogative.

Who, then, has the right to decide? In the first instance, it belongs to the parents—or to whoever has primary responsibility for the welfare of the child—to decide.[16] Obviously the parents depend in great measure on the information provided by the physician. Because of this responsibility, the role of the physician is second only to that of the parents.

Furthermore, when the parents' decision is no longer even questionably in the best interests of the infant, especially if the decision is to leave the infant untreated, society has the duty to intervene. Through what mechanism? Legislation, criminal prosecution, a child neglect hearing, review by hospital ethics committee, court intervention—only the circumstances and local legal regulations can help us decide which approach should be followed.

Even though concrete medical-ethical criteria have been suggested and despite the establishment of a pro-life legal context for this issue, it would be a mistake to suppose that the matter has been settled. The instance of Ryan Nguyen in Washington State is but one example of the complexities of this sort of case. The responsible medical authorities had determined that the infant's physical disabilities were so serious and his prognosis so poor that all aggressive treatment should be discontinued. Notwithstanding this professional evaluation, the child's parents disagreed and secured a lawyer who negotiated the infant's transfer to another facility where aggressive treatment was resumed.

The case is significant. As Arthur Caplan pointed out,

> If you can't say "no" in a situation where there is permanent and apparently irreversible kidney failure, an inability to feed properly and moderate to severe brain damage—a prognosis that is as grim as possible—then do we have any credibility talking about rationing anything in our health care system? If you can't say "no" here, then when can you say "no"?[17]

One final reflection: The context in which this question has been traditionally addressed in this country has been totally individualistic. What is the benefit to this newborn child? What are its burdens? But can we continue to attempt to reach this judgment without some reference to the general health care situation in this country, or indeed from a worldwide perspective? Can billions of dollars for neonatal care be justified when only marginal health gains can be achieved? When almost 1.7 million children worldwide die annually from vaccine-preventable diseases—half from measles—how can we justify spending enormous sums to achieve minimal quality of life for so few? Admittedly, we cannot simply cease our efforts to sustain the lives of this country's newborns with disabilities, for there will be no automatic transfer of funds to some international effort on behalf of the children of the world. But unless the developed nations of the world undertake some initiative on behalf of these suffering millions, it will be yet another example of the world's richest nations consuming a totally disproportionate share of the world's resources.[18]

STUDY QUESTIONS

1. One of the principal causes of physical and mental disabilities in newborns is genetic anomalies. What response has medical science made in the face of this problem?
2. The legal situation regarding disabled neonates reflects a national uncertainty regarding the rights and responsibilities of their parents as opposed to the responsibility of the society to protect some of its most vulnerable members. Explain and illustrate.
3. Not surprisingly, there are conflicting values and viewpoints in contemporary American society regarding persons with disabilities in general and infants with disabilities in particular. These surely influence the way Americans respond to their treatment. Explain some differences in points of view.
4. How does the position of the Roman Catholic Church on the issue of newborns with disabilities attempt to mediate these conflicting views and prioritize the values that are at stake?
5. Discuss the issue of "quality of life" as it applies to the dilemma of treating newborns with disabilities.

NOTES

1. See Centers for Disease Control at www.cdc.gov/nchswww/fastats/b.defects.htm; cf. also March of Dimes at www.marchofdimes.com/professionals/681_1206.asp.

2. See Clinical Support Technology (CST) at www.babycarelink.com/publicsite/opportunity.asp.

3. Cf. Chapter 4, "Abortion," the section Abortion for "Fetal Indications."

4. Raymond S. Duff and A. G. M. Campbell, "Moral and Ethical Dilemmas in the Special Care Nursery," *New England Journal of Medicine,* October 25, 1973, 890–94.

5. *Deciding to Forego Life-Sustaining Treatment: Ethical, Medical and Legal Issues in Treatment Decisions,* President's Commission for the Study of Ethical Problems in Medicine and Biomedical and Behavioral Research. Washington, D.C.: U.S. Government Printing Office, 1983.

6. Ibid., 28.

7. Public Law 98–457, *United States Statutes at Large,* vol. 98, part 2. For a contemporary critique of this legislation, cf. "Ethics and the Care of Critically Ill Infants and Children" by the Committee on Bioethics, in *Pediatrics,* July 1, 1996, 149–52.

8. Adopted June, 1992. AMA. Council of Ethical and Judicial Affairs: Code of Medical Ethics, 1998–99 Edition.

9. *Origins,* September 5, 1985, 192.

10. John J. Paris and Richard A. McCormick, "Saving Defective Infants: Options for Life and Death," *America,* April 23, 1983, 315. Cf. also Richard McCormick, "To Save or Let Die," *America,* July 13, 1974. For a full discussion of the distinction "Ordinary/Extraordinary Means," cf. below, Chapter Ten, "Death and Dying."

11. For an excellent analysis of the "quality of life" debate, cf. Richard C. Sparks, C.S.P., *To Treat or Not To Treat.* Mahwah, N.J.: Paulist Press, 1988, 155–225.

12. Pius XII, "Allocution to Physicians," November 24, 1957.

13. Cf. note 10; cf. also Sparks, note 11, 309–15.

14. For a discussion of "burden to others" as an appropriate consideration in calculating burden and benefit, cf. Sparks, note 11, 298–309.

15. John J. Conley, S.J., "Baby Jane Doe: The Ethical Issues," *America,* February 11, 1984, 84–85. Cf. also Richard McCormick, "Saving Defective Infants: Options for Life or Death," *America,* April 23, 1983, 313–17.

16. While this may be the theoretically and ethically correct answer, under the influence of the "Baby Doe" regulations, it seems to some that the present trend indicates that it is the physician in fact who usually makes the treatment decisions, rather than the parents. Cf. *New York Times,* September 30, 1991. For a contrasting view, cf. the citation at note 7 above from *Pediatrics.*

17. *New York Times,* December 27, 1994, A12.

18. Richard Nicholson, "What Is a Child Worth?" *Hastings Center Report,* January/February 1994, 5.

6 In Vitro Fertilization and Other Artificial Reproductive Technologies

THE MEDICAL-SCIENTIFIC DIMENSION

Nature

In vitro fertilization (IVF) is that process whereby fertilization is achieved *in vitro* (in the glass) and not *in utero*. It is accomplished through the intervention of medical technology, therefore, and not through normal sexual intercourse.

REASONS

Infertility

Fertility, the ability to bear a child, requires the capacity to produce mature gametes, or germ cells, to fertilize and to be fertilized, and to implant and carry to term. It has been estimated that even under ideal conditions, fertilization occurs in only one out of four acts of normal sexual intercourse.

In 1995 it was estimated that 7.1 percent of couples in the United States are infertile, that is, have been unable to bear a child after one year of normal efforts. About 40 percent of the time this has been due to male deficiencies, 40 percent due to female deficiencies, and 20 percent due to deficiencies originating in both parties. Among women twenty to twenty-four years of age, infertility has almost doubled since 1965. Although the percentage of married couples experiencing difficulty in conceiving has actually declined since 1965, the total number of infertile couples in this country has held steady due to the increased number of married couples in the child-bearing years.[1] In 1990 one million new patients sought treatment for infertility. It is estimated that 50 percent of these will not profit from any therapy available at this time.

In 1995, the Centers for Disease Control began collecting data for ARTS data. By the year 2000, slightly more than 400 clinics were responding to problems of infertility. In that year almost 100,000 ART cycles were reported, and 25,228 live-birth deliveries were the result.

The principal medical cause of infertility among women, according to medical experts, is Pelvic Inflammatory Disease (PID). This often leads to scarring of the fallopian tubes, the ovaries, and the uterus through infections caused by chlamydia (50 percent) and gonorrhea (25 percent). Also contributing to the problem are postponed childbirth, excessive athleticism and overexercise on the part of women (especially distance runners, dancers and joggers—which often leads to too-low body fat, inhibiting the production of estrogen), and substance abuse.

Other Reasons

Personal preference accounts for other instances in which a couple might turn to IVF. Thus health, the avoidance of genetic defects in offspring, career, convenience, and cosmetic concerns are, for some, sufficient reason to seek an alternative reproductive technology.

FORMS

The different forms of IVF can be understood either from the standpoint of the origin of the gametes or from the standpoint of the site of the pregnancy. When the gametes are provided by the natural parents, IVF is designated AIH (artificial insemination by husband). When provided by a donor, IVF is designated as AID (artificial insemination by donor). Based on the site of pregnancy, IVF can involve either the natural mother or a surrogate mother. It should be pointed out that the surrogate may provide simply the gestational but not the genetic component, or she may provide both.

It should be noted that artificial insemination is a broader term than IVF. Thus all instances of IVF involve artificial insemination, although the reverse is not true. For instance, in the case where an egg is provided by a donor, this could be fertilized in the donor through artificial insemination without recourse to IVF.

Laparoscopic Egg Collection

The process is initiated through the administration of hormones to stimulate egg production. Egg release is assured through an injection of the hormone hCG. As the egg-holding follicles ripen, physicians are enabled to monitor this by inserting an ultrasound transducer to permit observation of the pelvic organs. "Guided by these images, a needle is inserted through the vaginal wall and into a developed ovarian follicle; with gentle suction, the fluid inside the follicle is withdrawn along with the egg it contains. The procedure is repeated for each developed follicle, usually without requiring a separate vaginal puncture."

A culture medium is prepared in one or more petri dishes and the eggs are placed in it for a brief incubation period. Sperm are added after it has been determined that the eggs are sufficiently mature and fertilization follows. Approximately two days later, after some initial cell division, the fertilized egg(s) is returned to the uterus in the hope that implantation will occur.

Nonsurgical Methods

In cases where the woman is unable to produce eggs in order to achieve pregnancy, a donor must be found to provide them. One method, called nonsurgical embryo transfer or lavage,[2] requires that the couple choose a donor—preferably one who is exceptionally fertile—who is then impregnated by the husband's sperm. After approximately five days, the physician flushes the embryo out of the donor's womb and places it in the wife's uterus to be carried to term, hopefully. In those cases in which the wife is unable to sustain a pregnancy, the donor becomes a surrogate as well and carries the pregnancy to term. At birth, the child is presented to its father and his wife.

Other Artificial Reproductive Technologies (ARTS)

By the mid-1990s, the overall success rate for IVF continued below 20 percent, even though there were wide variations among programs and among patients. In its report for 2002, the CDC indicated that there were slightly less than 100,000 cycles attempted in that year, while somewhat more than 25,000 live-birth deliveries resulted, a success rate of around 25 percent. In 1984 Dr. Ricardo Asch of San Antonio developed a new procedure called Gamete Intra-Fallopian Transfer (GIFT). Without attempting fertilization in the laboratory, Dr. Asch inserted the sperm and egg directly into one of the fallopian tubes via a pipette. Ten years later, however, clinics employing GIFT were still achieving only the same 25 percent success rate as IVF. Clinicians then combined the laboratory elements of IVF with the tubal transfer procedure of GIFT, in this case transferring a zygote rather than the separate gametes. ZIFT (Zygote Intra-Fallopian Transfer), as it is called, failed to lift the level of success beyond 25 percent, however, and fewer clinicians are choosing this procedure because of the addition of an invasive procedure to the basic technique of IVF or GIFT. Since the late 1980s several other new procedures have been developed. Intracytoplasmic sperm injection (ICSI), for instance, involves the injection of the sperm directly into the egg by a microscopic needle. Partial Zonal Drilling (PZD), on the other hand, involves the drilling of a tiny hole in the protective shell of the egg *(zona pellucida);* the success rates of these procedures vary from one fertility center to another.

Since a single cycle of treatment of IVF can cost between $6,000 and $8,000, at the present the cost of this new technology per live birth is very high, given the low success rate of many clinics. Obviously the therapy is only for the wealthy or the well insured. In 1991 nine states required insurance companies to include this therapy in their coverage.

THE LEGAL DIMENSION

Legal Concerns

Many legal questions are raised as a consequence of IVF involving a donor or a surrogate, including the following:

- What is the offspring's relationship to the multiple "parents" it acquires through IVF? Does the child have a right to know its biological parent(s)? Does a biological parent have visitation rights or obligations toward the child?
- What are the obligations of a nonbiological parent toward the child in the event of divorce?
- Who owns the gametes kept in "banks"; who owns the frozen embryos? What if a divorce ensues—what is the correct legal disposition of these materials?
- In the case of donor gametes, does the child have a right to know who the biological parents are?
- May payment be made for the donation of gametes? For carrying a fetus through pregnancy? Are such contracts legal?
- Does everyone have a "right" to have a child? What is the source of that right? How absolute is that right? Does it include singles? Gay or lesbian couples? If not, on what grounds are they excluded?

Legislation

At the present time no national policy in the area of IVF has been established, either by statute or by judicial decision. The federal government did pass the Fertility Clinic Success Rate and Certification Act in 1992. By virtue of this legislation, data relating to the type, number, and outcome of clinics are collected from 383 U.S. fertility clinics and made available to the public. The regulation of ARTS has fallen to the states, however, providing them an opportunity to fashion a legal response to the new reproductive technologies. In New York State, for instance, on July 17, 1993, a new section of the Domestic Relations Law (DRL 121–24) took effect. After carefully defining its terms, the law declared that surrogate parent contracts (involving insemination or impregnation with the intention to surrender the child) were contrary to the public policy of the

103

state and, therefore, void and unenforceable (whether or not a fee is involved). If a fee is involved, all parties to the contract are subject to various fines. Finally, the law establishes the procedure to define the appropriate parental rights between the birthing mother and the father.

In dramatic contrast, the California Supreme Court (*Johnson* v. *Calvert*, No. S023721, May 1993) ruled that the genetic mother—"she who intends to bring about the birth of a child that she intended to raise as her own"—is the natural mother, rather than the birthing mother. The Court also recognized surrogacy contracts as binding, even when money provides the motivation for agreeing to bear a child.[3]

In England, as in some other European countries, it is legal to create embryos expressly for research, which is then restricted to the first fourteen days of life. This same time frame has been recommended in this country by the American Fertility Society. Since 1995, no experimentation on human embryos has been permitted by the federal government in any institution that receives federal funding for any purpose, including Medicare. Because it has contributed almost no funds to research in this new technology, the federal government has not been able to exercise any control through the introduction of guidelines for research.

Has the time arrived for the federal government to introduce some oversight? Lori Knowles thinks so.[4] She believes that the conjunction of reproductive technologies and genetic medicine ("reprogenetics" is her term) offers just such an opportunity. "Many policy makers and scientists," she says, "have acknowledged that we cannot leave the oversight of these techniques to the whim of individuals in the private sector."[5] What are the issues that clamor for this regulation? Valid research, safety for participants, and societal well-being are three areas that she cites. Knowles goes on to point out that:

> Research has shown that a technique used to inject sperm directly into eggs in fertility treatments can cause damage to the egg's chromosomes. This technique was used and the resulting embryos implanted in women before rigorous safety testing. Recent articles have indicated that there may be long-term health impacts for children conceived by in vitro fertilization—a technique that has become part of the reproductive medicine "mainstream."

Not only are there no policies governing these techniques, there are not even any serious conversations preparing for government oversight. Such an absence of scientific assessment and ethical evaluation leaves us with "little ability to explore the appropriate applications of future technology and develop policy to control it before it hits the market."[6] Why now? Why such a grave moment?

> The union of genetics and reproduction has moved us toward an era in which parents will have an astonishing variety of techniques available to conceive and gestate children and to select the attributes their children may have. [Such a situation] challenges our concepts of who we are, who we should be, and the kind of society in which we want to live. Clearly we should be talking about these issues.[7]

Her great concern, she explains, is that "human reproduction and genetic traits can become commodities when reproductive technology is regulated largely by the market."[8] Recent advances in the development and use of embryonic stem cells, in cloning, and in gender selection suggest that after almost three decades of clinical free-for-all we may have reached a point when the chance to sit together and hammer out meaningful policies and ethical assessments may have arrived.

The "Baby M" Case

Without a doubt, the legal decisions reached in the "Baby M" trial, initially litigated in Hackensack, New Jersey, constitute a landmark decision for the country. Though it has not answered all the legal questions and is legally binding only in New Jersey, the Court's views did begin the process of establishing legal precedent and opinion in this very complicated area. It should be pointed out that this case did not technically involve IVF, since both fertilization and gestation took place in the donor's body.

On March 27, 1986, Mary Beth Whitehead gave birth to a daughter, and so "Baby M" was born. By the terms of the contract she had signed with William Stern, Mrs. Whitehead agreed to be inseminated with Mr. Stern's sperm, to carry to term any offspring that resulted, and to deliver the child at birth to William and Elizabeth Stern. In return, she would receive $10,000—or $1,000 if a miscarriage or stillbirth occurred after the fifth month of pregnancy. Nothing would be paid to her if this occurred prior to the fifth month. Mr. Stern retained all rights to determine whether the pregnancy should be terminated and the fetus aborted.

After the birth of the baby, Mary Beth Whitehead changed her mind and the Sterns initiated legal action to secure the baby's custody—and the "Baby M" case began. For over a year the issues of the contract and the proper home for the child were argued in the New Jersey court of Judge Harvey R. Sorkow. His decision on April 7, 1987, determined:[9]

1. That the surrogacy contract was valid and enforceable.
2. That Mary Beth Whitehead's parental rights were terminated.
3. That the Sterns should be given sole custody of the baby.
4. That adoption by Mrs. Stern was in the baby's best interest.

This decision was immediately appealed to the New Jersey Supreme Court, which studied the record of the trial court and issued its unanimous decision on February 3, 1988. In its determination, the Court ruled:

1. That the surrogacy contract was invalid and unenforceable because it violated New Jersey statutes and public policy.
2. That Mrs. Whitehead's parental rights could not be justifiably terminated and hence the adoption by Mrs. Stern was invalid.
3. That both the natural father and the natural mother have correlative rights and claims to the child.
4. That the trial court's finding giving custody of "Baby M" to the Sterns was supported by the record.
5. That the determination of Mrs. Whitehead's visitation rights had to be reviewed by the court.
6. That surrogacy was not legally prohibited if voluntary and undertaken without payment; in addition, the natural mother must be given the right to change her mind and assert her parental rights.

By the end of 1987, three states (Arkansas, Nevada, and Louisiana) had enacted legislation that considers surrogacy. A large number of states have been considering bills on the question. It is interesting to see the great variety of approaches to this issue reflected in the proposed laws. Many states have used the occasion to redraw their artificial insemination laws at the same time.[10]

THE SOCIOCULTURAL DIMENSION

How do the attitudes, the values, the socially approved behaviors of contemporary American society influence our thinking and our behaviors about IVF?

Family

It has been long held that the family is the basic unit of American society. Until the present, the family was understood as constituted by husband and wife, who become father and mother to any children born to them. Does the dissociation of sociocultural parenthood from biological parenthood disturb one of the constitutive relations of our identity as individuals, as families and as a society? Some think so. In this view, the mechanics of IVF and surrogate mothering raise fundamental questions regarding who is parent/child to whom. The separation of biology from parenting disturbs our notion of lineage, it is argued. Quite apart from the question's legal ramifications, our sense of who we are is rooted in part at least in our belonging to a family. Will the introduction of reproductive technology further accentuate the fraying of family bonds and the isolation of the individual?[11]

Equality

Even though never fully realized, there is a strong, clear sympathy in the American spirit for the equality of all citizens. IVF is a procedure that will probably never be within the reach of the lower socioeconomic classes. Since many health insurers have opted not to cover IVF, it is hard to imagine how the poor will ever find this treatment option within their means.

Equally discriminatory, it has been pointed out, is the practice of surrogate mothering. The stand-in mother will always be selected from the ranks of the needy by the affluent, it is objected, never the other way around.

Respect for Life

The same deep-seated division that American society experiences at the present when confronted by the question of abortion surfaces in connection with IVF. Particularly sensitive are the way "surplus" reproductive material is handled and the question of experimentation on fetuses.

Government Interventionism

The advent of legal regulations with respect to IVF, whether by way of statute or of judicial decision, will involve the government in one of the most intimate and personal areas of its citizens' lives—reproduction. This development, seen by some as intrusion and by others as necessary regulation of a chaotic societal development, will surely have an important impact on family life.

A Feminist Perspective

Women do not have this constant production of gametes on a regular basis. Women produce gametes once a month and, in January, if a woman fails to conceive when she is trying to conceive, then she has lost September's baby. A woman does not have this random notion that no baby was there. Rather she has the notion that a particular baby, what would have been her baby, with certain dominant characteristics already settled, her September brown-eyed baby, is now gone....From the perspective of the woman, the whole notion of fertilization and what procreation is supposed to be about is so very different [from the man's]....From a woman's perspective, every woman has her own child. We do not bear the children of other people. We do not bear our husband's [sic] children. We do not bear a purchaser's children. We do not bear the children of the state....Pregnancy is an intimate social relationship. Our language discards [sic] that. Our language says children "enter the world." From where? We say babies "arrive." Women do not feel babies "arrive." They feel them "leave." Parenthood is an intimate social relationship wherever it develops and between whomsoever it develops. We need to find a perspective as a society that does not discard the

intimacy, nurturing and growth that grows [sic] between generations, but a perspective that supports, develops and encourages
that intimacy. We need to reject the very concept of surrogacy.
We need to reject the notion that any woman is the mother of a
child that is not her own, regardless of the source of the egg
and/or the sperm. Maybe a woman will place that child for adoption, but it is her child to place. Her nurturance of that child with
the blood and nutrients of her body establishes her parenthood
of that child.[12]

ROMAN CATHOLIC CHURCH TEACHING

Congregation for the Doctrine of the Faith

On March 10, 1987, the Congregation for the Doctrine of the
Faith issued its *Instruction on Respect for Human Life in Its Origin and
on the Dignity of Procreation*.[13] The document was not unexpected and
was a response from an official agency of the central administration of
the Catholic Church to many of the questions being asked of it in
connection with developing technologies in the field of human reproduction. After an introduction that set out some of the major viewpoints of the Roman Catholic teaching on anthropology, science, and
technology, the *Instruction* set forth its moral principles in the fields
of human embryology and reproductive technology.

Heterologous Artificial Insemination

In vitro fertilization is considered "heterologous" when at least
one of the gametes is donated by a third party. The congregation also
judged surrogacy according to the same criteria. In this connection,
therefore, the congregation declared:

1. Human procreation must take place within marriage. The "fidelity
   of the spouses in the unity of marriage involves *reciprocal* respect of
   their right to become a father and a mother only through each
   other." Hence third party participation through the donation of
   gametes or through surrogacy makes heterologous IVF morally
   unacceptable.

2. Additionally, "the child has the right to be conceived, carried in the womb, brought into the world, and brought up within marriage. It is through the secure and recognized relationship to his own parents that the child can discover his own identity and achieve his own proper human development." For this reason also, heterologous IVF is illicit.

3. Surrogate motherhood, similarly, is not morally licit since "it is also contrary to the unity of marriage and to the dignity of the procreation of the human person." It fails "to meet the obligation of maternal love, of conjugal fidelity, and of responsible motherhood; it offends the dignity and the right of the child to be conceived, carried in the womb, brought into the world and brought up by his own parents; it sets up, to the detriment of families, a division between the physical, psychological, and moral elements which constitute those families."

Homologous Artificial Insemination

In vitro fertilization is termed "homologous" when the parents themselves provide the gametes. In this connection the congregation stated:

1. "There is an inseparable connection, willed by God and unable to be broken by man on his own initiative, between the two meanings of the conjugal act: the unitive meaning and the procreative meaning....Fertilization is licitly sought when it is the result of a 'conjugal act which is per se suitable for the generation of children, to which marriage is ordered by its nature and by which the spouses become one flesh.' But from the moral point of view procreation is deprived of its proper perfection when it is not desired as the fruit of the conjugal act, that is to say, of the specific act of the spouses' union." For this reason, homologous IVF is morally unacceptable.

2. Additionally, "the one conceived must be the fruit of his parents' love. He cannot be desired or conceived as the product of an intervention of medical or biological techniques; that would be equivalent to reducing him to an object of scientific technology. No one may subject the coming of a child into the world to conditions of technical efficiency which are to be evaluated according to standards of control and dominion." For this reason as well, homologous IVF is not morally licit.

3. Furthermore, the congregation added, "the process of 'in vitro' fertilization and embryo transfer must be judged in itself and cannot borrow its definitive moral quality from the totality of conjugal life of which it becomes part nor from the conjugal acts which may precede or follow it."

4. Finally, "homologous 'in vitro' fertilization and embryo transfer is brought about outside the bodies of the couple through actions of third parties whose competence and technical activity determine the success of the procedure. Such fertilization entrusts the life and identity of the embryo into the power of doctors and biologists and establishes the domination of technology over the origin and destiny of the human person. Such a relationship of domination is in itself contrary to the dignity and equality that must be common to parents and children." For all these reasons, then, the congregation judged IVF in any form to be morally objectionable.

As its final comment, the congregation issued an "invitation with confidence and encouragement to theologians, and above all to moralists, that they study more deeply and make ever more accessible to the faithful the contents of the teaching of the church's magisterium in the light of a valid anthropology in the matter of sexuality and marriage and in the context of the necessary disciplinary approach." Such reflection is desired, the *Instruction* points out, because "the precise indications which are offered in the present instruction…are not meant to halt the effort of reflection, but rather to give it a renewed impulse in unrenounceable fidelity to the teaching of the church."[14]

THE MORAL DIMENSION

Moral Concerns

In a 1979 survey of the moral literature on the issue of in vitro fertilization,[15] the year following the birth of the first "test-tube" baby (Louise Brown) in England, Richard McCormick identified the following issues as matters of concern to various moral theologians:

1. Possible fetal damage
2. Embryo wastage
3. Harmful publicity
4. Genetic manipulation

5. Readiness to abort
6. Extension beyond married couple
7. Medical priorities—consumption of medical resources

Moral Evaluation

In his own reflection on the issue, McCormick singled out four concerns that needed to be resolved before IVF could be seen as a morally acceptable alternative to normal reproduction:

Technologizing Marriage

For McCormick, this concern finds expression in two different ways. Some who object to IVF base this opposition on the position of Pius XII regarding artificial insemination. The pope found this technology unacceptable, even when restricted to the married couple, because it separated the biological activity (fertilization, conception, childbearing) from the personal relation of the married spouses. The conjugal act, said Pius, has a natural and God-given design that joins the love-giving and the life-giving dimensions. From this, some theologians at the present time conclude that in vitro fertilization violates human dignity and the dignity of human procreation because it violates the integrity of the procreative process.[16]

In response, McCormick agrees that sexual union by its nature is both unitive and procreative. Therefore, he concludes, it is always a disvalue to separate these two dimensions of this union. It is not, however, an absolute disvalue and therefore it can be justified when there is a proper proportionality between its positive and negative consequences. Thus it always needs justification.

To label it a violation of nature is excessive, according to McCormick, since the child must still be the expression and embodiment of love. Sexual intercourse is not the only or necessary way of expressing this. To assert that the artificial insemination aspect of IVF is always an attack on the integrity of the procreative process seems difficult to establish plausibly. Many theologians, at least, do not perceive it as dehumanizing, according to McCormick.

This concern—technologizing marriage—can be understood in another way as well. As was mentioned above, excessive technology can depersonalize one of the most personal and intimate areas of human activity, the exercise of human sexuality in marriage. To introduce the elaborate procedures and regimens of an IVF clinic into the exercise of marital sexual intimacy runs the risk of dehumanizing one of the most personal and most intimate expressions of interpersonal communion. Small wonder that McCormick acknowledges this as a disvalue. In addition, there is the danger that the child may become a consumer item for which we enter into contracts and concerning which we make product choices regarding sex and stature, eye color and intelligence. And so great caution is necessary. But, concludes McCormick, this is not the same thing as a moral judgment that IVF is always a moral evil.

Abortion

Abortion can be a consideration in IVF technology from two standpoints. First, there is the question of the lost or discarded zygotes. Is this the moral equivalent of abortion? In addition, there is frequently, if not always, an understanding that the fetus will be aborted "if something goes wrong."

First, the problem of the zygotes. As a rule, clinics tend to withdraw and fertilize more than one egg when a laparoscopy is performed. It has been found through experience that the chances for a successful pregnancy are enhanced if multiple zygotes are implanted in the mother's womb following fertilization. Additional zygotes that remain unused can be frozen for later use if the first attempt proves unsuccessful. Obviously, this eliminates the necessity for successive laparoscopies. If the attempt is successful and pregnancy ensues, however, the question of what to do with the unused zygotes raises the abortion issue.

There are those who maintain that the remaining zygotes are persons with full rights. Therefore, in their eyes, simply to dispose of these unused zygotes is the moral equivalent of abortion and unacceptable. A second view sees these zygotes simply as human tissue and hence disposable at will without any moral complication whatsoever. Finally, some commentators consider the zygotes, although not persons, living human beings deserving respect and protection. How much, of course, is what is in dispute.

McCormick insists, as he does in all abortion debates, that the critical question is not the personhood of the zygotes. He points out that many who deny personhood to the zygotes insist that they be treated with respect and even awe. But is the loss of the unused zygotes the moral equivalent of abortion? McCormick's response is that we now know that many zygotes will be lost (roughly 50–60 percent) as a result of the couple's normal efforts to beget children. Since the loss of the zygotes in the latter case is not considered "causing abortions," it is not at all clear why the loss of zygotes in IVF should be viewed as abortion either, especially if roughly the same number of zygotes are lost in either case.

McCormick points out that IVF in connection with human research and IVF to achieve pregnancy are very different issues. In the former instance, the use of live zygotes for research and experimentation is excluded by an appropriate respect for nascent life. In the latter case, it is not necessarily excluded at all, and so McCormick objects to the use of the term "abortion" to describe IVF. This is not the same as to say that the question of the treatment of the unused zygotes is not without considerable weight, for it is truly a grave concern if one honestly values nascent life. Once again the requirement is that there be true proportion between the loss of the zygotes and the opportunity to beget children. Not all Roman Catholic theologians agree with McCormick on this point. They distinguish between the natural loss of zygotes in normal sexual relations (which no one causes) and that loss of zygotes resulting from attempts at in vitro fertilization when implantation fails. The individuals involved are morally responsible for the latter, they insist, but not for the former.

In his 1979 article, McCormick suggests a second sense in which abortion may be a consideration, namely, the routine expectation in IVF clinics that, should anything go amiss during pregnancy, the fetus will be aborted. Naturally this understanding would not be acceptable from a moral standpoint, as already explained under the discussion of abortion.

Harm to the Child Conceived through IVF

It was argued that the very IVF technology that gives life and human existence also exposes the individual so conceived to unavoidable risks, both mental and physical. Since the fetus is unable to give proper consent to assume this risk, it is morally wrong to expose it to this risk. McCormick replies that this objection is now moot since we know from experience that there is no greater risk to the fetus from the artificial reproductive technology than there is from normal conception. Hence we need only assure ourselves that the risks are roughly equivalent, rather than having to exclude all risks positively. He adds, however, that this evaluation does not absolve the original IVF researchers (Steptoe and Edwards) from all blame. They originally took this risk in genuine ignorance of what the consequences would be for the fetus. Indeed some experts insist that not enough preliminary animal research had been done and hence the risk to humans had not been evaluated sufficiently prior to actual experimentation.

Extension beyond Marriage

What McCormick had feared in 1979 has in fact come about. It had been observed by some critics then that successful IVF therapy utilizing gametes provided by married partners would not long remain so restricted. Third-party donors of egg or sperm and host wombs were in fact already in the planning stage when testimony was being given before the Ethics Advisory Board in Washington at that time. One researcher, in fact, admitted that he had already cloned three human eggs from testicular tissue. Such developments, moreover, were but a step beyond the already existing procedures involving artificial insemination by donor sperm. To these critics, these practices constituted "a radical attack on marriage, the family, human sexuality, personal identity and the lineage of the child." AIH was, in their view, "the wedge," and the principles alleged in its defense already justified AID in advance.

In reply, McCormick pointed out that any evaluation depended on what was understood by "the principles alleged in its (AIH) defense." If the principle understood was that "everyone has a right, indeed an absolute right, to have a child" or that "all means are licit to overcome sterility," then this principle needed to be rejected. If, however, "husband-wife IVF is a licit last resort to overcome sterility" was the principle envisioned, then this was quite another matter.

For McCormick, third-party participation is excluded from procreation because it violates the unity and exclusivity of marriage, within which procreation must take place—at least in the experience and understanding of the Christian faith community. In marriage, two people commit themselves to each other exclusively and permanently in a relationship of love, within which procreation and parenting will be carried on. As long as marriage means this within the Christian faith community, third-party participation will be seen as a violation of the unity and exclusivity of marriage. On the other hand, IVF without the intervention of third-party donors can be morally justified on the basis of the proportion between the consequences.[17]

In another context, McCormick quotes Daniel Callahan's summary of the negative social consequences of surrogacy:

1. It represents yet another mode of producing children that is less than desirable and at a time when we are not underpopulated.
2. It courts confusion about parentage with accompanying uncertainty about responsibility for the welfare of the child.
3. It introduces a cadre of women whose prime virtue is what we now take to be a vice—the bearing of a child one does not want and is prepared not to love.
4. It reduces women to their childbearing capacity, reducing a woman to a means.[18]

Response to the 1987 *Instruction*

In its concluding comments, the congregation invited moral theologians to continue a reflective dialogue concerning the many issues raised by the new reproductive technologies. As it pointed out, "the precise indications which are offered in the present instruction…are not meant to halt the effort of reflection, but rather to give it a renewed impulse in unrenounceable fidelity to the teaching of the church."[19] Theologians have not been slow to accept the congregation's invitation. The vast majority of moralists among Roman Catholics have expressed basic agreement with the *Instruction* regarding heterologous IVF and surrogacy. There have been some, however, who have taken exception to the congregation's rejection of homologous IVF.

1. According to the *Instruction,* the child "must be the fruit of his parents' love. He cannot be desired or conceived as the product of an intervention of medical or biological techniques; that would be equivalent to reducing him to an object of scientific technology."[20] Lisa Sowle Cahill responds that such reasoning is not, in fact, based

on "the actual experiences of married parents or of infertile would-be parents."[21] In the same connection Richard McCormick observes that neither prospective parents nor medical technologists would recognize their motives or their actions in this analysis.[22]

2. The *Instruction* objects that "homologous IVF and ET [Embryo Transfer] is brought about outside the bodies of the couple through actions of third parties whose competence and technical activity determine the success of the procedure. Such fertilization entrusts the life and identity of the embryo into the power of doctors and biologists and establishes the domination of technology over the origin and destiny of the human person. Such a relationship of domination is in itself contrary to the dignity and equality that must be common to parents and children."[23] Lisa Sowle Cahill observes that the *Instruction* "fails to be a convincing example of reflection on objective and universal human values because it substitutes assertions for nuanced arguments about what really constitutes respect for human 'nature,' 'dignity' and 'rights.'"[24] In a similar vein, McCormick asks, "Why exclusively the 'power' of doctors? Why not the 'loving care' of doctors? Why the 'domination of technology'? Why not the 'service and aid' of technology?" It is one thing for the congregation to be "rightly worried about the dehumanizing potential of technology." It is quite another to assert that the decision to introduce reproductive technology is an act devoid of parental love.[25]

3. The *Instruction* asserts that because "neither achieved in fact nor potentially willed as the expression and fruit of a specific act of the conjugal union," the generation of a human person through homologous IVF and ET is "objectively deprived of its proper perfection: namely, that of being the result and fruit of a conjugal act."[26] To this argument, McCormick replies, "Twice it [the congregation] refers to procreation by this technology as 'procreation deprived of its proper perfection.' That raises the interesting question: Is an act 'deprived of its proper perfection' necessarily morally wrong? If Catholic tradition is our guide, the answer is no. There are many actions, less than perfect, actions that contain positive disvalues that we regard as morally permissible in the circumstances. Indeed, the congregation itself, in allowing medical interventions that seek 'to assist the conjugal act,' allows for interferences that constitute something less than the perfect."[27]

Finally, the invitation of the *Instruction* to ongoing reflection, McCormick suggests, may lead "to a modification of some of the conclusions drawn by the Congregation for the Doctrine of the Faith. To exclude that in principle would be to attribute to the document greater decisiveness than it claims or can claim."[28]

In her assessment of the *Instruction,* Cahill praises the document for its reaffirmation "that there is a fundamental, experience-based, cross-cultural connection among what might be called the 'variables' of human reproduction: genetic parenthood, social parenthood and a commitment to interpersonal and parental partnership with the person with whom one cooperates in bringing a child into being."[29] McCormick would probably conclude, as he did in 1979, that no argument has been presented thus far that establishes clearly and with certainty that IVF procedures using the couple's own gametes are inherently and of necessity illicit when procreation through normal means—that is, through sexual intercourse—is judged impossible. If, therefore, the couple excludes the intention of aborting any handicapped fetus that might result from the procedure and if the risk to the child is kept acceptably low, the use of this alternative procreative therapy is morally acceptable.

PROCREATIVE LIBERTY

It seems fairly clear that over the past twenty-five years the principal criterion—if not the only one—for judging the moral acceptability of using IVF or one of the other reproductive technologies has been procreative liberty. This approach suggests that the only ethical consideration is the parents' desire for a child and their determination to use any available technology that will fulfill that goal. Procreative liberty offers the ideological framework, therefore, that would justify the right of adults to have a child for any purpose and by any means.

Is such an outlook an adequate approach to the use of reproductive technology? Thomas Murray thinks not. First of all, such a criterion suggests no consideration of the goods of the child created through such a technology. As he points out: "The decision to have a child [is a decision] to create a new person who will have interests, hopes, and concerns of her or his own. It is also a decision to initiate a vital, life-long relationship."[30]

Even more important, reproductive liberty as a criterion is unable to capture or promote values that are central to human flourishing. To be sure, adult autonomy and a woman's control over her reproductive functioning are genuine human goods. The right to choose cannot be gainsaid as an important issue, but the decision to have a child is much more than an exercise of an individual's autonomy. The decision to conceive, gestate, and give birth—indeed for both parents—is life-altering and opens the possibility for a much richer human flourishing.

> There are central human values that are either found only in the context of enduring, committed human relationships such as families, or that rely upon such relationships for their realization. Values such as love, loyalty, intimacy, steadfastness, acceptance, and forgiveness are crucial to well-functioning families, which are also the most robust settings in which to raise children to become confident, competent, loving, and emotionally resilient adults.[31]

Finally, it must be acknowledged that the decision to employ reproductive technology to conceive and bear a child must be for the child's welfare as well as for the parents'. As a human person, with full rights and human dignity, the child is called to human fulfillment through its relationship with God and with other human beings, just as its parents are. The possibility of accomplishing this must be clear to the parents and must be part of their decision to have a child in the first place.[32]

STUDY QUESTIONS

1. For what reason(s) might a couple make use of the new technologies that permit fertilization outside of the woman's body?
2. Describe the process used to procure the gametes and achieve fertilization "in vitro."
3. What legal issues have arisen in connection with in vitro fertilization?
4. The new reproductive technologies impact on a number of American values. Explain.

5. What is the authoritative teaching of the Roman Catholic Church regarding IVF? What reasons does it offer in support of its teaching?
6. What are the major moral concerns that arise in connection with IVF? Explain each.

NOTES

1. The New York State Task Force on Life and the Law, *Assisted Reproductive Technologies*. New York, 1998, 11–12.

2. Ibid., 54.

3. *Wall Street Journal*, May 21, 1993, B1. For a discussion of some of the legal issues involved in surrogacy contracts, cf. Martha Field, "Reproductive Technologies and Surrogacy: Legal Issues," *Creighton Law Review*, vol. 25, no. 5, November 1992, 1589–98.

4. Lori P. Knowles, "Reprogenetics: A Chance for Meaningful Regulation," *Hastings Center Report*, May/June 2002, 13.

5. Ibid.

6. Ibid.

7. Ibid.

8. Ibid.

9. *In re Baby M*, 13 FLR 2001.

10. Lori Andrews, "The Aftermath of Baby M: Proposed State Laws on Surrogate Motherhood," *Hastings Center Report*, October/November 1987, 31–40. Cf. also George J. Annas, "Baby M: Babies (and Justice) for Sale," *Hastings Center Report*, June 1987, 13–15.

11. See a discussion of this question in Ruth Macklin, "Artificial Means of Reproduction and Our Understanding of the Family," *Hastings Center Report*, January/February 1991, 5–11; Alexander Capron, "Whose Child Is This?" *Hastings Center Report*, January/February 1991, 35–38.

12. Barbara Katz Rothman, "Reproductive Technologies and Surrogacy: A Feminist Perspective," *Creighton Law Review*, vol. 25, n. 5, November 1992, 1606–07.

13. *Origins*, 16:30, March 19, 1987, 697, 699–711. In his 1995 encyclical *Evangelium Vitae*, Pope John Paul II reaffirms the congregation's condemnation of the use of embryos or fetuses for research or experimentation or to provide "organs or tissue for transplants in the treatment of certain diseases" (n. 63). *Origins*, April 6, 1995, 711.

14. *Instruction*, 710.

15. Richard A. McCormick, "Notes on Moral Theology," *Theological Studies*, March 1979, 97–106.

16. Ibid., 100.

17. Cf. also Richard A. McCormick, "Ethics of Reproductive Technology: AFS Recommendations, Dissent," *Health Progress,* March 1987, 33–37; Jeremiah McCarthy, "In Vitro Technology: A Threat to the Covenant," *Health Progress,* March 1987, 44–48.

18. Richard A. McCormick, "Surrogacy: A Catholic Perspective," *Creighton Law Review* 25:5, November 1992, 1621–24.

19. *Instruction,* 710.

20. *Instruction,* II, B, 4c, 706.

21. With Richard A. McCormick, "The Vatican Doctrine on Bioethics: Two Responses," *America,* March 28, 1987, 246.

22. Ibid., 247.

23. *Instruction,* II, B, 5, 707.

24. Cf. note 21, 246.

25. Ibid., 248.

26. *Instruction,* II, B, 5, 707.

27. Cf. note 21, 248.

28. Ibid., 247.

29. Ibid., 246.

30. Thomas H. Murray, "What Are Families For? Getting to an Ethics of Reproductive Technology," *Hastings Center Report,* May/June 2002, 42.

31. Ibid., 43.

32. The publicity given to several recent cases in which the parents' decision to have a child was based on its being part of the therapy for an existing child raises a serious question. Is such a decision morally acceptable since it seems to consider the new child as a means, not an end? Cf. John A. Robertson, Jeffrey P. Kahn, John E. Wagner, "Conception to Obtain Hematopoietic Stem Cells," *Hastings Center Report,* May/June 2002, 34–40.

PART THREE

Questions Concerning
Illness and Disease

Part Three deals with medical-ethical questions that involve illness and disease. Unlike the previous section, these conditions can occur at any stage in life. They are not diseases themselves but may be the causes of illness or disease. In each case, however, they take the reader to the frontiers of medicine as we go forward in the new millennium.

Genetic diseases, for example, are gradually being understood by the sleuths of medical science. The Human Genome Project has given an enormous impetus to medicine's ability to identify the causes of such conditions and has suggested an amazing new approach to dealing with illnesses that have their roots in the patient's DNA. In addition, scientists are also discovering that many common illnesses—cancers, cardiac diseases, diabetes—sometimes arise from genetic predispositions. The first experimental therapies on human subjects are even now under way in an effort to provide a radical cure for the damaged genetic material. It is exciting to live on the frontier!

Disease can also be the cause of the complete destruction of human organs and organ systems. A patient's heart or liver, kidney or pancreas can fall victim to serious illness—and with lethal results. In such cases the only remedy available to physicians is to replace the organ. Organ transplantation brings its practitioners to the very frontiers of medical technology and, when it succeeds, gives its beneficiaries another chance at life. What was a dream fifty years ago is sometimes today's therapy of choice.

Finally, this generation has witnessed the return of the term "plague" to common parlance. A worldwide pandemic, Acquired Immunodeficiency Syndrome, has already killed millions since it was identified in the early 1980s and will surely result in the deaths of many more millions around the world unless medical science can find a true remedy for this modern equivalent of the "black death." Just at the time that medical science believed that the use of antibiotics had truly delivered the human race from the killer plagues of earlier centuries, AIDS has arisen to challenge this notion. At this writing no one knows when or how medical science will solve this riddle, but even when it does many medical-ethical questions will remain.

These three subjects will be the focus of Part Three, then. Even as they call out for medical responses, they demand careful consideration from an ethical viewpoint since they raise value issues that cannot be ignored. More importantly, since they challenge a way of thinking that has become comfortable, they prepare us to challenge traditional views and established answers at this critical time when the questions themselves have changed.

7 Genetics

GENETIC SCIENCE

Introduction

According to Webster, *genetics* is that branch of biology that "deals with heredity and variation in similar or related animals and plants." It considers the natural variations and similarities in successive generations of living organisms. As an applied science, genetics has many uses. Thus it studies the possibility of developing improved varieties and strains of plants and animals through selective breeding. It is utilized, as well, in diagnosis, in forensics and in medicine.

Which organic structures play a central role in genetics? First, the *chromosome*. A chromosome is a thread-shaped structure, made up of DNA (deoxyribonucleic acid), that occurs within the cell nucleus as a discrete, microscopic unit. Chromosomes typically occur in pairs, and the number within each cell is constant for each species. In humans, chromosomes are found within the nucleus in every cell in the body (with the exception of red blood cells, which have no nucleus). Normally, twenty-three pairs exist in each human cell nucleus. One in each pair comes from each parent. Twenty-two pairs of chromosomes in humans are essentially alike in both males and females and are called "autosomes." The twenty-third pair determines sex and hence is distinguished in the male (XY) and female (XX).

A *gene* is a segment of DNA that occurs as a structural part of the thread-shaped chromosomes and codes for the production of inherited traits and characteristics. Transmitted from parent to child, genes determine such things as skeleton, tissue, and organs as well as many other physical and mental characteristics. Genes, too, occur in pairs, and many genes are found on a single chromosome. It is estimated that as many as 30,000 genes exist in each human cell nucleus. If chromosomes are imagined as strings of beads, then the genes would be the beads.

An *allele* is one of two or more alternative forms of a gene that occupy the same position on homologous chromosomes. Thus if ice cream were a gene, chocolate would be an allele.

Function of Genes

As already stated, genes transmit and determine hereditary characteristics. They contain directions that instruct the body to produce certain proteins that constitute the body's cell structures, hormones, and enzymes. They have been called the "building blocks of life" because they direct the body's production of chemicals necessary for life.

When an allele expresses a characteristic—and it is the only gene in the pair that is in that form—it is called dominant. When both genes in the pair must be in that form to express the trait, the gene is said to be recessive. Some human characteristics are determined by a single pair of genes, for example, hitchhiker's thumb or the ability to digest lactose. At other times, more than one pair is required to express a particular trait, such as skin color (six pairs). It should be recognized, of course, that many human traits and characteristics are determined also by nongenetic factors; body size, for example, is also influenced by environmental factors such as nutrition and climate.

Mutation

A change in genetic material is called a mutation. Mutations can result from a number of different causes, for instance, radiation or substance abuse. Mutations can be inherited and are often harmful. The defects they produce are caused either by dominant (Huntington's disease) or recessive (Tay-Sachs disease) alleles. Obviously, to inherit a disease caused by a recessive allele, cystic fibrosis for example, a child must receive the defective gene from both parents, and hence this class of genetic diseases occurs less frequently than those caused by a defective dominant allele, such as polydactyly. Approximately twelve hundred different genetic diseases have been traced to recessive genes. Just as physical characteristics can be determined either by single genes or by multiple genes, so can genetic disorders. An example of the latter would be spina bifida or cleft palate.

In addition, some anomalies are the result of chromosomal defects rather than defective genes. Thus an extra chromosome (trisomy) at the position of the twenty-first pair causes Down syndrome; at the eighteenth, it results in Edward's syndrome. A different problem results from the lack of an autosome. Usually such individuals do not survive till birth and thus constitute part of the number (40–60 percent) of human conceptions that end in a miscarriage. When a sex chromosome is missing (Turner's syndrome—XO) or an extra sex chromosome is present (Klinefelter's syndrome—XXY), the conceptus can survive but some defects usually result. At the present time, geneticists have identified more than four thousand inherited genetic diseases.

Besides causing genetic diseases, faulty genes have been shown to underlie many common organic diseases and mental ailments, particularly where a specific disease is known to be common within a family, such as coronary disease, cancer, diabetes, and Alzheimer's disease. In these cases, scientists are discovering that some alleles of some genes predispose an individual to the disease in question. Combined with environmental factors, particularly lifestyle, one is more likely to develop the disease than the rest of the general population.

Human Genome Project (HGP)

Under the auspices of the National Institutes of Health (NIH) in 1990, international teams of scientists began work on the Human Genome Project, a fifteen-year, three-billion-dollar undertaking funded by Congress. Its established goal was the identification and mapping of all the estimated 30,000 genes in the human genome (the long strands of DNA that make up the chromosomal inheritance of each individual). The project proposed to sequence—or arrange in order—the estimated several billion chemical code letters representing the "bases" that carry the genetic code in the DNA molecule.

By March 1993 approximately six thousand genes had been identified, but only a small fraction of the total number of genes had been sequenced. Simultaneously, scientists were announcing the identity of the genes which, when faulty, are responsible for such genetic diseases as amyotrophic lateral sclerosis (ALS), adrenoleukodystrophy (ALD), and type II diabetes.

In an effort to anticipate ethical problems arising from the Human Genome Project, a special program—the Ethical, Legal, and Social Implications Program (ELSI)—was established in 1992 and publicly funded. Thus it was hoped that attention to bioethical concerns might keep pace with scientific advances.[1]

The timetable for the Project was abruptly revised in 1998 when Dr. Craig Venter announced that he would complete his own decoding of the three-billion-letter human genome in three years. Since that time the race heated up, and the publicly funded researchers responded to the privately funded challengers by advancing their target dates from 2005 to 2003. The National Human Genome Research Institute announced the completion of the full human genome sequence in April 2003. Perhaps more serious than timetables, however, is the intent of the privately funded scientists to seek patent protection for the results of their research. Whether this will seriously impede the ultimate scientific success of the project, as the HGP researchers claim, is now being hotly debated. Critics insist that it is unethical to lay claim to own so much as a single gene.

Armed with this brief survey of some of the terminology and basic understandings employed in the science of genetics, the remainder of this chapter proposes to review four different clinical uses of genetic science, namely, genetic screening and counseling, genetic engineering, cloning, and stem cell technology. In each case, each of the five different dimensions (medical-scientific, legal, sociocultural, Roman Catholic Church teaching, and moral analysis) will be considered.

MEDICAL-SCIENTIFIC INFORMATION

Genetic Screening and Detection

Some of the principal methods of screening for genetic anomalies in fetuses have already been described in the chapter on abortion.

Testing or screening can be done on either the parent(s) or the fetus, clearly with different objectives in mind. In the case of adults, the screening can be in view of a reproductive decision or to test for a late-onset disease such as Huntington's disease. When a fetus is screened, the parents may be uncertain about continuing the pregnancy because of the risk of some genetic anomaly. Obviously, it is neither desirable nor possible to make mass screening programs available to the general public. Who, then, should be screened?

Four classes of individuals are usually identified as most at risk and, hence, prime candidates for genetic testing. Where a family history shows examples of a genetic defect in successive generations, the present generation will surely need to be concerned about its genetic inheritance. Another situation where the chance of genetic defect is heightened will be in a family where a previous pregnancy produced a child with a genetic disability. A third class of individuals who might well consider genetic testing includes those racial or ethnic groups among whom particular genetic defects occur with some frequency. Thus Cooley's anemia, when it occurs, is found most commonly among people of Mediterranean descent, while sickle-cell anemia occurs among African Americans. Tay-Sachs, on the other hand, is usually found within Jewish American families of eastern European origin, while cystic fibrosis is more common among whites of northern European origin. Finally, fetal testing for chromosomal abnormalities is recommended when a pregnant woman is over thirty-five.

Even though numerous tests have been developed to identify specific genes, the decision to use the test is not always a simple one. Take, for example, the current debate among geneticists and ethicists regarding the clinical use of the test for the gene (BRCA1, BRCA2) associated with breast and ovarian cancer. A woman who tests positive for this gene runs an 85 percent risk of developing breast cancer and a 50 percent chance of developing ovarian cancer. Those urging the continued restriction of the test to research argue that current strategies for preventing these cancers are of questionable value. Moreover, they cite the unknown psychosocial effects of a positive test result, plus the high risk of job and insurance discrimination. Proponents of the clinical use of the gene test, on the other hand, condemn the continued restriction as paternalistic and insist on the individual woman's right to know her genetic status, provided she understands the risks to which she may expose herself.

Although science has been developing various methods of testing for genetic defects, no established cure has been available for any genetic anomaly. What has been available is information and, in a few cases, a treatment. By analyzing the data developed through one or more of the various tests developed by geneticists, doctors and counselors can advise a couple whether their child has or is likely to develop a genetic defect. Based on this information, a couple may then decide what action to take with respect to a current or future pregnancy. Although not always explicitly mentioned, abortion is regularly viewed as one of the medical alternatives available when a fetus tests positive for a genetic disorder. The morality of such a decision was considered already in Chapter Four.

While it has not yet been established that any genetic defects can be cured, some can be treated. Phenylketonuria or PKU, for example, is caused when the child is unable to produce an enzyme needed to break down phenylalinine, an amino acid found in certain food products such as milk. When this occurs, phenylalinine builds up in the body and causes developmental problems because of damage to the brain. Because all newborns are now screened for PKU, however, it is possible to place an affected infant on a special diet that assures normal growth and development. Similarly, knowledge that their baby has a cleft palate defect helps prepare parents to deal with this disability and to plan whatever surgical intervention is deemed most advantageous for the infant. Testing for the Rh factor, finally, is another example where screening allows a genetic disease to be treated successfully.

Genetic Counseling

Frequently the counseling function is carried on by practicing physicians, often obstetricians or specialists in medical genetics, although Ph.D. geneticists are also sometimes involved. Diagnosis may be based upon a clinical observation of the affected individual(s), a detailed family history, laboratory tests (if such exist), prenatal diagnosis of the fetus (if one exists), and the examination of the remains of deceased relatives to determine if some pathology existed.

When the screening is directed at adults with a view to a reproductive decision, the counselor can only explain the outcome of the testing and the probable risk of inheritance by offspring, calculated according to the Mendelian laws and thus indicating only probabilities. The counselor can also inform the individual of the nature of the disease in question, its symptoms, gravity, prognosis for treatment, resources for support and cost. Finally, the counselor can discuss such medical alternatives as sterilization, adoption, and artificial insemination. Since this testing is often not covered by private insurers, the expense must frequently be borne by the individual. Although initially the availability of testing was limited to medical research centers at major educational institutions, it is now more broadly distributed throughout the country.

In the case of a pregnancy in progress, the counselor can discuss with the client the medical and legal alternatives that are available— keeping the child, abortion, and the availability of placement for the child. Ideally the counselor is expected to remain neutral concerning the values implicit in these choices to assure client freedom.

Genetic Engineering—Therapeutic

But scientists are not satisfied with simply testing for genetic anomalies. They are seeking cures, and since the cause of the defect is in the genetic material itself, the obvious solution is to replace or rebuild it. At the present time, scientists are developing two different categories of therapeutic genetic engineering. Germ-line gene therapy would involve interventions that affect the human germ (sex) cells— and hence all future generations of offspring from that individual. All other procedures are called somatic-cell gene therapy.

Through recombinant DNA studies over the past twenty years, scientists have succeeded in altering the genetic material in a number of nonhuman species. Thus, for example, they have inserted genes into bacteria that now produce insulin that can be used to treat diabetes. They have developed the capacity to combine the light-producing gene of a firefly with the genetic material of a tobacco plant so that the plant glows in the dark. They have produced a supermouse twice the size of normal laboratory mice.

As lab techniques have been developed using lower life forms, scientists are now taking aim at human genetic disorders. As knowledge and experience are accumulated, geneticists have begun to develop experimental therapies that will allow people born with defective genes to have "good" genes inserted—into their bone marrow, perhaps—that will produce the missing proteins or enzymes and cure their disease. In 1982, the President's Commission outlined four steps required to achieve successful somatic-cell therapy:

1. Clone the normal gene.
2. Introduce the cloned gene in a stable fashion into appropriate target cells by means of a vector.
3. Regulate the production of the gene product.
4. Ensure that no harm comes to the host cells.[2]

On September 14, 1990, a team of scientists led by Dr. French Anderson became the first to seek to meet these guidelines. After receiving approval from all of the oversight and regulatory bodies, they began gene therapy on a four-year-old child suffering from severe combined immunodeficiency (SCID) by introducing into her bloodstream some one billion cells, each containing a copy of a foreign gene. The scientists first extracted T-cells from the child's own blood. These were then exposed to a mouse-leukemia retrovirus, first rendered harmless and then endowed with a normal gene. The retrovirus, acting as a vector, invaded the T-cell and incorporated its genetic material, including the missing gene. The reengineered T-cells were then cultured, producing billions of copies that were infused back into the child's bloodstream, where the new gene began producing the missing enzyme, so that her devastated immune system might slowly begin to recover. A second child, nine years old, became the second patient to be offered this therapy on January 31, 1991.

For two years, the treatments were repeated every few months. At the end of that time, Dr. Anderson reported that his patients continued to show "strong signs of recovery" from their inherited disorder. "A full clinical report will be issued," he promised, "after completion of required tests and with a greater elapsed time of treatment."[3] In March 1993, Anderson—then at the University of Southern California—reported that both children had acceptable levels of the needed enzyme and were leading normal, healthy lives. Throughout the therapy the children continued to receive weekly injections of PEG-ADA, a drug that provides the missing enzyme. At the end of those two years of gene therapy, therefore, the research team judged that the children no longer required the therapy's continuance since their reengineered

132

cells were surviving and producing the ADA enzyme. Anderson admitted that the gene therapy had not produced a cure but claimed nonetheless that "if you put a correct gene into enough cells in a patient, you will correct the disease."

In his comments Anderson also pointed out that forty-seven protocols—involving ninety-two patients—had now received NIH approval, and clinical trials had begun on diseases as diverse as cystic fibrosis, cancer, and AIDS. Three patients were suffering from SCID and for them a cure was sought, not a treatment. In their cases, stem cells were the target of the therapy, rather than T-cells, which tended to die out after several months, thus requiring repeated treatments. Stem cells were withdrawn—from bone marrow in the case of an eleven-year-old girl and from umbilical-cord blood in the case of two newborn infants—then genetically altered and reinserted into the children's bodies. Since the stem cells are the source of all immune cells, including T-cells, it was hoped that the genetically engineered stem cells would produce a permanent supply of the ADA enzyme.[4]

At the present time, any activity involving therapeutic genetic engineering is experimental. The FDA has not yet approved any human gene therapy product for commercial use by clinicians. Even though the earliest trials began in 1990, little progress has been made in developing any therapeutic mechanism for general clinical use. In 1999 the entire enterprise suffered a major setback when eighteen-year-old Jesse Gelsinger died while participating in an experimental gene treatment for OTCD (ornithine transcarboxylase deficiency). Jesse suffered multiple organ failure four days into the therapy and died, perhaps the result of a severe immune response to the viral vector.

A second major setback occurred in January 2003, when the FDA called a temporary halt to all gene therapy trials using retroviruses as vectors in blood stem cells. The reason for this action was the news that a second child being treated in France for SCID had developed a leukemia-like reaction to the therapy. Despite requests for approval to renew clinical trials for lethal diseases, the FDA has failed to give a go-ahead—as of July 2003.[5]

Genetic Engineering—Eugenic

Correcting genetic anomalies is just one of the directions that recombinant DNA technology has taken. Suppose, instead of correcting the defect in an adult, one decides to modify the faulty genetic material at conception. Even further, suppose there is no defect at all. Suppose instead that one merely exercises selectivity in determining some physical traits. At this point, genetic engineering becomes eugenics. Suppose one decides to select one sex over the other. Researchers have developed a method of segregating X chromosomes from Y chromosomes. An egg can then be fertilized artificially to produce the desired sex. And what began as a technology to determine sex raises the larger question about selecting "desirable traits" in offspring. When the intervention will aim at increasing or improving some desirable trait or characteristic (e.g., physical size, IQ) it is spoken of as "enhancement genetic engineering," whereas the creation of an "improved" individual in a species or a new life form is termed "eugenic genetic engineering." There seems to be little doubt that such a capability will be developed. The question is whether it should be utilized.[6]

Cloning

Another fast-developing technology is cloning. Cloning involves genetic manipulation, and therefore it is an appropriate consideration in this chapter. It also holds out the possibility of being yet another artificial reproductive technology and therefore, from that standpoint, consideration of this technology would also have been appropriate in the preceding chapter.

The development of cloning as a scientific technology has inserted a dramatically new dimension to the discussion of the clinical applications of genetic science and of artificial reproduction. Admittedly, the ability to clone submammalian species has been around for some time. Still, no one had ever been able to take the next step and reproduce a mammal asexually. Indeed, in the minds of many scientists, it would never be possible. Imagine their surprise then, when Dr. Ian Wilmut at the Roslin Institute in Edinburgh, Scotland, announced the successful cloning of a sheep, Dolly. On February 23,

1997, Dr. Wilmut introduced his seven-month-old sheep to the scientific community and to the world.

What was equally astounding was the procedure that the Roslin scientists used to produce Dolly. Dr. Wilmut chose not to follow the previously developed method of separating the embryonic cells of a blastocyst into separate, identical single-cell zygotes. This latter procedure had been used successfully in the '70s in experiments with mice. By the late '80s this technique had been commercially adapted for animal breeding and came into wide use. No one had been quite prepared, however, when Dr. Stillman at George Washington University in the nation's capital announced that he had employed the same procedure successfully on humans. Even though he deliberately chose embryonic material that could not ever develop fully in utero (the zygotes did not survive beyond the thirty-two-cell stage), the procedure had been successfully employed in human reproduction. As Dr. Stillman explained, his only interest had been in adapting the procedure for the production of identical human zygotes. Interested or not, what he also did was initiate a huge public debate about the ethics of his achievement.

Dr. Wilmut's cloning procedure was radically different, however. In a procedure that has come to be called somatic-cell nuclear transfer technology, the scientist took the nucleus from a six-year-old sheep's mammary cell and inserted it into an egg from another adult sheep that he had previously enucleated. An electrical charge was next applied, causing the pores of the egg and cell to open, fusing the contents of the two and, voilà, an embryo. It may sound simple, but it took Dr. Wilmut and his team 277 attempts, of which only thirteen developed into embryos. Fortunately for her, Dolly was the sole survivor.

It may sound simple, but consider what had to occur. First, the adult cell nucleus had to fuse with the enucleated ovum. Since the original DNA had fully differentiated when it had become the nucleus of the mammary cell, it had to now dedifferentiate. This new embryo would then have to divide into daughter cells, which would be pluripotent stem cells with the capability of differentiating into specific tissues—muscle, skin, and so on. And it had worked! Witness Dolly!

It was only the beginning. On January 21, 1998, Drs. Stice and Robl, two University of Massachusetts researchers, announced that they had used a variation of the Roslin procedure to produce two

Holstein calves, using fetal skin cells. The new embryos were then frozen and shipped to Texas, where they found their surrogate mothers waiting for them. Forty percent survived, evidence that the technology was becoming more efficient. The two scientists had also replicated Dr. Wilmut's use of adult cells for this technology and the birth of additional cloned calves was announced as imminent.

In quick succession, the announcements multiplied. On July 22, 1998, a researcher, Dr. Yanagimachi, at the University of Hawaii, announced the birth of twenty-two cloned mice, seven of which were clones of clones. On December 9 of that same year *Science* magazine carried the announcement that scientists at Kinki University in Nara, Japan, had produced eight clones from a single adult cow's DNA, while less than a week later the fertility clinic at Kyeonghee University in Korea announced that somatic-cell nuclear transfer technology had been used successfully to produce human clones. The researchers arrested the zygotes' development at the fourth cell stage for "ethical reasons." Finally, on January 22, 1999, Dr. Wilmut was back in the news. At that time he described his plans to begin human cloning, not to produce complete human beings, but to clone human embryos in order to withdraw stem cells. That done, the rest of the embryo would be discarded.

It may be important at this point to contrast the condition of a cloned embryo from one created through sexual intercourse. The latter, it has been pointed out, has "at best a 28 percent chance of resulting in a human life, and perhaps as little as 14 percent—much less potential than many people are aware."[7] A cloned embryo, on the other hand, has almost no chance of developing into a normal, healthy child. As Hall has pointed out:

> the success rate in animal cloning experiments varies from species to species, but has always been very low, on the order of 3 or 4 percent. In primates, the animals closest to humans on the phylogenetic ladder—hundreds of cloning experiments have failed to produce a single viable embryo, much less a live birth.[8]

At the present time, it would appear that the vast majority of cloned embryos are genetically incapable of normal development, due to incomplete reprogramming of their genome. And so, based both on their genetic incompleteness and their lack of potential for a full life, cloned embryos are quite different from naturally conceived embryos. Whether this difference is sufficient to justify embryo research in which the destruction of the embryo is the intended outcome of the experiment will continue to be the focus of the stem-cell debate.

Human Stem-Cell Technology

In February 1999, two teams of researchers announced to the world that they had succeeded in isolating human embryonic stem cells, those elusive human cells that fleetingly appear in the ordinary development of a human being before the process of differentiation occurs. Dr. James Thomson of the University of Wisconsin (Madison) worked with human embryos that had been donated for the research by their parents through the IVF Clinic at the University. Dr. John Gearhart, a researcher at the Johns Hopkins University in Baltimore, isolated his stem cells from the germ cells of aborted fetuses. The precursors of the gametes, these germ cells are not committed to becoming particular organs. In both cases, the scientific procedure successfully isolated these pluripotent human cells and through chemical manipulation prevented them from differentiating into one of the 210 specific types of cells that evolve as the human organism develops from fertilization to birth.

These stem cells, then, are capable of multiplying indefinitely— "immortal" is the term used by some commentators!—and thus they became a potent instrument for human genetic experimentation. The two scientists know, for example, that if these cells are removed from their suspended state, they will develop into all the other types of human cells. At the present state of the research, this occurs randomly. The next step, therefore, will be to develop the mechanism that will allow the scientists to direct their pluripotent cells into becoming specific kinds of cells.

What could these stem cells be good for? The researchers cite a long list of possibilities—a fuller understanding of human embryonic development, a clearer appreciation of the multiplication of cancer cells, human tissue for testing new pharmaceutical products, a revolutionary new approach to human transplantation—all new, all exciting, all critically needed for clinical practice in the third millennium. The trick will be to control their differentiation. Then scientists will have islet cells to treat diabetes, nerve cells to restore brain function in Parkinson's or Alzheimer's patients, heart cells to restore cardiac function—the possibilities are enormous. Equally exciting is the fact that these cells can be genetically altered so that they will defeat the human rejection mechanism.

What scientific evidence is there to support these futuristic proposals? The technique works in mice! Introduced into a mouse's brain, stem cells become brain cells; inject stem cells into its heart and they become cardiac cells. The researchers are confident that these same reactions will occur in humans. Because these embryonic stem cells grow indefinitely in the right "nutrient soup," their supply will be inexhaustible. Dr. Thomson indicated that his research developed one trillion stem cells during the seven months of his initial research.

This new scientific breakthrough, therefore, requires researchers to harvest stem cells from newly created blastocysts, after which the remaining embryonic material will be discarded. Armed with these pluripotent cells, scientists can then develop the further technical mechanisms necessary to make this new technology available for clinical applications. For example, some scientists are already predicting that this new capability will make it easier to engineer a baby. By simply injecting the desired stem cell into the embryo, they say, it will spread throughout and produce the desired endowment. At the present, they recognize, NIH regulations prohibit such experimentation in people, but they are hopeful that these rules will soon be liberalized.

LEGAL ISSUES

Genetic Screening and Counseling

The only example of genetic screening on a national scale occurs in connection with PKU. By 1971, forty-one states had passed statutes requiring such testing of all newborns. At the present time all fifty states have enacted such legislation. A number of states have also passed laws mandating testing for sickle-cell anemia. Large-scale screening has also been undertaken by private groups. The most notable example has been the efforts of the Jewish American community of eastern European

138

ancestry, which has worked to reduce the incidence of Tay-Sachs among its members by 95 percent.

Genetic Engineering

A number of legal issues and concerns have arisen in connection with genetic engineering in general and with recombinant DNA technologies in particular. One issue that surfaced in the early 1970s was public—and scientific—concern arising from potential biohazards connected with recombinant DNA research. What new life forms were being produced in the laboratories, the public asked, and what risks did they pose to the general population? Particularly in communities located adjacent to the universities at which this research was being conducted, a public controversy arose that threatened the future of this scientific development. In response, the scientific establishment imposed a moratorium on this work until satisfactory guidelines could be developed. At the same time, municipalities such as Cambridge, Massachusetts, enacted legislation through which it sought to protect its citizens. At the national level, hearings were conducted in Congress, but no legislation was forthcoming. The executive branch did take action, however, and NIH issued guidelines that sought to allay fears and provide direction. A second wave of local legislation occurred in the early 1980s as commercial biogenetic corporations sought to locate within municipalities proximate to the major research universities. Again, Cambridge led the way in an effort to place adequate safety regulations on such corporations and thus protect itself from unnecessary risk.

Another area of legal concern has arisen in connection with the commercialization of genetic technology. Is it legal to patent living organisms? The question has been vehemently argued on both sides through the courts. In 1980 the Supreme Court determined that "anything under the sun that is made by man" could be patented. In May 1987 the U.S. Patent Office announced that it considered "nonnaturally occurring nonhuman multicellular living organisms, including animals, to be patentable subject matter."[9] This decision was attacked by a broad variety of groups—animal-rights advocates, cattle breeders, ethicists, and theologians. Still others have raised the specter of patenting genetically altered human beings, even though the regulation specified "nonhuman." Although the Patent Office has been petitioned to rescind its regulations, this is not likely to happen. As was already pointed out in connection with the Human Genome Project, privately funded researchers are patenting the results of their work—human cells, tissue—to justify the commitment of funds by their funding sources.

Cloning

The success of Dr. Wilmut's cloning of Dolly raised the possibility of cloning other mammals. Two procedures had made it possible—by separating the cells of an early blastocyst and producing identical embryos, or by using the Roslin procedure. Inevitably, the question was asked—and what of human cloning? Once Dolly hit the front pages, President Clinton took the initiative by asking his National Bioethics Advisory Commission (NBAC) to study the question and report back to him within ninety days. The commission returned to him with recommendations that human cloning as a reproductive technique should be prohibited for the next five years in view of safety concerns. Dr. Wilmut had required 277 attempts to achieve one success. At the present juncture, then, reproductive human cloning was seen as "irresponsible, unethical and unprofessional." The commission did suggest, however, that human embryo cloning might be permitted, provided that the embryos not be allowed to develop into babies.

The president accepted these recommendations and imposed these restraints on all such scientific research supported by public funds. Privately funded research, he urged, should observe the same restraints voluntarily. Debate followed swiftly in the Congress, although all attempts at restrictive legislation were beaten back. Meanwhile the FDA claimed jurisdiction over any publicly funded research that involved human cloning. It is not clear, however, that such claimed regulatory authority would be held up by the courts. For one thing, the FDA has simply asserted that it would require any investigator who would try to produce children through cloning— whether in the public or the private sector—to be held to the same requirements that apply to unapproved drugs. There clearly is not a neat match of definitions here—drugs and a cloned child. Moreover, the FDA announced its claim to jurisdiction and its interpretation of the law without following the standard procedures for administrative rule-making. Such a situation leaves the FDA and its claim vulnerable in the courts. Federal oversight of reproductive cloning is hardly guaranteed.[10]

In July 2002, President George W. Bush's follow-up Council on Bioethics issued practically the same report as Clinton's NBAC. Reproductive cloning, the Council determined unanimously, should not be permitted. Both public and privately funded research involving reproductive cloning ("cloning to produce children") should be banned since it is unsafe for both the woman and the cloned child and "there seems to be no ethical way to try to discover whether cloning to produce children can become safe, now or in the future." In addition, the Council cited additional reasons for banning reproductive cloning, namely, "the industrialization of reproduction, the danger of potential eugenics and other possible negative effects on society and on family relations."[11]

It is important to note the Council's additional reflections on reproductive cloning. In its unanimous response, the Council wrote "A child is not made, but begotten....A man and a woman give themselves in love to each other, setting their projects aside in order to do just that." While other forms of artificially assisted reproductive technology arrive at an end result that is not predetermined by the parents, cloning "introduces an entirely new creation story, one which challenges our 'continuing history' through human reproduction."[12]

By the summer of 2003, the only American jurisdiction that enacted restrictive legislation was California. The previous September, the governor had signed into law California's statute imposing a permanent ban on reproductive cloning, whatever the funding source. The rationale for the legislation was cloning's risk to the physical safety of both mother and child. In addition, it cited the threat of confusing familial relationships, the possible psychic harm to the DNA donor, and the commercialization of the family. At the same time, the California statute endorsed nonreproductive cloning because of its potential to alleviate the suffering of individuals, for example, with diabetes and Parkinson's disease. The law placed two conditions on researchers involved in this experimentation. The researchers had to be subject to state regulation, and their use of blastocysts had to be limited to embryonic material less than fourteen days old.[13]

If the federal government has so far resisted any legal prohibition of human cloning, such has not been the case outside the United States. The Council of Europe acted in January 1998 and established a universal ban on human cloning, judging it to be contrary to human dignity and an abuse of scientific techniques. It did permit, however, the cloning of human cells for research. UNESCO called for a universal ban on human cloning as an affront to human freedom and dignity. Similarly, the UN Commission on Human Rights called for a total ban on human reproductive cloning. In Canada, the Royal Commission on Reproduction and Genetic Technology, after a two-year study, recommended a complete ban on human reproductive cloning because it found that Canadians were "opposed to the commodification of people."

Stem-Cell Technology

Current federal law prohibits the use of public funds to support research that involves the manipulation of live human embryos or causes damage to them. The federal government has been debating the use of unborn children for experimentation for thirty years. In 1994 an NIH panel approved the creation of pre-embryos for research if there were not enough "orphaned" pre-embryos available following in vitro fertilization. The following year Congress replied by imposing a total ban on the use of public funds for embryo research, with the result that virtually all scientific studies of human reproduction and infertility have depended on private funding. For this reason the stem-cell research of Drs. Thomson and Gearhart was privately funded by the Geron Corporation.

On January 19, 1999, the Department of Health and Human Services (HHS) determined that embryonic stem-cell research did not fall under the 1995 congressional ban and, consequently, NIH was given the green light to fund the initial derivation of these cells from an embryo. On January 26, in testimony before a congressional subcommittee, Dr. Harold Varmus, director of NIH, described the process whereby that body would prepare guidelines that would direct the funding of this new area of research. On February 16, 1999, seventy members of Congress wrote a letter formally objecting to the decision of HHS to go forward with its funding and challenging the legality of the interpretation of the HHS lawyers.

Whatever the Congress believed, President Bush's Council on Bioethics astonished the scientific world by its recommendation. The Council, no longer with complete unanimity, urged a four-year moratorium on research cloning in order to permit additional research on existing stem-cell lines and on animal cloning. The Council also urged the public to become involved in the debate, pointing out that "human embryos have a special moral status and merit special respect because of their potential to become human beings. If research cloning were permitted but reproductive cloning banned," the Council's majority argued, "the government would have to require that any cells created through cloning eventually be destroyed and this would itself be …unsavory."[14]

Clearly, the issue of public funding has not yet been decided.

SOCIOCULTURAL INFLUENCES

Screening and Counseling

A reflection on the values and attitudes of American society on questions relating to issues in genetics has been noted in connection with newborns with disabilities and need not be repeated here. A few additional notes might be offered in connection both with genetic testing/counseling and genetic engineering.

Questions have been raised about testing and engineering from the standpoint of *equality*. If these procedures are expensive and not covered by insurance, then they will not be available to all, but only to those well-off enough to be able to afford them. Is that fair? Are we not simply widening the health care gap between those covered by insurance and the uninsured? The question may well be asked: Who is speaking up in this society for the poor? Is this a justice question? How is the common good of American society related to the availability of decent health care?[15]

Mandatory screening—for example, for PKU or for sickle-cell anemia—raises questions of the *invasion of privacy*. The debate is similar to the current controversy over mandatory testing for AIDS. Will insurance companies or employers be able to require testing? Employers, certainly, will be interested in eliminating individuals who would push up their health-insurance and workmen's-compensation costs. Insurance companies will want to limit their risks as well. What about these conflicting concerns? Whose right should prevail? The answer is not yet in sight. In fact, it is not even being discussed by the general public, who will surely be most affected. Serious concerns involving the privacy of personal medical information have been voiced already, however, in connection with the Human Genome Project and have been an issue considered by the ELSI program of the HGP.

As *family size* has decreased, the pressure for "perfect" children has increased. This is not only reflected in the rejection of defective children through abortion, but as biotechnology develops the capacity to predetermine traits and characteristics, the temptation to "engineer" one's offspring will increase.

In modern genetics, the American *respect for academic freedom and for scientific research* runs up against a growing *concern for ecology and the environment.* It is one thing to develop new life forms in the relative safety of the laboratory, but quite a different thing to release them into the atmosphere. This conflict of values is clearly reflected in the growing number of legal actions seeking to block research activities that could possibly place the community and its environment at risk.

As can be readily understood, these are but a few of the many questions raised by the scientific advances that provide headlines each day in the press. Genetics will continue to challenge this society to clarify and prioritize its values for a long time to come.

Genetic Engineering

As already pointed out, American society holds high the *freedom of academic researchers* to pursue scientific inquiry wherever it leads. This tradition, Americans believe, has played a major role in contributing to the advanced state of scientific knowledge in this country. Any attempt at interference by external agents generates strong objections from academics and researchers. And yet, scientific research is costly, making financial support an ever present concern. When funding is denied, therefore—especially by the major funding source of all scientific research, the federal government—researchers may find their work seriously impeded or even halted. The funding issue is central, therefore. It is important for a second reason, its supporters insist. Government oversight is critically important, they point out, if this scientific effort is to avoid the extravagances and abuses that this research may engender. Since it involves human life, this exercise of review and reasonable restraint is crucial. Absent the funding, absent the oversight.

Equally important to many Americans is the *value placed on human life*. Witness the results of the surveys cited in connection with cloning. It is precisely this conflict of values, therefore, that pits the great medical benefits promised by stem-cell research against the dignity and worth of a living human organism, the embryo. It is hard to say which will prevail, however, given the degree of commitment of both sides. The political lobbying of the biomedical community and the pharmaceutical industry is well known in Washington; so too is the demonstrated power of the pro-life community. Only a seer would predict the outcome.

Cloning

Public opinion would appear to have a chilling effect on all reproductive human cloning at this time. Any scientist who ignored this would face wide public disapproval. A 2003 Gallup poll showed that 86 percent of all Americans believed that reproductive human cloning should be illegal while the previous year 90 percent judged that it was morally wrong. The *Washington Post* editorialized that it was alarmed at scientists' "purposely causing conceptions in a context entirely divorced from even the potential of reproduction."[16] Commentators point out, however, that similar public opposition was voiced when IVF was first introduced, and "never" quickly became "why not?"

A number of societal values will be challenged, however, if cloning is utilized as a reproductive technology. Dr. Wilmut himself rejected this use, arguing that it could lead to serious relational problems between adult (parent?) and clone. For one thing, there seems to be serious concern that the child will be held hostage to follow in the footsteps of the adult. Will there be psychological restraints on the clone, denying the clone the right to an open future, establishing a "genetic bondage" as one commentator called it? Would the cloned individual feel genetically destined to the same future? Would clones have a diminished sense of individuality? Would cloning undermine the basic elements of a loving, nurturing family? If widespread, what would become of the expected acceptance of each child as a unique individual? Would cloning undermine human dignity by threatening the child's later sense of self and autonomy, which, as one commentator points out, a vast body of research in developmental psychology has demonstrated to be vital for psychological health? There are many who answer "yes" to these queries.

On the other hand, it has been pointed out that Americans seem to look upon reproductive decisions as some inherent right that only affects the adult making the decision—whether or not to use in vitro fertilization, a surrogate mother, and now cloning. The trouble with this tendency to claim absolute reproductive freedom as an inalienable right—as the right of every individual adult to be free of any other consideration beyond the decision to have a child—is that the focus is lost forever for the child. As an increasing number of commentators have noted, the question ought to be: Is IVF good for the child? Is arranging for a surrogate to carry the pregnancy to term good for the child? Now another, even more crucial question arises: Will cloning be good for the child? If America's experience with IVF can teach us anything, it ought to be that we must not sacrifice the clone's welfare by insisting on the adult's reproductive freedom as the only consideration.[17]

Stem-Cell Technology

The use of cloning as an artificial reproductive technique is only one of the benefits that scientists foresee for the new technology, however. Human embryos, it is argued, can provide embryonic stem cells that offer the possibility of curing numerous human illnesses. Given the widespread American conviction that medicine can eventually cure all ills, there surely is a strong bias in this country in favor of new technologies that promise the eradication of so many serious diseases. Americans may stop short of approving cloning as an artificial reproductive technology—at least for the time being—but the other medical applications that may be spawned by this exciting new research are sure to be widely applauded.

What of the fact that zygotes, embryos, fetuses will be destroyed by the research that discards these human organisms in order to harvest their stem cells? It is not difficult to see how the same arguments that Americans have accepted for or against abortion will reappear as responses to this new research involving human embryos. And the same central question will be repeated: What value do you place on the pre-embryo (blastocyst) or the embryo? Scientists propose to create living human beings, whatever the stage of pregnancy may be, without any intention of allowing them to achieve their natural full development. To approve stem-cell research would constitute an open invitation to researchers to cause human conceptions purposely without any thought of human reproduction. As one critic of the NBAC recommendations commented, it is OK to clone them, as long as you kill them![18]

ROMAN CATHOLIC CHURCH TEACHING

In February 1987 the Congregation for the Doctrine of the Faith released its *Instruction on Respect for Human Life in Its Origin and on the Dignity of Procreation*. While the document was principally concerned with the new IVF technology, the congregation also offered some views that touched on questions relating to other aspects of genetic science.

Eugenic Genetic Engineering

Each human person, in his absolutely unique singularity, is constituted not only by his spirit, but by his body as well. Thus, in the body and through the body, one touches the person himself in his concrete reality. To respect the dignity of man consequently amounts to safeguarding this identity of the man *"corpore et anima unus,"* as the Second Vatican Council says (*Gaudium et Spes*, 14.1). It is on the basis of this anthropological vision that one is to find the fundamental criteria for decision making in the case of procedures which are not strictly therapeutic, as, for example, those aimed at the improvement of the human biological condition.[19] ...Certain attempts to influence chromosomic or genetic inheritance are not therapeutic, but are aimed at producing human beings selected according to sex or other predetermined qualities.

These manipulations are contrary to the personal dignity of the human being and his or her integrity and identity. Therefore in no way can they be justified on the grounds of possible beneficial consequences for future humanity. Every person must be respected for himself: In this consists the dignity and right of every human being from his or her beginning.[20]

Therapeutic Genetic Engineering

The legitimacy and criteria of such procedures have been clearly stated by Pope John Paul II:

A strictly therapeutic intervention whose explicit objective is the healing of various maladies such as those stemming from chromosomal defects will, in principle, be considered desirable, provided it is directed to the true promotion of the personal well-being of the individual without doing harm to his integrity or worsening his conditions of life. Such an intervention would indeed fall within the logic of the Christian moral tradition.[21]

Cloning

While no formal or authoritative declaration regarding cloning has yet been issued by Vatican authorities since the appearance of Dolly on the international scene, the church's moral evaluation of this new technology is not hard to guess, whether cloning is used as a reproductive technology or as an intermediate step to secure stem cells for research or therapy. In its 1987 *Instruction on Respect for Human Life in Its Origin and on the Dignity of Procreation,*[22] the Congregation for the Doctrine of the Faith based its teaching about IVF on the following principles, which apply equally well to the use of cloning as a reproductive technique:

1. Human procreation must take place within marriage through the loving exchange that constitutes the marriage act.
2. The child has the right to be conceived, carried in the womb, brought into the world, and brought up within marriage. It is through the secure and recognized relationship to his own parents that the child can discover his own identity and achieve his own proper human development.

148

3. It would violate the human dignity of the child to be brought into
the world through the intervention of medical or biological techniques, thus reducing him to the object of scientific technology.

In his testimony before a congressional committee on February
12, 1998, Cardinal William Keeler of Baltimore spoke for the
American Catholic bishops. He condemned the treating of a human
being—the human embryo—as an object, as a means to someone
else's end, rather than a being endowed with a unique, inherent dignity. He pointed to the recommendation of the NBAC that human
cloning be permitted as long as the clone is not implanted in a
woman's uterus to be the most obvious indication of the dehumanizing effect of cloning. Finally, he quoted Leon Kass, who criticized
human cloning for "turning begetting into making, procreation into
manufacture...[thus] making man himself simply another one of the
man-made things."[23]

Stem-Cell Technology

The use of cloning as a technique for acquiring stem cells from
the early blastocyst, which would then be discarded, would surely
come within the church's condemnation of abortion. Since, as Vatican
II has taught, the safeguarding of human life must begin from the
moment of conception, to terminate the life begun at fertilization can
never be morally defended, even for the most laudable medical goals.
Since the gift of life brings with it the accompanying gift of being created in God's image and likeness, the destruction of that life for scientific purposes can never be morally justified

Pope John Paul II speaks directly to this issue in his encyclical
letter *Evangelium Vitae* (The Gospel of Life):[24]

This evaluation of the morality of abortion is to be applied also
to the recent forms of intervention on human embryos which,
although carried out for purposes legitimate in themselves,
inevitably involve the killing of those embryos. This is the case
with experimentation on embryos, which is increasingly widespread in the field of biomedical research and is legally permitted in some countries....This moral condemnation also regards
procedures that exploit living human embryos and fetuses—

sometimes specifically "produced" for this purpose by in vitro fertilization—either to be used as "biological material" or as providers of organs or tissue for transplants in the treatment of certain diseases. The killing of innocent human creatures, even if carried out to help others, constitutes an absolutely unacceptable act. (63)

Thus it is implied that the Roman Catholic Church offers no objection to the aims of such research and the many therapeutic possibilities envisioned by the researchers. What the church objects to, however, is the misuse of the living human organism which that research generates. Dr. Thomson began with blastocysts, produced through in vitro fertilization and "left over" in the fertility clinic at the University of Wisconsin. For the church, a human blastocyst is a living human being. It deserves the same respect and reverence as an embryo, a fetus, or a newborn baby. Its human development is primitive or, better, foundational. From this hollow ball of cells will develop a fully human being. To remove the embryonic stem cells from this living organism and then discard what is left is as much an abortion as any other termination of human life that is in the process of becoming. The fact that this is taking place outside a woman's womb does not change the moral character of the deed. No matter how lofty the motives, the act cannot be morally approved.

The Johns Hopkins researcher, Dr. Gearhart, began his experiments from a different starting point. He chose the dead fetal tissue that was the result of an abortion and from this material developed his stem cells. Although he did not cause the abortion, he approved of the result of the abortion by its use. He could not have carried out his research without the abortion's having taken place. If one person commits an immoral action and a second person knowingly profits from it, is not the second person participating in the immoral act in some way? Does it not amount to approval of it? If you know that I've stolen $100,000 and you borrow $10,000 from me, does that not now involve you implicitly in my immoral act? Obviously for those who hold that abortion is morally acceptable, this whole argument falls to pieces. What we are concerned with here is the position of the Catholic Church regarding abortion, and its condemnation of abortion needs no further demonstration.

Another important consideration, though more of a practical than moral nature, is the caution needed when approaching overly publicized therapies like stem-cell technology. What clinical support for such therapies has evolved so far? One report[25] indicates that a double blind study of the impact of fetal stem cells on Parkinson's sufferers reported that none of the forty participants benefited from the therapy. In fact, 15 percent showed "rapidly worsening symptoms." In their comments on the experiment, Caplan and McGee noted that the current technique for employing fetal cells in treating Parkinson's victims ran a high risk of causing disastrous harm to the patients. Their conclusion was that the clinical value of fetal cell implants up to that time was "hype." It is crucial, they insisted, to weigh one reality against another and to sort out potential benefits from actual ones.[26]

THE MORAL DIMENSION

Screening/Counseling and Engineering

A number of *moral concerns* (i.e., concern for moral values) can be identified both in connection with genetic testing/counseling and with genetic engineering.

Genetic Screening/Counseling

Will the desire to eliminate genetic disorders dry up our sense of *compassion?* Will we continue to care for and support those individuals that slip through whatever genetic safety nets we construct? These will be among the most vulnerable and most dependent members of our society. Will our yearning for the perfect cancel our patience with the imperfect? As has been noted:

> It is vital that the growing desire to have "normal" babies does not erode our acceptance and care of those who have disabilities, otherwise the advances made through the Americans with Disabilities Act will be nullified.[27]

151

Childbearing decisions are inherently *private*, but they are not exclusively so. Does society, for instance, have the right to insist on testing marriage license applicants for genetic defects in virtue of its public health function? How far does this right extend? Does society have the right of self-defense in the sense of requiring certain individuals to refrain from childbearing? Denmark, to cite one example, refuses to issue a marriage license to individuals with certain types of genetic defects. Is this morally justified? Or should it be up to the individual to decide whether or not he/she wishes to be screened, whether or not to know the results of the screening, whether or not to know that he/she has a genetic defect? And then, further, should the individual be able to decide whether or not to have children who might inherit the defect?

Another area of ethical and legal concern regarding genetic privacy arises from the establishment of DNA data banks. It has been suggested that the current rules protecting the confidentiality of medical information are inadequate to preserve an individual's genetic privacy. Unless new, enforceable privacy rules are developed, it is argued, the rapid advance in genetic information threatens to undermine the security of personal information.[28]

And what of the information gained from testing, mandatory or otherwise? Who has the right to share this knowledge? Who "owns" the information? Should it be absolutely *confidential* or does some other person(s) also have the right to know—a spouse or other family member, the family doctor, one's insurance company, one's employer, one's landlord, a government agency? Anecdotal information has begun to accumulate to indicate that those who test positive run the risk of becoming the victims of discrimination—in employment, in the delivery of health care and social services, and in the matter of insurance coverage.[29] This was certainly the experience of the African American community in connection with sickle-cell testing.

For many, *abortion* is always—at least implicitly—a consideration when genetic flaws are found in a fetus through screening. Is abortion for fetal indications ever justified?[30] The screening process itself is subject to error and the counselor may misinterpret genetic data. When one is dealing with the screening of adults, one is able to talk only about the possibility of passing the anomaly to offspring, about percentages. When one is screening a fetus, however, the implications are quite different! Moreover, when first introduced, prenatal screening could detect only serious, lethal conditions. Given the advances in both prenatal diagnosis and molecular genetics, however, our ability to uncover "many normal variants and social predispositions" will be enhanced, and "if they are either present or absent, depending on the wishes of the parents, the fetus could be aborted."[31] Will the development of screening technology simply increase the reasons for abortion?

Genetic counselors are supposed to remain *neutral* and simply provide information.[32] Is this possible? Can one's own values be kept out of the counseling process? Is it desirable? Often, great emotional and interpersonal stress results when the counseling process must deal with positive indications. Who will provide support and help the client process the information?

Finally, as noted earlier, not all will have the technology available. Will this *discriminate* unjustly against the poor and the unfortunate? Surely we can agree that the commitment of our common resources should be for our common good and hence be generally available. In another sense, discrimination will be a natural temptation—given our past and present history of racism—as group differences are brought to full public awareness by the Human Genome Project. The obvious challenge will be to acknowledge these differences while at the same time insisting that they have no relevance when it comes to "respect for individual dignity and *equality of right*."[33]

It is essential to recall the experience of the eugenics programs in the first half of this century, both in this country and in Germany. Remembering the genetic discrimination that arose then from a simplistic but unscientific genetic determinism should help avoid that fatal blunder in the present situation.[34]

Genetic Engineering

No serious moral questions seem to be raised by genetic engineering on human subjects for *therapeutic* purposes. Initially, of course, the procedures will be experimental, and hence all of the conditions for informed consent in such a situation must be met. The question of cost must be faced as well, for it raises an ethical concern in relation to availability.[35]

Initially, only somatic-cell gene therapy was the focus of scientific experimentation and ethical reflection. Recently, however, germ-line gene therapy has received attention from scientists, and this raises more complex ethical concerns since the therapy would affect not only the patient but that individual's offspring as well.[36]

This issue is not a concern only for ethicists. Scientists themselves are concerned about the potentially enormous implications of germ-line engineering. In the latter part of 2000, the American Association for the Advancement of Science addressed the question of "inheritable genetic modification." Before any further research would be attempted, they urged, two conditions needed to be met. First of all, broad public discussion needed to be initiated concerning the "safety, efficacy, and social implications" of the technology. Equally important, a system of public oversight needed to be put in place to regulate both public and privately funded research. Their concerns went unheard, however. Within the year, a fertility clinic announced it had initiated a procedure that altered the genome of babies born through this technology. In the absence of any oversight in this country, at least one commentator is concerned that this technology will evolve into

> a highly individualized marketplace fueled by an entrepreneurial spirit and the free choice of large numbers of parents that could lead us down a path, albeit incrementally, toward a society that abandons the lottery of evolution in favor of intentional genetic modification. The discoveries of genetics will not be imposed on us. Rather, they will be sold to us by the market as something we cannot live without.[37]

By joining genetic modification and germ-line gene transfer, we thus come to a crucial crossroads. How far could we permit the possibility of "ever-accumulating genetic enhancement" to proceed? Would we become "post-human" beings—creatures descended from but different from human beings?[38] Should we allow this to happen? What will happen to human dignity and human nature? What are our obligations to future generations, to unborn human beings?

These questions speak only to intentional germ-line gene transfer. What if it should happen accidentally? One scientist describes a worrisome possibility.

At present, instead of trying to fix genes, so-called gene therapy floods the organism with extra copies of a normal gene (each usually carried in by a vector) in the hope that these correct genes will start pumping out the missing proteins and overwhelm the deficiencies of the uncorrected genes. But as it turns out, it is very difficult to get the new genes into even approximately the right places, and it is very difficult to get them to go forth and multiply. To ensure that even a small percentage sticks and persists long enough to have some effect, researchers must flood the organism with even more new copies of the correct gene-plus-vector. As a result, the stuff goes all over the place. This gives rise to gonadal bio-distribution and to the possibility of inadvertent germline GT [gene transfer].[39]

At the risk of putting the brakes on gene-transfer research, King urges the need to rethink gene delivery completely and, if necessary, change direction. At the very least, she argues, this would allow the field to "begin to address the questions raised by its progress."[40]

Eugenics, however, is a different matter. Negative eugenics would propose to eliminate undesirable characteristics, while positive eugenics would seek to preselect desirable traits. Who will decide which qualities are desirable? The procedures, especially at the outset, will be experimental. What value would justify such experimenting with human beings? Simply the parents' preference for a son? For a child with blue eyes? With a 150 IQ? Or might some societal value justify the selection of traits? Which? Whatever the reason, the procedure raises the question of technologizing reproduction and childbearing—an issue already dealt with in the context of in vitro fertilization.[41] As already pointed out, the Roman Catholic Church rejects all eugenic interventions as contrary to the dignity and integrity of the human person.

What about nonhuman life forms? Their development through genetic engineering needs to be dealt with in terms of proportionality. What risks are involved? What benefits are anticipated that might be in proportion to the risks? Simply to resolve the issue by reference to the "bottom line" is, of course, not a satisfactory moral analysis.

Cloning

Any moral evaluation of cloning for reproductive purposes must deal with the values involved in such a situation. Obviously, the development of yet another artificial reproductive technology offers individuals the possibility of producing offspring when all other procedures are impossible or not desirable—for example, to avoid a genetic defect when one of the parents is a carrier. But at what a price? Certainly for the near term, the chances of harm to the clone will be enormous. Add to this the negative impact this technology will almost certainly have on the cloned individual. How can an appreciation for parenthood, filiation, family relations survive in our society? What of the psychological stress that being cloned will impose on the cloned individual? After all, this was the major reason President Clinton's NBAC recommended a moratorium on human cloning. It was an argument repeated by President Bush's Council on Bioethics in 2002. Surely all of this will have such serious negative impact on society that it will be hard to justify using this procedure for reproductive purposes by a single couple. From this viewpoint, this will pit the common good of society against the reproductive freedom of the individual. Unfortunately, if our past experience in this country is a reliable teacher, the latter will probably prevail.

Human dignity is also a precious value that will be threatened by this new technology. Society has always viewed the human person as unique and unrepeatable. Identical twins aside, our fundamental human individuality affirms our worth and our value. The production of a clone, its basic commodification, endangers our sense of the wonder and mystery of human becoming arising from the mutual love of two parents who call us into being through their physical union in the conjugal act. It threatens our understanding of our individual lives as gifts from God, who bestows on each of us this free and gratuitous likeness to himself.

Obviously, for someone evaluating reproductive human cloning from within the Christian experience, the moral question is easier to resolve. The deep conviction of this faith community is that bringing a child into the world is one of God's greatest gifts to married couples. In a sense, God invites them to be cocreators of new life. To procreate in any other way, therefore, is viewed by this faith community as fundamentally unacceptable, as morally objectionable.

For any community, the fundamental moral question, of course, is the moral status of the blastocyst or pre-embryo. As was argued in connection with abortion, this is a living organism and incontrovertibly human, otherwise how could it provide scientists with human stem cells? To kill it, to cause its death cannot be justified, even for the loftiest human motives, even to make possible a revolution in the treatment of human diseases and in the wide expansion of organ transplantation. The end, as always, never justifies the use of immoral means.

A counterargument might be offered by scientists. The blastocyst is a hollow ball of human embryonic cells. Within the first two weeks, prior to the appearance of the primitive streak, it is not possible to tell which cells will develop into the placenta (to be discarded at birth) and which will become the embryo. Therefore it cannot be determined whether the cells withdrawn for this research come from the future placenta or from the embryo-to-be. But this response misses the point. The moral quality of the act comes from the killing of the blastocyst, not from the biological character of the cells. To terminate the life of this living human being is what is objected to—whether it is on day three or day six or at any time during its development into a fully human person.

A few further bits of information from some scientific developments that are continuing may make this moral objection moot. It may not be necessary to use embryonic stem cells. On January 22, 1999, the *New York Times* described the research of Dr. Vescovi, a scientist working in Milan. His studies in mice have purported to demonstrate that specialized stem cells—for example, skin stem cells, which normally only produce skin cells—can be transplanted into another kind of tissue and produce cells of that tissue type. Thus neural stem cells can be transplanted and develop marrow cells in a mouse whose marrow cells had been destroyed by radiation. So far this procedure has only been observed in mice, but if it can be replicated in humans, then human-skin stem cells can be used to restore human bone marrow. It would have another advantage. Since all of the biological material would come from the same person, it would bypass the rejection mechanism of the immune system.

One further observation. Dr. Thomson revealed that his work produced in excess of one trillion stem cells during the seven months of his research. Surely if stem cells can divide indefinitely, there may be no real need to continue harvesting them from blastocysts.

And finally a caution. All of the studies done so far by Drs. Thomson and Gearhart have been funded by the Geron Corporation, and the research has been licensed commercially to that corporation. If this research does indeed result in a biomedical bonanza, it may well happen that this moral dilemma will be resolved by a bottom-line argument rather than by an ethical one.

STUDY QUESTIONS

1. Explain the role of genes as the basis for the structures and functioning of the human organism, as well as for the many defects and anomalies that beset human beings.
2. What response has medical science made to the problem of genetic disease and defects?
3. What aspects of this rapidly growing branch of biological science (genetics) have triggered a legal response?
4. What is meant by dominant and recessive genes? What practical difference does this make in determining either physical traits or genetic anomalies?
5. What moral concerns are connected with genetic counseling? With genetic engineering?
6. In reflecting on the many advances in genetic science, what analysis would you make of the viewpoint expressed in the slogans "We must not play God!" and "We mustn't fool with Mother Nature"?
7. If cloning permits otherwise infertile couples to have genetic children of their own (DNA from father into enucleated egg of mother), what is so bad about that?
8. How would you respond to the charge, "By objecting to scientific progress achieved through stem-cell technology, the Roman Catholic Church is once again demonstrating its antitechnology prejudice."

NOTES

1. Sharon J. Durfy, "Ethics and the Human Genome Project," *Archives of Pathology and Laboratory Medicine* 117, May 1993, 466–69. For a challenging discussion of the relationship between the notion of genetic disease and the new genetic knowledge developed through the Human Genome Project, cf. A. L. Caplan, "If Gene Therapy Is the Cure, What Is the Disease?" in *Gene Mapping*, eds. G. Annas and S. Elias. Oxford University Press, 1992, 128–41.

2. *Splicing Life*, the President's Commission for the Study of Ethical Problems in Medicine and Biomedical and Behavioral Research. Washington, D.C.: U.S. Government Printing Office, 1982, 42.

3. John C. Fletcher and W. French Anderson, "Germ-Line Gene Therapy: A New Stage of Debate," *Law, Medicine and Health Care*, Spring/Summer 1992, 29.

4. For an overview of human gene therapy technologies, cf. Manal A. Morsy et al., "Progress Toward Human Gene Therapy," *JAMA* 270:19, November 17, 1993, 2338–45.

5. See http://www.genome.gov/10001087 and also http://www.genome.gov/10001621.

6. At a Hastings Center meeting considering "Clinical Priorities in the Application of Human Genome Research," while some argued for an uncrossable line between the therapeutic use of genetic technology and enhancement techniques, at least one participant argued in favor of developing human characteristics—such as needing only three hours' sleep a night or having a highly retentive memory. *Hastings Center Report*, January/February 1993, 4. Cf. also A. L. Caplan, cited above, note 1.

7. Stephen S. Hall, "Eve Redux: The Public Confusion over Cloning," *Hastings Center Report*, May/June 2003, 11–15.

8. Ibid., 13.

9. *Time*, May 4, 1987. In 1988 the U.S. Patent and Trademark Office awarded the first patent for a genetically altered animal, the Harvard mouse. Since that time many more additional animal patents have been awarded, while several hundred patents for animal and human genetic material are awaiting approval. On May 18, 1995, at a Washington press conference, leaders of the major religious faiths indicated their intention to petition the government to institute a moratorium on the issuing of new patents for genetically altered animal and human genes, cells, organs, tissues and embryos. Their stand will doubtlessly place them in direct opposition to the biotechnology industry, which views patent protection for genetically altered material as essential to its ability to raise capital for its ventures. Cf. *New York Times*, May 13, 1995; The Tablet (Brooklyn), May 27, 1995.

10. Rebecca Dresser, "Human Cloning and the FDA," *Hastings Center Report*, May/June 2003, 7–8.

11. Alissa Lyon, "The Cloning Report: Left of Bush but Still a Ban," *Hastings Center Report*, September/October 2003, 7.

12. Ibid.

13. Margaret R. McLean, "Red Light, Green Light: The California Cloning and Stem Cell Laws," *Hastings Center Report*, November/December 2002, 7.

14. Lyon, 7.

15. Cf. final chapter for a more complete discussion of this issue.

16. October 2, 1994.

17. Paul Conner, O.P., "The Indignity of Human Cloning," *The National Catholic Bioethics Quarterly* (Winter 2002): 635–58.

18. Thomas A. Shannon, "Human Embryonic Stem Cell Therapy," *Theological Studies* 62 (December 2001): 811–24.

19. Actually, the congregation is quoting Pope John Paul II, from his address to those attending the Thirty-Fifth General Assembly of the World Medical Association, October 29, 1983. *Origins*, 16:30. March 19, 1987, 700.

20. Ibid., 703.

21. Ibid., 702.

22. Ibid., 711.

23. Cardinal William Keeler, "The Problem with Human Cloning," *Origins*, Vol. 27, No. 36, 599.

24. *Origins*, April 6, 1995, 711.

25. *New England Journal of Medicine* 10 (2001): 710–14.

26. Arthur Caplan and Glenn McGee, "Fetal Cell Implants: What We Learned," *Hastings Center Report*, May/June 2001, 6.

27. Kenneth Garver and Bettylee Garver, "The Human Genome Project and Eugenic Concerns," *American Journal of Human Genetics* 54 (1994): 155. In the summer of 1998, the AMA's Council on Ethical and Judicial Affairs delivered a lengthy report on "Multiplex Genetic Testing," that is, a "package" of genetic tests for different anomalies administered in a single testing session. The council expressed serious concerns in connection with the problems presented for adequate informed consent and the difficulties attached to patient counseling. *The Hastings Center Report*, July/August, 1998, 15–21.

28. This was precisely one of the issues that led to the establishment of the ELSI Program by the leaders of the Human Genome Project. Cf also George J. Annas, "Privacy Rules for DNA Data Banks," *JAMA* 270:19, November 17, 1993, 2346–50.

29. *American Medical* News, February 10, 1989, 29. Cf. also Lisa S. Parker, "Bioethics for Human Geneticists: Models for Reasoning and

Methods for Teaching," *American Journal of Human Genetics* 54 (1994): 139; Harry Ostrer et al., "Insurance and Gene Testing: Where Are We Now?" *American Journal of Human Genetics* 52 (1993): 565–77.

30. For a full treatment of the abortion question, see Chapter Four; for another view of the issue cf. also Frank A. Chervenak et al., "When Is Termination of Pregnancy During the Third Trimester Morally Justifiable?" *Bioethics Reporter*, vol. 1, 1985, 515.

31. Cf. Garver, note 26, 155.

32. The National Society of Genetic Counselors in its 1992 Code of Ethics affirms that genetic counselors must strive to "respect their clients' beliefs, cultural traditions, inclinations, circumstances and feelings…[and] refer clients to other competent professionals when they are unable to support the client." Parker, note 28, 139.

33. Ibid., 144; cf. also H. Edgar, "Outside the Community," *Hastings Center Report*, November/December 1992, 32–35. In September 1997 the Task Force on Genetic Testing issued its final report to the National Human Genome Research Institute. While too lengthy to be summarized here, it called attention to many of the concerns regarding genetic testing expressed in this chapter.

34. Cf. Garver, note 26, 153–4.

35. Cf. James F. Gustavson, "Gene Therapy: Ethical and Religious Reflections," *Journal of Contemporary Health Law and Policy* 8:163 (1992) 183–200.

36. Cf. note 2; cf. also Nelson A. Wivel and LeRoy Walters, "Germ-Line Gene Modification and Disease Prevention: Some Medical and Ethical Perspectives," *Science* 262, October 22, 1993, 533–38; A. L. Caplan, cited above, note 1.

37. Mark Frankel, "Inheritable Genetic Modifications and a Brave New World," *Hastings Center Report*, March/April 2003, 32.

38. Greg Kaebnick, Editorial, *Hastings Center Report*, March/April 2003, 2.

39. Nancy King, "Accident and Desire: Inadvertent Germline Effects in Clinical Research," *Hastings Center Report*, March/April 2003, 25–26.

40. Ibid., 28.

41. Cf. Chapter Six.

8 Organ Transplantation

THE MEDICAL-SCIENTIFIC DIMENSION

History

There is evidence of attempts at transplantation since the dawn of medical history. Thus, for instance, as early as 600 B.C. in India there is evidence of the attempt to accomplish skin grafts on the same person. In the seventeenth century there is evidence of an effort to transplant tissue from one person to another, and in 1682 the first bone transplant is recorded. In the same period (1668) a Bologna book was published describing the procedure for accomplishing a blood transfusion. In 1881 the first modern skin transplant is reported, while 1905 saw the introduction of corneal transplantation. In Europe, prior to World War I, efforts were made to transfer organs (kidneys) from nonhuman species (apes, pigs, goats) to human recipients.[1] At approximately the same time (1920s) skin grafts between identical twins were attempted. In 1943 the hemodialysis machine was developed.

In 1951 a Boston physician, Dr. Hume, achieved notoriety with his transfer of a kidney from a cadaver to a living recipient who survived for six months. The first successful nephrectomy from a living donor was performed in Boston by Drs. Murray and Merrill in 1954. The kidney was removed from an identical twin and given to his brother. The recipient, Richard Herrick, married and began a family. He died eight years later from a heart attack that was apparently related to the kidney condition which originally occasioned the organ transplant. In 1959 a successful kidney transplant was performed in which the donor was not an identical twin. In 1962 the first successful cadaveric kidney transplant was achieved, and the following year saw similar success in the first transplantations of liver and lung.

The major problem faced in transplant surgery has been the rejection of the donated organ by the recipient's immune system. In March of 1961, azathioprine was discovered, the first powerful immunosuppressive drug. This development witnessed a dramatic improvement in transplant results as well as a sharp rise in surgical attempts to transplant organs. In December 1967 the first heart transplant was accomplished in South Africa by Dr. Christiaan Barnard. The recipient lived only two weeks but the procedure was declared a success. The early enthusiasm for this new development dampened, however, as the rejection problem continued to baffle surgeons. In 1979 organ transplantation received an enormous boost with the discovery of cyclosporine. Scientists discovered that this drug, developed from certain fungi, neutralized the body's "rejection mechanism" without shutting down the immune system completely.

With the introduction of cyclosporine in 1980, organ transplantation surgery took a quantum leap forward and remains a fast-changing field as today's experiments become tomorrow's routine procedures. It is no surprise, therefore, that the waiting list for transplanted organs grew from 13,766 in 1988 to an estimated 79,446 at the beginning of 2002. Approximately six thousand people die each year waiting for donated organs.[2]

Categories of Donors

Living donors contribute approximately 25 to 30 percent of the organs secured for transplantation. Among the organs contributed by living donors are the kidney, bone marrow, and parts of organs, such as the liver, the lung, or the pancreas.

The source for the remaining 70 to 75 percent of organs recovered for transplantation is cadavers. Skin, bones, corneas, and most major internal organs are able to be recovered from cadavers and transferred to living recipients.

Recovering Organs

Theoretically four major approaches for recovering organs have been described in the literature.[3] The first is *sale*. A person could agree with another individual or with an institution to donate a nonessential organ for a price during that individual's lifetime, or some or all organs on the occasion of death with the price becoming part of the estate to be left to the person's heirs.[4] Although illegal in the United States, such an approach has evolved, particularly in less developed countries and—not unexpectedly—specifically among the poorest segments of the population.

A second approach for recovering organs is through an *assumed consent* (or required harvesting) system. It is understood in Belgium and in a number of other European countries, for example, that anyone admitted to a hospital is a potential organ donor, should death ensue.

By law, then, the authorities are permitted to remove organs for transplantation at the time of death, unless the individual has expressly indicated an unwillingness to donate these organs. Belgium, for example, reported a 119 percent increase in donations in the first three years after implementation of the law.[5]

Another approach is *voluntary donation*. This has been the approach in the United States up to the present time. The general population has been asked, through the educational efforts of the sponsoring organization (e.g., The Eye Bank), to donate organs at the time of death for the benefit of fellow citizens. Mechanisms such as living wills or notations on one's driver's license are recognized as the means whereby one can indicate the intention to donate organs.

Closely related to this system is the method established by law in New York State and in many other jurisdictions. Since January 1, 1986, the *"required request"* law in New York mandates that hospital administrators certify in the case of every death that occurs in the hospital that the family of the deceased was asked to donate the organs of the deceased for transplantation or for research. In addition, the record must show which organs were donated or what the reason for the refusal was, if the family was unwilling to approve the request. In the same year the federal government endorsed "required request" legislation nationally.

Availability of Organs

The ideal organ donor is the individual who is relatively young, has suffered no organic disease, and has died as a result of a fatal auto accident, head trauma, or brain tumor. It is estimated that between twenty and twenty-five thousand individuals meet this description each year. At the present time only 15 percent of these individuals end up as organ donors. At the same time, as transplant procedures improve and survival rates increase, the gap between the number of available organs and the number of individuals seeking transplants widens.

As already mentioned, it has recently been estimated that there are over 79,000 individuals awaiting transplantation for kidney, heart, liver, pancreas, lung, heart-lung, and other solid organ replacement. Between 1997 and 2001 organs were harvested from approximately five to six thousand donors, while it is believed that potential donors may be almost four times that number. Although actual recovery efforts range between 37 percent and 59 percent, experts consider that it is realistically possible to increase effectiveness so that 80 percent of available donors will actually become involved.[6]

At any given time, for example, between seven to ten thousand individuals are waiting for donor kidneys. Because renal dialysis is able to keep these patients alive while a donor is being sought, this is the longest waiting line. Fewer are waiting for heart or liver donors, since these individuals die first, if the wait is lengthy.[7]

The continuing shortage of organs has led some transplant physicians to seek new sources for donation. Although a determination of "brain death" has traditionally been required for individuals on life support to be an organ donor, the *New York Times* has reported that some physicians are now transplanting organs from individuals declared dead when their hearts stop beating. Another innovative technique has been initiated by the Regional Organ Bank of Illinois. In this case, when an individual dies in the emergency room or is declared DOA, physicians may infuse a preserving fluid into the abdomen of the cadaver to keep the internal organs suitable for transplantation. Family members of the deceased are then approached with the request for authority to take the organs. This procedure has been criticized by several ethicists because it raises "difficult questions about the definition of death and when it occurs." Such an aggressive approach has struck others as an example of "the almost predatory degree to which we are trying to get organs."[8]

At the present time, some private insurance carriers cover "medically necessary" transplants. Coverage under Medicaid varies widely from state to state and is constantly changing. The federal government covers all costs for kidney transplants. This is cost-effective since the cost of dialysis is higher than that of a kidney transplant. It also covers the cost of liver transplants for some children. In most states, Medicaid covers transplantation of kidneys, hearts, livers, and bone marrow. Medicare covers all of these, though with some restrictions. Since 1986, Medicare has covered the cost of heart transplantations that are "medically necessary."

THE LEGAL DIMENSION

In the 1950s the courts emphasized and encouraged both voluntarism and informed consent in connection with organ transplantation. Both at the state and federal levels, they ruled that adults could donate to relatives. Donation by minors was approved with the consent of parents and with judicial approval. In 1954 the court approved the kidney transplant between the Herrick twins at Peter Bent Brigham Hospital in Boston.

In 1968 the Uniform Anatomical Gift Act was developed by the Commission for Uniform Acts and three years later it had been adopted by all fifty states. It set forth the conditions for informed consent and recommended voluntarism to provide the organs needed for transplantation. In 1984 the National Organ Procurement Act[9] was passed by Congress. This statute prohibited the sale of organs and rejected the proposal to introduce routine harvesting in this country. It provided for the establishment of a national transplantation network. The United Network for Organ Sharing has fullfilled this function since 1987 under contract to the Department of Health and Human Services. All transplant centers and organ procurement organizations must be members of this network. In addition, each potential transplant recipient must be registered and appropriate information on each donor and recipient must be provided to the network.[10]

In 1986, the Omnibus Budget Act (PL 99–509) marked the beginning of the federal government's endorsement of required-request legislation. The law requires all hospitals receiving Medicaid/Medicare aid to establish a working relationship with one or more OPOs (organ procurement organizations). It also mandates a required-request operation and participation in the OPTN (Organ Procurement and Transplant Network).

In 1985 New York State passed its "required request" law. As already explained, this statute mandated the establishment of a procedure in every hospital in the state whereby the family of anyone who dies in a hospital would be asked to approve the donation of the deceased's organs. If this request is denied, this fact and the reason for the refusal must be recorded. A full report must be made annually detailing the results of the requests. Similar laws have been enacted in numerous other jurisdictions.

On March 26, 1998, Secretary Donna Shalala of the Department of Health and Human Services announced a new federal regulation regarding organ distribution. She challenged the transplant network, the nonprofit United Network for Organ Sharing, to devise a new system that would provide a wider sharing of organs and an enhanced priority for the sickest patients. In this way she sought to eliminate the narrow geographic limitations that had crept into the distribution system. She called for uniform national criteria for earning a place on a transplant list and a ranking system that ensured that those who were equally sick were given similar status. In response to her challenge, a final rule was developed by the transplant community and implemented by the Department of Health and Human Services on March 16, 2000. This rule set out as its goals "(1) standardized criteria for placing patients on transplant waiting lists, (2) standardized criteria for defining a patient's medical status, and (3) allocation policies that make most effective use of organs, especially by making them available whenever feasible to the most medically urgent patients who are appropriate candidates for transplantation"[11]

Compensation Revisited

Even though the National Organ Procurement Act of 1984 excluded the sale of organs, it would seem that Congress was willing to revisit this question.[12] In 2001 two bills were introduced into

Congress to deal with the national dearth of organs for transplantation. Avoiding all mention of sale, the proposals would offer modest "incentives"—such as through tax credits or funeral expenses—to increase the supply of transplantable organs. Even though limited to pilot efforts and to cadaveric organs, this break with the American tradition of voluntary donation would surely open the way for more aggressive forms of compensation and for extension to "inter vivos" (live donors) donations.

The medical establishment was quick to respond to the congressional initiative. The American Medical Association, at its 2002 convention, voted in favor of similar pilot studies, provided that appropriate oversight be included and that they be limited to cadaveric organs. The decision was based purely on a benefits/harms calculus, which was quickly criticized as an ends-justify-the-means argument. Ultimately, whether or not these pilot studies receive a congressional green light remains up in the air and so, until that hurdle is overcome, the nagging problem of long lines of organ-seekers will characterize the American transplant scene.

THE SOCIOCULTURAL DIMENSION

Methods of Harvesting

Of all the methods of procuring organs for transplantation, the method most in harmony with the American spirit seems to be *voluntarism*. This system seems best to coincide with the American ideals of *freedom* and *altruism*.

The availability problem, however, runs up against the fundamental American valuing of *equality*. Whatever the system is for making organs available for transplantation, it ought not favor the powerful and the rich, nor be based on class or privilege.

While the American *entrepreneurial spirit* might seem to favor the concept of selling organs, this approach seems to have little support among the public, even though it is recognized that some portion of blood received for transfusion is provided by paid donors. Somehow the concept of financial gain for this life-saving donation has appeared reprehensible to the American people.

Racial/Ethnic Differences

Several reports have noted that African Americans wait almost twice as long for an organ as whites, but different explanations are offered for this divergence. For instance, there have been almost no African American or Asian donors listed in the Bone Marrow Registry until relatively recently. No match would be available for people of color, therefore, until a significant number of minority donors come forward to be included in the registry. Efforts are currently under way to achieve this and they are meeting with some success.[13]

Acceptability by Major Religious Groups

According to officials at the New York Regional Transplant Program, "...research by the American Council on Transplantation has found that a majority of religions support transplantation." Their survey ranges from "Amish" to "Protestantism," and responses are generally in favor of the donation of organs. It would seem, therefore, that no major religious body would object on religious grounds to organ transplantation, recognizing at the same time that religious communities such as the Jehovah's Witnesses and some orthodox Jewish groups do not approve participation in organ transplantation by their members.

ROMAN CATHOLIC CHURCH TEACHING

Position of the American Catholic Bishops

In the *Ethical and Religious Directives for Catholic Health Care Services*,[14] the following directives are noted:

(63) Catholic health care institutions should encourage and provide the means whereby those who wish to do so may arrange for the donation of their organs and bodily tissue for ethically legitimate purposes, so that they may be used for donation and research after death.

(64) Such organs should not be removed until it has been medically determined that the patient has died. In order to prevent

any conflict of interest, the physician who determines death should not be a member of the transplant team.

(65) The use of tissue or organs from an infant may be permitted after death has been determined and with the informed consent of the parents and guardians.

THE MORAL DIMENSION

A number of concerns regarding moral values can be identified in connection with organ transplantation. In order to simplify the moral analysis, these will be considered both at the microlevel and at the macrolevel.

Microethical Concerns

In connection with organ transplants from living donors, several ethical issues deserve consideration.[15] Obviously the *free, informed consent* of the donor is a major concern. Since living donors normally come from within the same family as the recipients, the possibility of pressure, if not coercion, is very real. Every effort, then, must be made to preserve the freedom of the donor.

A second consideration is the *justification of the "mutilation."* Obviously there must be a reasonable proportion between the loss to the donor and the benefit to the recipient. If cadaver organs are available and the chance of success is basically the same, it seems difficult to justify live donation.[16]

When organs are harvested from cadavers, it is necessary to be *sensitive to the feelings of the family* and to show *respect for the body* of the deceased. For this reason, then, those required by law to seek family approval for donation need special preparation for making this delicate request.

Naturally, in either case—whether the donation originates with a live or with a cadaver donor—from the standpoint of the recipient, all of the requirements for *informed consent* must be met.[17]

Macroethical Concerns

Two questions sum up macroethical concerns.[18] First, will there be a *fair and equitable distribution of the organs;* who will receive the donated organ? Then, second, is this a *reasonable use of limited resources* for health care? With respect to the former question, it should be pointed out that the medical organizations responsible for organ transplantation have only recently begun to establish nationally accepted criteria to identify recipients for organ donation. Each transplant center has been relatively autonomous in making these choices.[19] The moral concern in this connection, then, is that whatever criteria are established be fair and equitable. The ability of the wealthy and the influential "to push to the head of lines" is not pure fiction. In matters of life and death, which is almost always the situation in organ transplantation cases, the temptation is greater than usual. This, then, is a concern that is frequently raised.

The second major issue involves the utilization of limited resources. Obviously, the expenses involved in organ transplant therapy are very high. This area of medicine requires a major commitment of personnel and facilities on the part of health care institutions. At a time when ordinary health care remains unavailable for so many in our society, the question of priorities must be faced. The question is not at all simple and uncomplicated, but that should not prevent us as a nation from wrestling with the dilemma and identifying our priorities.

STUDY QUESTIONS

1. What general approaches have developed to obtain organs for transplantation? From what sources do donor organs come?
2. What legal provisions have been enacted in connection with this new technology?
3. Would you expect this transplantation technology to be readily acceptable in American society or not? Explain your reasons.
4. Does the Roman Catholic Church support or reject transplant technology? What reasons does it offer for its position?
5. What are the macro-/microethical concerns that are associated with organ transplantation?

NOTES

1. Because of the shortage of organs for transplantation, xenografts are still being attempted. A discussion of a baboon-to-human liver transplantation is offered by Dr. Thomas Starzl in the January 9, 1993, issue of *The Lancet* (341:8837): 65–71.

2. See *www.txorgansharing.org/Vital_statistics.htm;* cf. also Stuart J. Younger et al., "Ethical, Psychosocial, and Public Policy Implications of Procuring Organs from Non-Heart-Beating Cadaver Donors," *JAMA* 269:21, June 2, 1993, 2769. Cf. also *New York Times,* March 27, 1998.

3. See discussion and critique of methods in Arthur L. Caplan, "Organ Transplants: The Costs of Success," *Hastings Center Report,* December 1983, 23–32. Cf. also R. A. Sells. "Resolving the Conflict in Traditional Ethics Which Arises from Our Demand for Organs," *Transplantation Proceedings* 25:6, December 1993, 2983–84.

4. Cf. also M. J. Hanson, "A Pig in a Poke," *Hastings Center Report,* November/December 1992, 2; Fred Rosner et al., "Ethical and Social Issues in Organ Procurement for Transplantation." *New York State Journal of Medicine* 93:1, January 1993, 30–34.

5. Cf. Rosner, note 4, 31.

6. R. W. Evans et al., "The Potential Supply of Organ Donors: An Assessment of the Efficiency of Organ Procurement Efforts in the United States," *JAMA* 267:2, January 8, 1991, 239–46.

7. ABCNEWS.com reports that deaths of individuals on transplant waiting lists tripled between 1990 and 1999. Cf. also reported deaths of patients on the solid-organ waiting list registered with UNOS (United Network of Organ Sharing): 1988—1,537; 1989—1,732; 1990—2,080; 1996—4,022; 2002—5500. Cf. Angelina Korsun, "The Organ-Tissue Donation Process," *The Mount Sinai Journal of Medicine* 60:1, January 1993, 37–40. Cf. also Roger W. Evans, "Organ Procurement Expenditures and the Role of Financial Incentives," *JAMA* 269:24, June 23/30, 1993, 3113–18.

8. *New York Times,* June 2, 1993, A15. In this connection, cf. Renee C. Fox and Judith P. Swazey, "Leaving the Field," *Hastings Center Report,* September/October 1992, 9–15; Stuart J. Younger, note 2, 2769–74.

9. Public Law 987–507, 42 USC #273.

10. Fred P. Sanfilippo et al., "Factors Affecting the Waiting Time of Cadaveric Kidney Transplant Candidates in the United States," *JAMA* 267:2, January 8, 1992, 247–52. Cf. also Andrea A. Zachary, "Is There Racial Bias in Transplantation?" *Journal of National Medical Association* 85:11, 821–23.

11. Department of Health and Human Services, 42 CFR Part 121, 1.

12. Donald Joralemon and Phil Cox, "Body Values: The Case Against Compensating for Transplant Organs," *Hastings Center Report* January/February 2003, 27–33.

13. Angelina Korsun, note 7, 40. Also note that race can introduce biological factors that complicate organ transplantation. These include different rates of ABO blood groups within races and differences in compatibility of complex antigens. As a result, organs from black donors will have a better chance of matching with black recipients than with white. When donation rates are lower—as in the African American community—fewer organs will be available for blacks than whites.

14. *Origins* 24:27, December 15, 1994, 459.

15. These are issues involved in individual, concrete cases.

16. Thomas Starzl, "Will Live Organ Donations No Longer Be Justified?" *Hastings Center Report,* April 1985, 5.

17. Cf. Chapter Twelve.

18. These are issues affecting organ transplantation in general.

19. In 1991, the UNOS guidelines established a regional distribution system in preference to a national system.

9 Acquired Immunodeficiency Syndrome

THE MEDICAL-SCIENTIFIC DIMENSION

The Disease

The virus that causes acquired immunodeficiency syndrome (AIDS) is called the human immunodeficiency virus (HIV). HIV is a retrovirus, that is, one which is reverse transcribed into the individual's DNA. The virus thus incorporates itself into that person's basic human genetic material permanently. Because of this, it has the capacity to reproduce itself rapidly and in large quantities. In addition, it can no longer be eliminated from the cell by therapeutic means.

Most viruses—the common cold, as an example—stimulate the host organism's immune system to develop antibodies to neutralize the virus's activity. Although HIV also does this, the antibodies are unable over the long term to have this normal neutralizing effect due to the integration of the virus into the host DNA. HIV continues its destruction of T-4 cells and gradually destroys the body's immune system. The disease can therefore progress until it reaches a stage that meets the CDC definition.[1]

Because no therapy exists to eliminate the virus completely from the infected individual, that person remains infectious and can communicate the disease to others through the various mechanisms of transmission, namely, through sexual contact and through the blood, and perinatally from mother to fetus. Thus anyone participating in high-risk behavior with an infected person runs the risk of becoming infected. How high is the risk?

> Anyone having unprotected sex with a person who has engaged in high-risk behavior since 1977 runs the risk of having been

174

infected. The odds of infection are one in a hundred for a single act of unprotected intercourse (i.e., without effective use of a condom). Homosexual men and female sex partners of infected drug users run a far higher risk: a 66% to 75% chance of becoming infected themselves.[2]

Even though HIV has been isolated from a large number of body fluids, for example, blood, semen, vaginal secretions, saliva, tears, breast milk, cerebrospinal fluid, amniotic fluid, secretions, and excretions, there is no epidemiologic evidence that it can be transmitted except through blood, semen, vaginal secretions, and breast milk.

Definition

AIDS was originally defined by the Centers for Disease Control as the acquired immune deficiency associated with one or more of a number of life-threatening opportunistic infections, for example, Pneumocystis carinii pneumonia (PCP), tuberculosis, or Kaposi's sarcoma. This description, however, has been enlarged and extended to a much broader range of symptoms ranging from minor, nonspecific symptoms to persistent lymphadenopathy (enlargement of lymph nodes) accompanied or not by more serious symptoms, to markedly deficient cell-mediated immunity associated with infections (opportunistic or not) other than those included in the original CDC definition of AIDS, and/or other types of cancers such as lymphoma or squamous cell carcinoma.[3]

Anti-HIV Drugs/Vaccine

By the spring of 1993 three antiviral drugs had been licensed to combat HIV: Zidovudine, or AZT, Didanosine, or ddI, and Zalcitabine, or ddC. These three all combat HIV by blocking the action of an enzyme, reverse transcriptase, which the virus uses to reproduce. A new drug, U-90,152, also attacks this enzyme molecule but at a different site. Clinical trials of this drug, in a class of compounds called bisheteroarylpiperazines, or BHAPS, began in March 1993.

175

In December 1995, the FDA approved Saquinavir (Invirase), the first protease inhibitor, and a new generation of anti-AIDS drugs came into being. In combination with two other drugs (AZT and 3TC) this so-called drug "cocktail" quickly proved effective in reducing many patients' viral loads to undetectable levels. As scientists continued their struggle to eliminate the virus entirely from the bodies of infected individuals, a new family of drugs was added to the "cocktail"—nucleoside reverse transcriptase inhibitors. In combination with the previously developed drugs, these now form the basis for the best results from available antiviral therapies.

This therapy has been used not only for patients with confirmed cases of AIDS but also for individuals in the earliest stages of HIV infection. The side effects of the therapy have often been extremely stressful and the regimen very demanding. Since these drugs succeeded in many cases in eliminating any detectable virus, naturally the question arose whether there were undetected pockets of HIV in the body that could give rise to reinfection. Had the drugs completely eliminated the virus? It turned out the answer was "no!" Scientists discovered that HIV persisted in the so-called memory T-cells of the immune system.

As already explained, because the HIV incorporates itself into the cell DNA, it is not accessible to the traditional vaccine produced from antibodies. Another characteristic of HIV equally frustrating to medical researchers is its tendency to mutate as it spreads from one individual to another, thus altering its protective coat. As in the case of influenza, so with HIV—a vaccine that would be effective against one strain would be of little value against mutated variants. Researchers are seeking to identify stable elements in the viral core that will be common to all strains of HIV and which can then be attacked by a vaccine. It is generally acknowledged, however, that the availability of a vaccine for widespread use—the only effective means of protecting the general population—is still years away, from the most optimistic point of view.[4]

Progress of the Disease in the Individual

As mentioned earlier, the virus attacks the body's immune system. As this defense system is gradually exhausted and the T-cell count drops below 200, the individual becomes an easy victim of infections that would ordinarily have been resisted. Called "opportunistic infections," these include—among others—Pneumocystis carinii pneumonia, tuberculosis, and varieties of cancer, such as Kaposi's sarcoma.

In the early years of the epidemic, once those infected with the virus had reached a condition that met the CDC definition for AIDS, their rates of survival varied. Some died within weeks of this initial diagnosis, while others managed to resist for a longer period. Men seemed to survive longer (the average is fourteen to eighteen months) while women succumbed sooner (six to eight months). One's prior health seems to have been a significant factor in this process. Thus persons with AIDS who previously suffered from such conditions as hepatitis A, parasitic infections, or sexually transmitted diseases such as syphilis moved more rapidly into the final, lethal descent into AIDS. Another factor that seemed to hasten the process was the use of recreational drugs or stimulants such as amyl nitrate ("poppers").[5] That scenario continues true today, except in developed countries. For those who have access to the new combination-drug therapy, the progress of the disease will be very different, since the new drug "cocktail" is able to reduce the viral load to levels that are undetectable. Because this treatment is so new, however, it is not possible to predict the long-term consequences of this therapy.

Will everyone exposed to the disease who develops seropositivity—that is, who tests "positive" for the virus—inexorably pass through the various stages of the disease until a condition that meets the CDC definition is reached? This question is still being debated. In 1988 then-Surgeon General Koop predicted that 20 to 30 percent of those infected by the virus would develop a CDC-defined illness within five years. Beyond that time he was unwilling to make a prediction.[6] Infectious disease experts believe now that if left untreated, all individuals infected with HIV will sooner or later fall victim to some lethal, terminal infection as a result of the destruction of their immune system. Now that multiple-drug therapy has become available in developed countries of the world, however, it is possible to suppress the viral load to a point that it cannot be detected. It would seem that in such cases the individual will not progress to full-blown AIDS.

One final characteristic of the disease remains to be noted. The virus is not only lymphatropic but neurotropic as well. It attacks the central nervous system as well as the immune system. Although it had been noted early on that many AIDS patients suffered from apathy and forgetfulness and tended to withdraw into themselves, these were judged to be indications of depression, a common enough reaction among persons infected with such a lethal disease. It is now known, however, that many, "perhaps a majority of AIDS victims experience a progressive deterioration in cognitive functions with subacute encephalitis."[7]

Transmission of the Disease

According to the CDC and other public health officials, although the HIV has been isolated in a wide variety of body fluids, as noted above, there is no epidemiologic evidence for the transmission of the disease except through blood, semen, vaginal secretions, and breast milk. We now know also that even though the immune system suffers damage in most individuals (90 percent) in the first three to five years of HIV infection, the full effects of the disease may be delayed for as long as ten years. How the new "drug cocktail" will affect this time frame is not yet clear. While the new combination-drug therapy may succeed in eliminating any detectable viral load, the HIV is not completely eliminated, and so, if that therapy is ended, the virus retains the ability to reactivate and thus infect new cells.[8]

Despite almost twenty-five years of public health education in the United States, others *will* get AIDS, unfortunately, whether through sexual activity or through blood. Although the increase within the gay population had leveled off, it is still true that needle sharing among addicts and anal intercourse among homosexual men are the principal ways Americans are infected with AIDS, with the result that roughly 80 percent of the disease's victims have been male. But it is equally certain that AIDS is being spread among the heterosexual population through intercourse between IV drug abusers and bisexual men and their partners. At the 1998 World AIDS Conference, it was estimated by a CDC official that the number of new HIV infections in the United States would increase by approximately forty thousand a year.[9]

This had been the AIDS picture since 1993 when the number of new AIDS cases peaked at 80,000 and then decreased annually. The situation changed in 2002 when the CDC reported for the first time in a decade that the incidence of new AIDS cases increased slightly over 2 percent. Though the overall increase in cases was small, the only affected group in the U.S. AIDS population was gay men. The director of the AIDS Center at the CDC noted, "Our biggest concern is what appears to be a resurgent epidemic in gay men, particularly among younger men."[10] Since an increase in HIV infection translates into new AIDS cases, the 7.1 percent increase in new HIV infection among gay and bisexual men—an increase for the third consecutive year—may mark a disturbing turning point in this country's AIDS epidemic.[11]

At the present time, a relatively small percentage of AIDS cases result from sexual intercourse between men and women not in the high-risk groups. Small, perhaps, but how big is the risk? Can one be infected by a single act of sexual intercourse if one's partner happens to be infected? Scientists cannot say. In a study of eighty spouses of individuals infected through contaminated blood, some victims picked up the disease from a single sexual encounter, while others have remained free of infection despite hundreds of sexual exposures to an infected spouse. There is no doubt, however, that the risk is increased through unprotected sex and through multiple sexual partners. In the latter case, besides the obvious increase in the numerical possibility of infection, some scientists believe that other sexually transmitted diseases increase susceptibility to AIDS.

Extent of the Epidemic

Worldwide

As of December 31, 2002, the Joint UN Program on HIV/AIDS estimated that 42 million people were living with HIV/AIDS. Five million new cases occurred in that year, the UN said, while slightly more than three million individuals died from AIDS worldwide. Ominously, the report noted that women were becoming increasingly affected by HIV so that now almost 50 percent of the total number are women. To put a human face on these cumulative statistics, it was pointed out that in Africa two children become orphans every thirty seconds.[12]

USA

At the beginning of the epidemic, the NIH estimated that approximately one million individuals were infected among people in the high-risk groups. In 1986 the surgeon general placed the total infected with the AIDS virus in the USA at 1.5 million. Large numbers, it was noted, were asymptomatic and probably unaware of their status; yet they were capable of infecting others through the identified channels of transmission. In 1998 the CDC revised that estimate to 800,000 Americans who are HIV infected. At the 2003 National HIV Prevention Conference in Atlanta, authorities called attention to the increase in newly diagnosed cases and suggested that almost one million Americans were now living with HIV/AIDS.[13]

Several developments in the AIDS epidemic are particularly ominous. At the beginning of the AIDS decade (1982) women constituted only a small percentage of reported cases—6 percent. By 1992 this figure had almost doubled—11 percent. In 1998 it was estimated that 25 percent of all new infections occurred among women. Naturally this statistic is closely related to the increase in AIDS among heterosexuals. While there were only 133 heterosexual contact cases in the fall of 1985 (118 women and 15 men), by 1992 the number had soared to 11,936 (7,249 women and 4,687 men).[14] Particularly upsetting is the sense that "interest in women with HIV appears to be secondary to the potential for vertical transmission of HIV to children and horizontal transmission to men." This sexist dimension of the AIDS epidemic is borne out by the fact that many of the AIDS-related infections peculiar to women (e.g., cervical cancer and pelvic inflammatory disease, or PID) were excluded from eligibility for disability payments until the revision of the definition of AIDS in January 1993.[15]

The second frightening statistic is the increase of HIV infection and AIDS cases among teenagers. Exact figures regarding HIV infection are not easily acquired, but in three recent years the cumulative number of individuals in the thirteen to twenty-four age group increased 77 percent. Nearly half of the reported cases have been located in New York, New Jersey, Texas, California, Florida, and Puerto Rico. At the 2003 Conference in Atlanta, it was pointed out that HIV from intravenous drug use had increased by 15 percent among youth and young adults, with the greatest increase among thirteen- to fifteen-year-olds.

Until recently the majority of cases of teenage AIDS has been restricted to males, minorities, and older adolescents, but that too is changing. In 1990, one out of five hundred college students (on nineteen campuses) tested HIV positive. A year later among Job Corps participants, the ratio was one in three hundred. The ratio based upon gender is also changing. In 1992, Surgeon General Antonia Novello announced that the ratio of female to male patients with AIDS doubled in the prior four years from 17 percent to 39 percent. Not everyone agrees about the reasons for these developments, but one thing seems clear to public health officials—AIDS education is not working for teenagers. Either the message is not being heard or the youngsters believe "it can't happen to them." The fact is that "HIV, the virus that causes AIDS, is spreading unchecked among the nation's adolescents, regardless of where they live or their economic status." Ten years later, the CDC statistics for 2002 indicated that 50 percent of the new HIV infections (40,000) were younger than twenty-five years of age.[16]

THE LEGAL DIMENSION

The response of the legal profession to the AIDS crisis has been slowly emerging and developing throughout the course of the epidemic. As the courts responded to challenges, a body of legal doctrine has been evolving. Many of these challenges pit the interests of public health against the individual's right of privacy and other fundamental civil rights. Very briefly, we will identify some of the major questions that have evolved to date and the direction—if any—being taken by the courts.

Children in the Classroom

This issue has evolved from a number of challenges concerning the appropriateness of placing AIDS-infected children in the classroom.[17] In a number of school districts, parents of other children have objected to the presence of infected students because of the perceived risk to their children. However, in the absence of behavioral problems and the attendant risks they might bring, it would appear that the courts have concluded that it is not justifiable to exclude these children from the classroom. This view is based on the conviction regarding the individual's right to a public education in the classroom. It should be noted that an alternative form of education may be required as the disease progresses and the child's ability to participate in the class decreases.

In their consideration of the question, the lower courts responded to objections such as the danger of an infected child biting a classmate or spreading infection through skin lesions by judging these risks to be minor and theoretical. An individual, in the view of the court, can protect himself from such dangers by appropriate protective steps.

This issue was resolved in more general terms in June 1998 when the United States Supreme Court voted (five to four) to uphold a lower court's decision that a woman with asymptomatic HIV infection met the definition of disability under the 1990 Americans with Disabilities Act. The court stopped short of ruling flatly that HIV infection is automatically covered under that law, but many legal commentators believe all or almost all HIV-infected individuals could claim the law's protection.[18]

Employment

Had the court issued its decision earlier, many legal conflicts involving the workplace could have been avoided. It is not difficult to understand the pressures on business people in the marketplace. Employers claim many reasons for wishing to exclude AIDS-infected employees from their workforce—pressure from other employees, loss of customers, increased costs for medical coverage and disability payments. Now that AIDS has received a "disability" designation, all of the legal protections for this class of citizens becomes available to those infected with AIDS. In June 1993 the Equal Employment Opportunity Commission (EEOC) ruled that employers may not refuse to hire people with disabilities because of fears that they will raise insurance costs. By establishing this policy in order to enforce the 1990 Americans with Disabilities Act, the Commission opened the way for disabled workers, including those with AIDS, to sue employers who they believe have violated this policy.[19] Even this, however, is no guarantee that they will not fall victim to unjust practices in the marketplace.

THE SOCIOCULTURAL DIMENSION

The major sociocultural aspect of the AIDS question that will be considered is the attitude of the general population toward those infected with AIDS. As already indicated, the vast majority of AIDS sufferers belong to two subcultures in our society, namely, homosexual and bisexual males and IV drug abusers. For a number of reasons these individuals have a negative image in America. Of course, this is not a universal attitude, but there is enough antipathy toward gays and addicts in American society to impact the way that persons with AIDS are viewed. Additionally, society's compassion may have been diminished because of the belief that the infected person's condition is the result of that individual's freely chosen behavior. This gives rise to the blame-the-victim syndrome—"it's their own fault." Finally, because the behaviors that occasioned the infection in the first place are judged morally unacceptable by most mainline churches, an additional stigma is placed on individuals infected by AIDS, in the eyes of many.[20]

As already mentioned, one concrete effect of this public attitude toward persons with AIDS is discrimination—in housing, in employment, in the availability of social services. A second outcome seems to be public reluctance to foot the bill for AIDS. The private health care industry (hospitals, insurance providers, and pharmaceutical companies) has been engaged in a pass-the-buck strategy that seeks to drop the bill in the lap of a reluctant federal government. The result has been added suffering and mental anguish for AIDS patients as they find themselves increasingly unable to afford the cost of their health care. Typically, individuals with AIDS who are insured through their employers become too ill to continue working. With the loss of their jobs, they lose health care insurance as well. In most cases Medicaid coverage is unavailable until a poverty level of $2,000 is reached. Thus the disease not only ravages their bodies; it devours all their material resources as well. Clearly, the availability of AIDS "cocktails" makes long-term employment—and hence insurance—available once again.

183

ROMAN CATHOLIC CHURCH TEACHING

In 1987, in the course of his American tour, Pope John Paul II spoke to a group of persons with AIDS:

> God's love has many aspects. In particular, God loves us as our Father. The parable of the prodigal son expresses this truth most vividly. You recall that moment in the parable when the son came to his senses, decided to return home and set off for his father's house. "While he was still a long way off, his father caught sight of him and was deeply moved. He ran out to meet him, threw his arms around his neck and kissed him" (Lk 15:20). This is the fatherly love of God, a love always ready to forgive, eager to welcome us back.
>
> God's love for us as our Father is a strong and faithful love, a love which is full of mercy, a love which enables us to hope for the grace of conversion when we have sinned....
>
> God loves you all, without distinction, without limit. He loves those of you who are elderly, who feel the burden of the years. He loves those of you who are sick, those who are suffering from AIDS and from AIDS-related complex. He loves the relatives and friends of the sick and those who care for them. He loves us all with an unconditional and everlasting love....[21]

In their general meeting of November 1989, the American Catholic bishops issued a formal statement on the question of AIDS. Entitled "Called to Compassion and Responsibility: A Response to the HIV/AIDS Crisis," this document[22] highlighted five challenges:

- *Compassion*—"The truly compassionate individual works at his or her own cost for the others' real good, helping to rescue them from danger as well as alleviate their suffering....People with AIDS are not distant, unfamiliar people, the objects of our mingled pity and aversion. We must keep them present to our consciousness as individuals and a community, and embrace them with unconditional love....Compassion—love—toward persons infected with HIV is the only authentic gospel response." [23]
- *Integrity*—"By their very existence as male and female, by the complementarity of their sexuality and by the responsible exercise of their freedom, man and woman mirror the divine image implanted

in them by God....All this requires that we understand ourselves and live not just naturalistically, as it were—as bundles of bodily drives and instincts—but in a manner which respects the integrity of our personhood, including its spiritual dimension. Through the grace of the Spirit, that can be done."[24]

- *Responsibility*—"It is a matter of grave concern that, while many homosexual persons may be making changes in specific sexual practices in response to HIV/AIDS, fewer may be choosing to live chaste lives....The church holds that all people, regardless of their sexual orientation, are created in God's image and possess a human dignity which must be respected and protected....It envisages a pastoral approach which urges homosexual persons to form chaste, stable relationships....Intravenous drug use also plays a large role in the spread of HIV....[I]t is important to see substance abuse as an actual or potential disease for some persons—a disease, however, for which there are treatment and hope....Education and treatment aimed at changing behavior are the best way to control the spread of HIV among intravenous drug users and to prevent passage of the virus to their sexual partners and to children in the womb."[25]

- *Social Justice*—"Discrimination against those suffering from HIV or AIDS is a deprivation of their civil liberties. The church must be an advocate in this area, while also promulgating its own nondiscrimination policies in employment, housing, delivery of medical and dental care, access to public accommodations, schools, nursing homes and emergency services....Individual privacy and liberty are highly valued in our society. Liberty, however, carries with it the obligation not to harm or interfere with others. If HIV-infected persons have rights which others must respect, they also must fulfill their fundamental ethical responsibility to avoid doing harm to others."[26]

- *Prayer and Conversion*—"Our response to persons with AIDS must be such that we discover Christ in them and they in turn are able to encounter Christ in us. Although this response undoubtedly arises in the context of religious faith, even those without faith can and must look beyond suffering to see the human dignity and goodness of those who suffer. Without condoning self-destructive behavior or denying personal responsibility, we must reject the idea that this illness is a direct punishment by God....[I]n its ministry to and for persons with HIV/AIDS, the church calls everyone to conversion, offers sacramental reconciliation and human consolation, seeks to assist all those who suffer, proclaims faith's explanations of suffering, sin and death in the light of the cross and the resurrection, and accompanies those who suffer on their journey of life while helping them face death in the light of Christ."[27]

THE MORAL DIMENSION

Microethical Concerns—Patient Oriented

Discrimination

As pointed out earlier, the groups at high risk for AIDS— accounting for the vast majority of the cases reported in the U.S.—are male homosexuals or bisexuals and IV drug abusers. Discrimination is a reality in the lives of these people for two reasons—first, because they belong to these particular subcultures in our society, and second, because they have AIDS. It has been suggested that the AIDS crisis offers an opportunity for continuing the ancient condemnation of homosexuality. AIDS becomes a metaphor for that sin. As a result, the two groups at high risk are in danger of being marginalized and criminalized in our society, and despised to the point of being victimized by antigay crime.

Obviously, such hate-inspired violent behavior must be rejected and condemned by anyone claiming a gospel outlook. But homophobia and "addictophobia" are not the only sources of discrimination against persons with AIDS. Their disease itself has led them to be shunned, rejected, and vilified. Over the last two decades their homes have been burned, their children ejected from school, their employment terminated, their insurance canceled. Dental clinics have refused to care for their teeth and embalmers have refused to prepare their bodies for burial. As noted earlier, discrimination based on disability is illegal. It is also immoral. While it is understandable to fear a deadly illness that one does not fully comprehend, this ignorance does not justify violent or discriminatory behavior against those infected. Such behavior denies a fellow human being the basic dignity, the fundamental respect that is that individual's due as a creature made in God's image, as a brother or sister redeemed by Jesus and called to membership in his kingdom. While an individual has the right—indeed, the obligation—to avoid and protect himself from unnecessary or reckless

186

exposure to the infection, this must not be done in a way that dehumanizes or victimizes those in our society already infected.

Confidentiality

Closely related to the problem of discrimination is the question of confidentiality. A basic principle of medical ethics—and indeed of Christian morality—is respect for persons. From this principle flow the patient's right to privacy and the physician's obligation to confidentiality. It is a prima facie obligation, one which is presumed to bind unless a more compelling duty conflicts with it. The problem of confidentiality in the case of AIDS involves a conflict between the patient's right of privacy and either (1) the public health concerns of responsible medical authorities, or (2) the right of the patient's spouse or partner to avoid infection.

First, the public health question. At the present time, it does not seem that a convincing case has been made for the need to know the identity of persons with AIDS, even though the tracking of the disease by public health authorities through a statistical record appears quite legitimate. Since no follow-up for medical or counseling purposes is envisioned, there does not seem to be an adequate reason for submitting these names to the authorities. In addition, as has often been observed, unless confidentiality is assured, it is doubtful that many of these individuals will participate in the screening programs that have been set up.

The second conflict, noted above, puts the patient's right to privacy against the spouse or partner's right not to be infected with AIDS. What does the physician do when he learns that the patient does not intend to tell the other party of the infection—when, in fact, he intends to take no precaution to protect his partner, whether in sex or in drug use, from infection? If the physician is unable to convince the patient to change his mind, then the doctor has the obligation to share this information with the other party. Although privacy is an individual's right, it is not an absolute value, and when it conflicts with the principle of justice, with the right of an innocent person to be spared direct grave injury, that is, infection by an incurable disease, it must give way. The doctor, therefore, must advise the patient what will be done and then intervene. It should be noted, however, that the legal

187

status of such an intervention varies in the individual states. As of January 1, 1989, the doctor would be legally protected in New York State, but that circumstance will vary from state to state.[28]

Obligation Not to Spread the Disease

The final patient-oriented moral concern refers to the infected individual's obligation not to spread the disease to other persons. Because of the very nature of AIDS, it would be a grave injustice to communicate the disease deliberately and knowingly to someone else. The infected person, therefore, must use every reasonable means to avoid this.

Microethical Concerns—Physician Oriented

Obligation to Care for the Patient with AIDS

What is the obligation of a physician to undertake the care of a patient with AIDS? May a doctor ethically refuse to care for such an individual? Refuse treatment to an AIDS patient? Edmund Pellegrino says "no" and offers four reasons:

1. Care of the sick is at heart a moral enterprise. A sick person is exquisitely dependent and vulnerable. The inequality of knowledge and power of physician and patient establishes a fiduciary relationship between them based on trust. This alone allows and justifies the invasion of the patient's privacy and autonomy by the physician. To refuse treatment violates this fiduciary relationship.
2. Medical care is not a commodity, a marketplace issue. It is never simply a matter of price, quality, or distribution, and hence a physician is not free to deny care to a patient in need of it.
3. Medical knowledge is nonproprietary. It is not the private possession of the physician. Rather, doctors enter into a covenant with society for a social purpose, through which they have access to all knowledge gathered from all patients by all physicians. The skill based on this knowledge, therefore, may not be refused a member of the society in need of it. In addition, it has been pointed out that medical education is largely publicly supported and, there-

fore, society has a right to expect physicians to respond positively in a public emergency.

Additionally, the medical professional has entered a covenant with society to provide a service that inherently involves some risk. This covenant cannot be nullified, therefore, simply because some danger is now present—any more than a fireman can refuse to enter a burning building or a police officer refuse to seek to apprehend a criminal because of personal danger.

4. The Hippocratic oath, not in its explicit content but in its symbolic meaning, is a covenant that applies to all physicians. It is a promise to act on all patients' behalf who seek that assistance and so is morally binding.[29]

Inappropriate Treatment

The physician who agrees to treat AIDS patients may be confronted with the dilemma of inappropriate treatment from two different directions. First of all, there is the question of unapproved therapies or those that are still in the experimental stage of development. Just as physicians caring for cancer patients were once confronted by the request to administer laetrile, even though the substance was found to have no therapeutic value by medical authorities, so AIDS patients may ask their doctors for assistance in using illicit or useless therapies—a victim of Kaposi's sarcoma may request cyclosporine, for example.[30] While a physician should refuse to cooperate when benefit is nonexistent or overshadowed by risk, it is quite a different matter when clinical field trials of the substance are being conducted at the time of the request.[31] Such a dilemma was not uncommon when AZT first began to be used. News of rumored remedies spreads quickly among those condemned to die from a lethal disease. This has been particularly true of the grapevine that exists in the homosexual subculture. It was not unheard of, even, for some participants in experimental programs to share a portion of their medication with friends not included in the test. In such situations it would be much more difficult morally for the physician to demur.[32]

The second instance of inappropriate treatment arises from a different situation entirely. How should/must a physician treat a request to use "all available means" in the treatment of the disease? What does "do everything possible" mean in the context of AIDS?

When it becomes clear that further treatment of Pneumocystis carinii pneumonia (PCP) will only delay death and prolong the intensive care of the sufferer, must the care be given? Since good ethics begins with good medicine, it seems quite clear that no physician need offer—or indeed consider—a therapy that is clearly useless. If a particular treatment offers no possible benefit to the patient, there is no obligation to offer it as an option. But how does one judge a particular therapy "useless"? What percentage of success is required before a treatment is "useful"? How long must the effort be made till the therapy can be judged "futile"? Although these are medical judgments rather than ethical ones, that distinction does nothing to make the decision easier for the physician. It is particularly in situations like these that the doctor's emotional attitudes toward the addict or the homosexual patient may be crucial. Will the same therapy, for instance, be prolonged for the hemophiliac patient and terminated as "futile" for the IV drug abuser?

Other aspects of this difficult question are no different for AIDS patients than for other terminally ill individuals. For instance, the patient may ask that "all means be used" without knowing clearly or accepting how close he is to death. He may not appreciate what resuscitation or the use of a respirator involves. He may simply be pleading not to be abandoned in his dying and, in view of the addict's and the homosexual's experience of social rejection and marginalization, it is not hard to understand this fear.

Informed Consent

One aspect of the informed consent question has particular urgency in the care of patients with AIDS, namely, competence. It is clear now that the human immunodeficiency virus attacks the central nervous system as well as the immune system. This, understandably, raises the possibility of a neurological basis for lessened capacity. Drugs used in the treatment of AIDS also may affect cerebral functioning. The competence in question requires that the patient be able to deal with the information provided by the doctor, appreciate the gravity of his condition, and reach a decision based upon personal values. The question of informed consent to DNR (Do Not Resuscitate) orders offers the physician a particular challenge. Even though the principles involved are identical to those affecting any terminally ill patient, the doctor must exercise "exquisite sensitivity" in view of the mental state of many AIDS victims who see themselves as rejected and abandoned by society.[33]

Because the loss of competency is often quite gradual and subtle, the best way for the AIDS patient to be sure that his wishes will be carried out is to appoint a surrogate or proxy, ideally with durable power of attorney status. Although normally a family member would be selected for this responsibility, in the case of AIDS patients conflicts often arise with family members over lifestyle. Hence a friend or companion more familiar with the patient's values and preferences may often be chosen ahead of a family member. This has led to conflicts with family members claiming a legal right to make these decisions.

Macroethical Concerns

It has been pointed out that many, even most, of the moral issues surrounding AIDS are social justice issues rather than questions of sexual behavior.[34] They pit the concern for the common good against the rights and interests of the individual with AIDS. It is not possible to offer any absolute principles in advance that will decide which side should prevail. Only a careful reflection on each issue will permit us to judge which competing value should be chosen. In any event, "measures which purport to serve the common good but undermine individual dignity frustrate the basic good which public order strives to protect: the human dignity of that society's members."[35]

Mandatory Testing

Before considering the moral issues that arise in conjunction with testing, some preliminary understanding of the testing technology can be helpful. At the present time, the two most commonly used tests are the enzyme-linked immunosorbent assay (ELISA) and the Western blot test. Both technologies seek to establish the presence of antibodies produced to fight the human immunodeficiency virus in the blood.

They are not, therefore, tests that diagnose the presence of HIV but rather of seropositivity. When used alone, the ELISA test complicates the screening by producing false positives—"as many as ninety out of a hundred...in a healthy blood donor population."[36] False negatives too are possible, since the body does not produce a detectable volume of antibodies immediately after exposure to HIV. Since "a 'window' of up to four weeks may occur before the antibody appears,"[37] the ELISA test may give rise to unwarranted security when administered close to the time of exposure. Prudence, therefore, dictates that the testing be repeated within six months. False positives are eliminated by following up the ELISA test by the Western blot test. When the two tests are used in conjunction, there is a much greater degree of authority given to the results.

At the present time mandatory testing for individuals in specific groups has been instituted for those entering military service or the foreign service. In addition, legislation in some jurisdictions requires HIV testing in connection with certain public acts—for example, on the occasion of receiving one's marriage license. Is this morally justifiable? Clearly such tests can be morally justified only by some proportionate medical or public health objective, for they clearly breach the individual's right to privacy.[38] It is incumbent, therefore, on any institution or jurisdiction that wishes to require testing to establish the proportionate benefit to justify such an invasion of privacy.

Mass Screening

The problems of discrimination and confidentiality have already been considered in the analysis of patient-oriented microethical concerns. But what of mass screening? This approach to public health problems is not new. Not that many years have elapsed since our last experience with a similar effort, the screening of African Americans for sickle-cell trait in the early 1970s. Because of the "negative social consequences to the people the test was supposed to help,"[39] that testing was abandoned.

Voices have been heard calling for a similar program to test for the HIV antibodies. Since up to now there is no follow-up program envisioned that would seek to accomplish a change in behavioral patterns and, more importantly, since there is no therapy that might be administered for the benefit of those who test positive, there has seemed little justification for mass screening of the general population. Whether the success of multiple-drug therapy administered as early as possible after infection occurs will change this situation still remains to be seen.

Quarantine

Based on what was said earlier, it is clear that there are elements in American society who believe that persons with AIDS and those who test seropositive should not be allowed to mingle with the general population.[40] There are, indeed, examples of this approach in recent public health history.[41] The 2002–03 outbreaks of SARS and monkeypox in this country are concrete examples. Would isolation or quarantine be morally justifiable as a response to AIDS? In the absence of the actual commission of a crime or without virtual certitude that a criminal or highly dangerous act will be committed, it is unethical to isolate or incarcerate an individual. The quarantine of HIV-infected individuals would surely be immoral. In addition, in view of the numbers of Americans thought to be seropositive and the permanent character of the infection, quarantine would require the detention of almost a million people for the rest of their lives. Even if this were possible logistically, it would be so abhorrent to our libertarian orientation as a society as to be unacceptable. In view of the recent Supreme Court decision regarding HIV/AIDS as a disability, it is hard to believe that quarantine would be any more acceptable legally.

Funding

It was estimated in 1986 that the cost of the average hospital bill for an AIDS patient would be $140,000, approximately the same as the cost of a heart transplant. More recently, the amount has been set at $83,000. In 1994 the average annual cost of care for an adult with AIDS in the United States was estimated at $32,000.[42] The estimated total cost for the first nine thousand victims to die in California of AIDS was 1.25 billion dollars. Typically, most AIDS patients are hospitalized two or three times during the course of the illness, and each hospitalization costs three times more than it does for the average patient.[43] Who is going to pay for this health care?[44] Where will the funds come from to pay for the health care of AIDS victims? Since during the course of the disease most AIDS patients are unable to continue in their jobs and then lose their health insurance with their employment, the funding can only come from public funds.

It has been suggested that the federal government finance health care costs for AIDS through the Social Security Act and Medicare, much as it does end-stage renal disease. But the objection has been heard: "Why should the public pay for the health care of individuals who freely assumed risk for the disease through their behavior?" And since in many cases the behavior is illegal, the objection may be seen to have even more weight. In response it should be pointed out that the reality of life is that we live in community—albeit at times fitfully, imperfectly, even reluctantly. We cannot extricate ourselves; we must share the risks and the burdens, as well as the benefits. In the Judeo-Christian tradition, of course, we *must not* try to extricate ourselves. We *are* community.

STUDY QUESTIONS

1. What is the cause of AIDS? How does it gain access to the human organism? Describe its effects.
2. The AIDS epidemic is now more than twenty-five years old. In what ways has the epidemic evolved over this period?
3. Describe some of the legal reactions that have evolved in response to AIDS. What is the current legal status of these issues?
4. What are the major points of the Roman Catholic Church's response to the AIDS epidemic? Why is discrimination so frequently encountered by people with AIDS?
5. The ethical issues that arise in connection with AIDS are so numerous that they constitute, in the view of some observers, a "review course in medical ethics." In what ways can the ethical issues be organized for ethical analysis? What are the principal ethical questions that have been identified and what do you personally believe concerning each?

NOTES

1. John Mills and Henry Masur, "AIDS-Related Infections," *Scientific American*, August 1990, 50–57.

2. William C. Spohn, S.J., "The Moral Dimension of AIDS," *Theological Studies*, March 1988, 96.

3. At the present time, the CDC lists over two dozen opportunistic infections that threaten an individual with an HIV-weakened immune system. Some are bacterial infections; others arise from viral, protozoal, or fungal infections. Finally, there are malignancies and neurological conditions that may accompany a low T-cell count. See www.aidsmeds.com; also Mathilde Krim, "AIDS: The Challenge to Science and Medicine" (Special Supplement), *Hastings Center Report*, August 1985, 3.

4. In May of 1997, AIDS researchers admitted that the development of a complete AIDS vaccine may take as long as twenty years. *New York Newsday*, May 26, 1997.

5. Cf. Spohn, note 2, 93–94.

6. Ibid., 96.

7. *Hospital Ethics*, January/February, 1986, 2.

8. *New York Times*, November 14, 1997. Cf. also *Time*, January 25, 1988.

9. *New York Newsday*, June 28, 1998. The possibility of becoming HIV infected from one's physician or dentist has been the focus of a major public debate. Three studies in *JAMA* indicate that it is far more likely for medical personnel to become infected from their patients than vice versa. To date only Kimberley Bergalis's dentist has been linked to AIDS in patients. *Time*, April 26, 1993, 17. Cf. also Lorys F. Oddi, "Disclosure of Human Immunodeficiency Virus Status in Healthcare Settings," *Journal of Intravenous Nursing*, 17:2, March/April 1994, 93–102.

10. *Newsday*, July 28, 2003.

11. Ibid.

12. For a further analysis of AIDS statistics, cf. *New York Times*, June 24, 1998. Cf. also Jonathan Mann et al., "Toward a New Health Strategy to Control the HIV/AIDS Pandemic," *The Journal of Law, Medicine and Ethics*, 22:1, Spring 1994, 41–42.

13. See www.cdc.gov/hiv/stats.htm.

14. Centers for Disease Control, "HIV/AIDS Surveillance Report," January 1992, 1–22.

15. *New York Times*, July 1, 1998. Cf. also Ungvarski and Ballard. "Nurses, Consumers, Activists and the Politics of AIDS," in *Policy and Politics for Nurses*, 2nd ed., Philadelphia: W. B. Saunders, 1993, 677–97.

16. *NIAID Facts and Figures,* January 2004; cf. also *NY Newsday,* July 29, 1998; *Newsweek,* August 3, 1992.

17. David Kirp's volume, *Learning by Heart: AIDS and Schoolchildren in America's Communities,* portrays the very divergent experiences of AIDS children in nine school districts throughout the country in the early years of AIDS. New Brunswick: Rutgers University Press, 1989.

18. *New York Times,* June 26, 1998.

19. *Time,* June 21, 1993, 14.

20. As recently as ten years ago, same sex relations were illegal in twenty-four states and only three states protected the civil rights of gay individuals (*Time,* April 26, 1993, 28.) In 2003, however, the United States Supreme Court (*Lawrence* v. *Texas,* 02–102) ruled that intimate consensual sexual conduct was part of the liberty protected by substantive due process under the 14th Amendment (41 S.W. 3d 349).

21. John Paul II, "A Meeting with AIDS Victims" (September 17, 1987): *Origins,* October 15, 1987, 313–14.

22. *Origins,* November 30, 1989, 421, 423–34.

23. Ibid., 426.

24. Ibid., 427.

25. Ibid., 428–29.

26. Ibid., 430.

27. Ibid., 431.

28. Cf. also Bernard Lo, "Ethical Dilemmas in HIV Infection: What Have We Learned?" *Law Medicine and Health Care,* 20:1–2, Spring-Summer, 1992, 92–103; N. Holly Melroe, "'Duty to Warn' v. 'Patient Confidentiality': The Ethical Dilemmas in Caring for HIV-Infected Clients," *Health Care Issues* 15:2, September 1990, 58–69.

29. Dr. Edmund Pellegrino, Professional Workshop, "The Ethical Aspects of AIDS," The New School, 1987. Cf. also Rodney Hayward and Joel Weissfeld, "Coming to Terms with the Era of AIDS: Attitudes of Physicians in U.S. Residency Programs," *Journal of General Internal Medicine,* January 1993, 10–18; Pascal James Imperato et al., "Medical Students' Attitudes Toward Caring for Patients with AIDS in a High Incidence Area," *New York State Journal of Medicine* 88, May 1988, 223–27.

30. Abigail Zuger, "Professional Responsibilities in the AIDS Generation," *Hastings Center Report,* June 1987, 18. Cf. also Lo, note 28, 92–96.

31. Cf. Zuger, note 30, 18.

32. Cf. Lo, note 30, 92–96.

33. Cf. Pellegrino, note 29.

34. Cf. note 2, 90.

35. Ibid.

36. Cf. note 3, 9.

37. Cf. note 2, 93.

38. Cf. Josephine Ryan, "Clinicians and HIV Infection: Social Policies and Professional Issues," *Health Care Issues* 14:10, October 1989, 42–44; LeRoy Walters, "Ethical Issues in the Prevention and Treatment of HIV Infection and AIDS," *Science* 239, February 5, 1988, 599–600.

39. Carol Levine and Ronald Bayer, "Screening Blood: Public Health and Medical Uncertainty" (Special Supplement), *Hastings Center Report,* August 1985, 11.

40. Cf. Ryan, note 38, 40–42.

41. Deborah Jones Merritt, "The Constitutional Balance Between Health and Liberty" (Special Supplement), *Hastings Center Report,* December 1986, 2–10; Ruth Macklin, "Predicting Dangerousness and the Public Health Response to AIDS," ibid., 16–23.

42. Cf. Mann, note 12, 46.

43. *Hospital Ethics,* January/February 1986, 3–4.

44. Cf. David L. Long. "AID$—Fighting the Economic Epidemic," *Nursing Management* 18:9, September 1987, 66–71; Dennis P. Andrulis et al., "The Provision and Financing of Medical Care for AIDS Patients in U.S. Public and Private Teaching Hospitals," *JAMA* 258:10, September 11, 1987, 1343–46; editorial, "The Economic Impact of AIDS," ibid., 1376–77.

PART FOUR

Questions at the End of Life

Part Two, the first section that considered specific medical-ethical questions, began with issues that arose at the beginning of life. Part Four considers several questions at the final end of the life spectrum. Part Four investigates two subjects—first, the issue of death and dying, and second, the question of euthanasia. The two are related, of course. In fact, the second builds on understandings laid out in the more general investigation of the human experience of death.

Death is a statement of fact; an event has occurred. Life has ended. Dying describes, rather, the process of passing from life to death. It may be swift and unexpected, almost instantaneous. In other cases it may be slow and painful, extending over weeks and months— even years. Whatever form it takes, it raises many questions—medical, legal, and of course, moral. Much has changed about dying in America; the same is not true about death.

Euthanasia adds a particular character to the experience of dying—death is deliberately caused. This question has begun to engage the attention of Americans across the land. Without a doubt, euthanasia is an issue that is on the threshold of dividing the nation in the same way that abortion has caused convulsions in our national conscience. Whichever side one takes in this controversy, there is no doubt that it will force upon us once again the need to choose between values that are central—even sacred—for us all.

10 Death and Dying

THE MEDICAL-SCIENTIFIC DIMENSION

What are the medical-scientific issues that we need to address as we seek to deal with the question of death and dying? While many of these questions have other dimensions—legal, philosophical, theological—they are surely issues of clinical practice in the delivery of health care.

1. What is death? What does dying mean?
2. When does death occur? How can the fact of death be determined?
3. What obligations does a physician have with regard to health care for the terminally ill and the dying?
4. What are the rights—and the obligations—of the patient in the process of dying?
5. Who has the right to make health care decisions, particularly when they involve life and death? The patient? The family? The physician? All three?

One's understanding of death is, of course, influenced by one's understanding of life. What it means for a human being to die is necessarily understood in the light of what it means to live humanly. The nature of human life, its origins, its purpose, its destiny—all of these questions necessarily influence the meaning death has for us. But these are not issues that shall concern us yet.

Instead, we need first to raise the question: When does death occur? And since in our culture a doctor is almost always involved in this judgment, how can a doctor say, "The patient is dead"? How does a physician determine that death has in fact happened? Traditionally,

201

death has been deemed to have occurred when all cardiopulmonary function has irreversibly ceased. Other indicators—color, rigidity, decay—might confirm the fact, but a person is normally judged dead when the lungs cease providing oxygen to the blood and the heart stops circulating the blood through the body.

What had served so admirably as a test to determine death for so long, however, suddenly became inadequate in many cases with the advance of medical technology. The availability of machines that can take over the functioning of the human heart and lungs made it often impossible to tell whether all spontaneous cardiopulmonary function had ceased permanently. A new mechanism for determining death became necessary.

Brain Death

In 1968 an interdisciplinary Ad Hoc Committee of the Harvard Medical School was established to propose new criteria for determining death. The committee acknowledged that there were two reasons that motivated this search for more contemporary guidelines. The first, as already noted, was the advent of medical technology that masked one's loss of spontaneous functioning. The second was the developing technology of organ transplantation. If a mortally injured person could be maintained indefinitely on a ventilator, for example, how could that individual's death be declared so that his organs might become available for transplanting?

The committee set out, therefore, to define what it called "irreversible coma" and to describe the characteristics of a permanently nonfunctioning brain. Its conclusions were published in the *Journal of the American Medical Association* on August 5, 1968,[1] and they described a condition that has since come to be known as "brain death." The terminology has changed in the intervening years and "coma" is no longer the correct medical term to describe the condition that we now know as "brain death."[2] The committee described the four tests to determine this condition as follows:

1. *Unreceptivity and Unresponsivity* to externally applied stimuli. Thus "even the most intensely painful stimuli evoke no vocal or other response, not even a groan, withdrawal of a limb or quickening of respiration."

2. *No Movements or Breathing*—neither spontaneous muscular move-ments nor spontaneous respiration over the period of at least one hour.

3. *No Reflexes*—the absence of elicitable reflexes, e.g., of the pupil of the eye to a direct source of bright light, indicates the absence of central nervous system activity.

4. *Flat Electroencephalogram*—this is judged to be of great confirma-tory value when the first three clinical indicators are present (except in the case of hypothermia or when central nervous system depres-sants have been used). The committee judged that this test—as well as the other clinical tests—should be repeated twenty-four hours later. (This time frame has since been reduced.)

The committee pointed out that when all four criteria are pres-ent, this neurological assessment indicates that all cerebral and brain-stem function has ceased. Some commentators have proposed that as long as the neocortex, which controls higher functioning such as speech and reasoning, has ceased to function, brain death may be declared. This view has not been accepted, however, and total brain-stem activity as well as all cortical functioning must have ceased for a determination of brain death.

In 1981 the President's Commission for the Study of Ethical Problems in Medicine and Biomedical and Behavioral Research issued a report that updated and reaffirmed the validity of the Harvard criteria for determining brain death.[3] Most states now recognize, either by statute or through judicial decisions, that death may be determined on the basis of the irreversible cessation of all functions of the brain.

The Physician's Responsibility

Does the determination of terminal illness and the onset of the dying process alter the physician-patient relationship in any way? What obligations does a doctor have to provide health care for the terminally ill and the dying? On March 16, 1986, the Council on Ethics and Judicial Affairs of the American Medical Association issued a new set of ethical and professional guidelines to deal with this question.[4] Again in April 1992 this same council issued its statement, "Decisions Near the End of Life," to deal with the questions of physician-assisted suicide, active euthanasia, and the withholding/withdrawal of life-sustaining treatment for individuals who are neither terminally ill nor permanently unconscious.[5] Although these are not binding on individual doctors, they offer general direction to medical practitioners. The guidelines deal with the terminally ill, those for whom death is imminent. The guidelines also include for the first time those permanently incapacitated, that is, those in irreversible coma but not clinically "terminally ill."[6] (It is estimated that at the present time, approximately 15,000 to 25,000 Americans are in a persistent vegetative state.) In this context, the AMA said that life-prolonging medical treatment, "including medication as well as artificially or technologically supplied respiration, nutrition, and hydration," need not be continued.

Physicians, according to the AMA, could ethically cease or omit treatment in order to permit a terminally ill patient whose death is imminent to die. The doctor, to be sure, is not under an obligation to stop treatment, but such a decision is now professionally acceptable. In any case, the physician should not intentionally cause death, in the AMA's view, although whatever is medically necessary to alleviate severe pain may be done. If the patient is mentally competent, the patient should make this decision. If not, the patient's family or legal representative may decide.

Even though this issue might seem resolved, many commentators believe that it will continue to raise many questions.[7] A number of reasons have been suggested:

1. *A technological imperative* arises from medicine's technological advances and its capacity to sustain vital organ function in critically ill patients. The problem is compounded by society's unrealistic expectation that modern medicine can cure or reverse even the most severe diseases.
2. *The inability to predict recovery* accurately for specific patients.
3. Until recently, *a reimbursement system* that calculated financial return to both doctors and hospitals on how much "care" and intervention was provided.
4. *Increased concern with possible malpractice* or even criminal liability if the physicians did not follow this technological imperative.
5. *Inability to distinguish* aggressive treatment from maintenance or comfort care, when all hope of cure is gone.
6. *Lack of sufficient knowledge* of intensive medical care on the part of some physicians caring for the critically ill.[8]

Granted these pressures to continue aggressive treatment, must physicians acquiesce in refusals of treatment, especially in life-threatening situations? What norms or criteria might guide a physician in responding to such a patient decision? Suppose the refusal were irrational, even though the patient is legally competent? What if there is a good chance of a cure if treatment is accepted, while death is certain if it is refused? Can a physician ethically agree to participate in such a decision? Can an individual demand what amounts to medical malpractice from a doctor? Must the refusal of treatment always be honored, or is medical paternalism ever justified? Can a physician ever rightfully reject a patient's decision and simply impose therapy?

Some of these questions will be discussed in the chapter on informed consent; others are still being debated by medical ethicists and health care providers. At least in theory, however, the conviction has grown in this country that once a free, rational decision is made by an adult patient to forego treatment, a physician has no alternative but to honor this. This is not the same as to say that a doctor must violate his own conscience or his professional standards of practice; hence the possibility of transferring the patient to another physician always exists, at least theoretically.

Moreover, as has often been pointed out, sometimes the patient is not really asking to be allowed to die but rather some other message lies hidden in the words—a protest against helplessness, or a cry for autonomy and self-determination. Deciphering this code, however, is where medicine moves away from science and becomes art.

Who Decides?

Although it has been generally accepted for some time that the right to make health care decisions lies with the competent adult patient[9]—indeed, that it is a constitutional right[10]—in practice this is not always the way it works out. Medical paternalism and/or patient passivity often conspire to take the decision out of the patient's hands. More of this later, when we consider informed consent. There is no doubt, however, that it is surely the legal right and the responsibility of the adult, competent patient to accept or refuse any or all medical treatment recommended by that patient's physician, even when that treatment is necessary to sustain the patient's life. Similarly, when an adult is no longer competent to decide, this right does not cease but in fact passes to another who is called on to exercise this decision on behalf of the incompetent patient.[11]

The legal identity of the surrogate may be fixed by any mechanisms recognized by law (by "living will" when legally binding or by durable power of attorney for health care decisions) or by judicial decision. If a proxy is not legally established, one is normally chosen from those who have known the patient well and presumably have the patient's best interests in mind, beginning with the individual's family. The surrogate is morally bound—but not always legally bound—to honor the patient's wishes if these have been expressed prior to the loss of competence.

Consent for minors is given by parents or guardians, but the minor patient may be invited to give assent if that individual is capable of understanding the situation.

THE LEGAL DIMENSION

Why the Fact of Death Is Legally Significant

It is not difficult to realize that the fact of death has fundamental legal consequences for the individual—the individual is legally a person no longer; all rights cease. There remains only the need for a respectful interment to be arranged by the family—a task that in another age was undertaken by the church and, before that, by the state.

Other legal consequences for other individuals also flow from the fact of death—the payment of insurance, perhaps also an inheritance tax, the passing of one's assets to one's heirs, the marital status of one's spouse are some examples. Small wonder that the law makes clear provision for recognizing a physician's judgment that death has in fact occurred.

Since the state also recognizes that respect for life is of common benefit to society, it is also of interest to the state to determine that life has ended due to natural causes, or by accident, or through criminal intent.

National Policy

Thus far, most legal determinations regarding death and dying have been left up to the individual states. No federal policy exists in regard to any of the questions raised by this issue. No federal laws have been passed; no judgments have been handed down by the Supreme Court that would determine when death has occurred or what rights one has in making health care decisions, especially in terminal situations. At the state level, however, considerable activity has occurred in relation to these issues.

The consideration of the *Cruzan* case by the U.S. Supreme Court in 1989 offered the possibility of a precedent-setting decision on this question at the national level. The Court, however, chose to uphold the decision of the Missouri Supreme Court, and so the determination remained at the state level.

The Congress has, however, attempted to clarify the question of patient rights in a more general way. Enacted in 1990 and effective December 1, 1991, the Patient Self-Determination Act (PSDA) seeks to assist all citizens in understanding their rights regarding health care decision making as governed by state law (whether statutory or through judicial decision). The Act's major provisions require that:

1. Each state develop a written description of its laws governing an individual's rights to make decisions about medical care, including the right to accept or refuse medical or surgical treatment. In addition, the right to make advance directives (e.g., living will, durable power of attorney) must be explained.
2. Every health care institution (hospital, hospice, nursing home, home care, HMO) receiving federal funds, such as Medicare or Medicaid, must give this written information to all individuals receiving medical care from that institution.
3. Every health care institution document in each individual's medical record whether an advance directive has been executed.

The Act, therefore, leaves to the individual states the jurisdiction to make laws about patient rights and advance directives or not. The Act's goal was simply to make sure that all Americans are informed of their rights under state laws in the hope that more patients will receive medical care that is responsive to their needs and wishes.[12]

"Living Will" Legislation

While these issues have thus far not been determined at the national level, considerable activity has occurred in state legislatures and courts. The desirability and the need for enabling legislation in support of a "living will" have been debated for some time.[13] Although the name may differ from one jurisdiction to another, it is basically a document indicating what medical treatments and therapies are to be used/not used to prolong life in the event of a terminal illness, once competency is lost.

The American Catholic bishops initially opposed this legal development out of fear that it might promote a "euthanasia mentality" or might be a threat to the same right in the case of those who executed no such declaration. When courts began issuing judgments (cf. *In re Eichner*[14]) that threatened the traditional church teaching permitting the refusal of life-support treatment that was judged extraordinary, the American bishops changed their strategy and instead issued "Guidelines for Legislation" for the information of those preparing legislation on life-support treatment.[15]

Another concern that emerged and supported "living will" legislation was a growing awareness that radical right-to-lifers, some law-enforcement authorities, and some health care providers had adopted an extreme vitalism that threatened to negate an individual's right to refuse treatment.[16] In view of such militancy, "living will" legislation was judged to be one remedy that might secure an individual's right to decide.[17]

"Living will" legislation was first enacted in California in 1976, but few states followed suit until 1984. By the following year, thirty-six jurisdictions had passed statutes recognizing these declarations, and eventually only two states remained without a "living will" statute. In these states—New York and Nebraska—a "living will" has no legal status. Although it may be a valuable expression of a patient's wishes, it may also be legally set aside by a surrogate.

Durable Power of Attorney for Health Care

For some time it has been possible legally to delegate authority to a proxy to handle one's business affairs, should one become incompetent.

This same authorization is now sometimes extended, either through legislation or by court opinion, to health care decisions. By the beginning of 1985, three states (California, Pennsylvania, and Colorado) had made this possible, and at the present time all fifty states permit some form of durable power of attorney, although the rules may vary considerably from state to state. Many commentators recommend this approach over the "living will" since it allows a more flexible response to the concrete situation that may not have been anticipated when the "living will" was written.

Court Decisions

While legal developments in this connection have almost all evolved on the state level, the activity has been considerable. Since the *Karen Ann Quinlan* case in 1976, almost seventy-five right-to-die cases have been decided in the courts at the appellate level or in federal district courts. Although not all courts have judged the issues in precisely the same way, Alan Meisel suggests that a legal consensus has evolved that embraces the following points:

1. Competent patients have a common-law and constitutional right to refuse treatment.
2. Incompetent patients have the same rights as competent patients; however, the manner in which these rights are exercised is, of necessity, different.
3. No right is absolute, and limitations are imposed on the right to refuse treatment by societal interests.
4. The decision-making process should generally occur in the clinical setting without recourse to the courts.
5. In making decisions for incompetent patients, surrogate decision-makers should apply, in descending order of preference, the subjective standard, the substituted judgment standard, and the best interests standard.
6. In ascertaining an incompetent patient's preferences, the attending physician and surrogate may rely on a patient's "advance directives."
7. Artificial nutrition/hydration is a medical treatment and may be withheld or withdrawn under the same conditions as any other form of medical treatment.
8. Euthanasia and assisted suicide are morally and legally distinct from foregoing life-sustaining treatment.[18]

As Meisel is careful to point out, a consensus is not "a monolithic body of law." There are dissenting voices on the question, but the majority view is clear and firmly in possession at this time.

In January 1988, New York State enacted a DNR (Do Not Resuscitate) statute that permits a patient, whether personally or through a proxy, to request the attending physician to indicate in the medical record that the individual wishes that no resuscitation be attempted in the event of cardiac arrest. New York's Health Care Proxy statute two years later is another example of legislation regulating patient decisions about health care in a terminal situation. Similar legislation has been enacted in many jurisdictions and reflects society's ongoing effort to assure patient autonomy in the face of revolutionary advances in intensive care medicine. In addition, these laws mirror our uneasiness and concern regarding the protection of the most vulnerable groups in our society—the incompetent, the senile, the newborn, the physically and developmentally disabled.

While court decisions have consistently supported the termination of life support in cases involving a persistent vegetative state or a terminal situation, there may be a developing legal view in which the courts reject such a request for termination of life support when these medical conditions are not present. Several state supreme court decisions over the past decade have raised this issue but have left undecided any definitive answer, for example, this decision from California:

> The [California] court declared that a decision based on the patient's prior wishes or best interest must be supported by clear and convincing evidence, rather than the less demanding preponderance of the evidence. The court determined that the latter standard was acceptable when applied to terminally ill or permanently unconscious patients, but that the stricter standard should govern when conservators seek to forgo nutrition and hydration from conscious patients still able to perceive the discomfort and other symptoms that dehydration and starvation could produce. According to the court, applying a lower standard of proof to cases involving conscious patients could be "unconstitutional because it would give inadequate protection to the patient's right to life and the state's interest in preserving life."[19]

What remains to be determined, then, is how the courts will interpret the "best interest" standard for incompetent but conscious patients, who are not considered either permanently vegetative or in a terminal situation.

The Right to Die

During the years that have followed the *Quinlan* decision in 1976, an expression has crept into the literature and into the public discussion of end of life decisions—the "right to die." Just what does the expression mean and what basis is there for claiming such a right?

As it turns out, the phrase can refer to many different concepts and hence any claim to such a right must first clarify the sense in which the expression is intended. Thus it may refer to:

1. The natural and inevitable death that awaits all things that enjoy life.
2. The right to refuse medical treatment that can neither cure nor improve one's condition even though this may necessarily include the acceptance of a heightened chance of death.
3. The right to refuse medical treatment in order that death will follow. Obviously this involves a choice of death.
4. The right to require another's positive assistance in effecting one's death, in addition to the termination of treatment. This is the alleged right to assisted suicide or to be made dead by another, to be mercifully killed.
5. The right to select "the manner, the timing, and the circumstances of one's death." One thus exercises control over one's own destiny.
6. The right to choose "what one regards as the most humane or dignified way to die," including the right to obligate others to assist and thus participate in one's plan.[20]

Does a right to die exist? Who can claim such a right—whatever the precise meaning that is given to the expression? Does everyone enjoy such a right? Or must one be in a dying mode—irreversibly dying and thus in a terminal state? Is it sufficient that one is gravely ill or disabled, but clearly not dying? Must one be competent to exercise such a right, and in fact make such a claim—a logical conclusion if the basis for the right is personal autonomy? What then of the incompetent—the elderly senile, those in a persistent vegetative state, the mentally ill? What of those who have never been competent? Can proxies exercise this right for those who have lost competence? It should be evident that the answers to these and other questions will not be reached easily or soon!

In his reflection on this question of a right to die, Leon Kass asks what has led to the assertion of such a right at this time in our history. Fear, he answers—fear of an unacceptable lengthening of one's dying due to the intervention of medical technology, fear of living too long with neither purpose nor meaning to life, fear of the depressing experience of senility and dependence on others, fear of the loss of control over our lives and destinies, fear of being a burden on others. And despite all these fears, he asserts, there is no philosophical basis for a right to die. Indeed, it is the right to life that forms the basis and foundation of all other human rights—a right that is inalienable, flowing from human nature itself. In Kass's view, then, there is neither a right to commit suicide nor a correlative right to demand another's assistance in achieving death. Similarly, he can find no basis for claiming such a right in the law—neither in the original Constitution nor in the Bill of Rights. He does admit, however, that some of the language in the *Cruzan* decision indicates the possibility of claiming a basis for a right to die in the due process clause of the Fourteenth Amendment.[21]

In summing up his fundamental concerns about this question, Kass singles out three serious dangers:

1. The right to die or to assisted suicide will surely be read to include an obligation on others to kill or to help cause death. Who will be the euthanizer? To whom will the state extend its present monopoly on the legal use of lethal force?
2. There will be no way to restrict this right to those who knowingly and willingly seek death. It will surely be extended to the incompetent—either explicitly or in its actual practice, as has happened in Holland. There will be no way for society to protect these most vulnerable of its members.
3. The ethical center of the health care profession—the commitment to healing and to "do no harm"—will "be lost forever and, with it, patient trust and physician self-restraint."[22]

THE SOCIOCULTURAL DIMENSION

The Meaning of Death

What values are reflected in the practices and attitudes of our society regarding death and dying? Our cultural environment always affects our values; the practices of our society in some way influence our behaviors. In the matter of death and dying this is just as true as it is in any other aspect of our lives.

Consider the contemporary scene for a moment. What are typical American values? Youth, health, fitness, life—these are paramount. At times it seems that little else matters. How do we deal with death and dying then? So often we simply deny them, and when we cannot deny them, we ignore them. Surely we do not talk about them! Death is a taboo subject for conversation. It does not fit into the range of topics we typically discuss with our children or with our friends and associates. When a grandparent dies, children are told: "Grandpa's gone to heaven." We do not take them to the wake—"Children cannot understand." When a pet goldfish floats upside down in the fish tank, children are told: "He's gone to goldfish heaven"—undoubtedly with grandpa nearby.

One of the reasons we are able to avoid a confrontation with death is that in many cases we have "quarantined" our dying members—our relatives, our friends, our neighbors—in special situations reserved for those who are dying or are likely to die. We find them in retirement villages, in "golden-age homes," or in nursing homes or hospitals. No longer do we keep at home those among us who are dying. At the present time, 85 percent of our generation will die in hospitals. And so our children—and we with them—can be oblivious to what it means to die. If we never see anyone die, we will have little understanding—and less feeling—for what dying is all about. One comes to know death from observing the preceding generation cope with it. Because this has been absent from our experience, we cannot expect to recognize death as the natural culmination of life. For us, death is the enemy, the one to be overcome and defeated, never the one to be welcomed as the point of passage from life to life.

Aging, too, is guilty by association, and so we tend to deny it, reject it, or disguise it as long as we can. In order to maintain this facade, we call death by other names. In our mourning rites we present the body as living—in dress, in cosmetic decoration, in setting. Some of our cemeteries present themselves as virtual country clubs; our funeral homes often resemble luxury motels. Thus death is not the visitor expected at life's end. Rather death is viewed as failure, defeat, and for so many, the source of anxiety and depression.

So often in our culture, then, dying is to be resisted, avoided, denied. No longer a natural process at life's end, dying becomes a mistake, a miscalculation, a cause for resentment. Modern medicine is hailed for its imagined unlimited capacity to reverse the aging and the dying process, for death is a cheat, a villain, a scoundrel. We deny the reality of death, its naturalness, its inevitability. Life is what counts. When death cannot be avoided, it must be condemned. Small wonder, then, that we experience great difficulty in coping with death. Its meaning, its value, its possibilities—all are so often forgotten because only life has value.

ROMAN CATHOLIC CHURCH TEACHING

If the previous comments truly reflect the prevalent cultural mood in this country, it surely does not resonate well with the traditional Christian understanding of death.[23] "In death, life does not end; it changes" is what the church sings in its funeral liturgy. Since Vatican II, the Roman Catholic Church has made the resurrection—of Jesus and of his followers—the theological focus of this final eucharistic celebration before interment. Since the council, it has laid aside black vestments for white, and it intones "alleluias" over those gathered for the occasion. Hope and joy in the midst of loss and sorrow is the formula it uses as it seeks to affirm the meaning and value of death.

These liturgical practices are a natural consequence of the church's understanding of life and death. This understanding was enunciated in an American setting by a committee of the American Bishops' Conference, when the Pro-Life Committee issued a set of *Guidelines for Legislation on Life-Sustaining Treatment*.[24] Many of the same points have been given fuller expression by Pope John Paul II in his 1995 encyclical, *Evangelium Vitae* (The Gospel of Life).[25] The following is an analysis of the major principles that reflect the church's teaching.

Theological Foundations

1. Life is a gift of God, a loving God, a creator God.
2. Human life deserves particular respect, has inherent dignity, value, worth because each human being is made in the image and likeness of God.

3. The value and worth of each person have been reaffirmed through the death and resurrection of Jesus Christ, and each of us is called to share eternal life with him.

Moral Principles

1. Life is a sacred trust over which each enjoys a special stewardship, but not absolute dominion.
2. Positively, each individual has a moral responsibility to safeguard and protect life; negatively, any direct attack on innocent life is forbidden.
3. Because of the personal nature of the obligation to preserve one's health and life, the decision in all health care matters belongs to the (adult, competent) individual, not in isolation but in solidarity with family and community.
4. Suffering, a fact of life, is a physical evil. It can, however, have a special significance for the Christian who sees in suffering the basis for a special relationship with Jesus in his suffering and death.

Practical Consequences

1. One's obligation to preserve life is not absolute, for physical life—although a basic and fundamental good and the condition for all other human goods—is not an absolute good or value. Rather, one is bound to use only whatever means are proportionate to this end.
2. Thus, one is not obligated to use "extraordinary" or disproportionate means, namely, those that entail burdens that are greater than the benefits they bring.
3. In arriving at health care decisions, one normally should seek counsel and support from one's physician and family.
4. Though suffering may have special meaning for the Christian, one may always use whatever means are available to eliminate or reduce pain and suffering, even if the painkillers themselves carry some risk of shortening life. One may never, however, directly or intentionally cause death to end suffering.[26]
5. Health care should never be denied an individual simply because of age, disability, the terminal character of the illness, incompetence, or mental incapacity.

A Controverted Issue

One issue that remains unresolved is the question of the administration of artificial nutrition and hydration. What is the nature of such treatment—is it medical treatment or is it rather an example of the basic care that is due any human being? When it is not provided, does that denial become the cause of the patient's death? Is the patient being "starved" to death?[27] This is a particularly nagging question when the person has not been declared to be in imminent danger of death. Conflicting—even contradictory—answers to these questions have been given by ethicists, moral theologians, and even bishops.[28] While the legal consensus seems to agree that tube feeding is a form of medical treatment, this has not ended the ethical debate, as is evidenced in the most recent *Directives* issued by the American bishops.[29]

THE MORAL DIMENSION

Moral Values

What ethical or moral values are involved in issues of life and death—in my life and death or in anyone else's?

- *Autonomy*—A primary value is personal autonomy. But what is the extent of this autonomy? Does my life "belong" to me? Absolutely and utterly? To dispose of as I wish? Or is life rather a gift, over which I am given limited dominion or "stewardship"?
- *Human Dignity*—In part, this is the basis for personal freedom, enabling me to make moral decisions. Does this personal dignity give rise to the freedom to take my own life? To end life? To choose death? To request, or even require, help from another to accomplish this?
- *Value of Human Life*—Is there such a thing as a life not worth living—by reason of illness, distress, pain, or physical or mental disability? Does the loss of one's ability to contribute to society affect that individual's worth or value? Does it diminish one's dignity as a human being?

Obviously, these values can at times be in conflict, and it is this conflict of values that has given rise to the developing national debate over euthanasia.

A Christian Reflection

In its reflection on human living and human dying, the Christian faith community has consistently affirmed its convictions regarding these realities. First, life is the gift of a loving creator. This creative love establishes and grounds the value and worth of each person's life. Thus I have value because God loves me, prior to any achievements or accomplishments on my part.

Further, with this gift comes the responsibility to protect it. While I have dominion over my life, rooted in my personal freedom, it is neither absolute nor complete. Thus, for Christians, the concept of responsible stewardship describes how I am accountable before my creator for my health and life.

Positively, therefore, I am obliged to conserve and protect my life, to use all means that are proportionate to this end. These include such natural means as nourishment, rest, clothing, shelter. Similarly, the means developed by medical science to preserve or restore health should also be utilized.

But are we obliged to use absolutely all means? Must I do everything? And if not absolutely all, then *which* means? How can I decide my moral responsibilities and obligations in this respect? The terminology "ordinary and extraordinary means" has been developed within the Roman Catholic tradition to clarify an individual's positive obligation to safeguard life and health. Thus any means is considered ordinary when the benefit *to me* is greater than (or at least equal to) the burden. Conversely, any means that involves burdens greater than the benefits *to me* is designated as extraordinary. It is not morally obligatory, although a person is free to use it.[30]

Note particularly the phrase "to me." This indicates the personal and individual character of this calculation of ordinary/extraordinary means. What may be a benefit or a burden for one person may not be viewed the same way by another individual. The ability to bear pain, to endure dependency, or to cope with reduced functioning or confinement—all of these may be viewed quite differently by different individuals. The terms "ordinary/extraordinary," therefore, do not have any determined content. No specific therapy or treatment can be designated ordinary or extraordinary (in the moral sense) for *all* patients. This designation can only be calculated and determined according to the degree of benefit or burden for the individual involved.

This being so, if my positive obligation is to preserve life and health, the negative responsibility obliges me never to take my own life, either personally or through another. In other words, I may never place an act that has as its immediate intent the ending of my life, without any other purpose. Thus innocent human life—yours, mine, anyone's—may never be directly attacked, never directly terminated, even by the individual himself or herself.

Finally, when it is established that I am dying, I am free to forego medical interventions that merely prolong dying. I may also request drugs to alleviate pain, even if there is some risk that they may shorten my life.

Who Decides?

Because of my fundamental human dignity and in view of my personal freedom, the responsibility to make these life-and-death decisions is mine. They should not be made alone, however, nor in isolation, but within the community of my family and friends. I depend, too, on the information that my physician alone can provide and so my doctor has an important role in this decision-making process. In the end, however, it is I who must stand before the Lord and be accountable for my decision.[31]

What of the dying individual who is no longer competent, who can no longer exercise that freedom? Does the right and obligation to make health care decisions cease with the loss of competence? Should anyone ever be able to make such a proxy decision for another? Should anyone else ever be allowed to make treatment decisions on behalf of a dying person? There are those ethicists who answer "no." The issue is too grave, too fundamental, they explain, for anyone to rightfully make such a decision for another. In effect, then, the right to decide is lost with the loss of competence according to this view.

This is not the common view, however. If it is true that I have the right to make health care decisions for myself, then that right survives, even when I cannot exercise it. That right would be empty and futile unless someone else could exercise it for me, once I lose the capacity to decide. Hence a proxy decision is sometimes both necessary and desirable.

What norms should the proxy follow? If I have left instructions, then the proxy is morally (but not always legally) bound to follow these. If I have left no directions, then the proxy is asked to choose what I would have decided—and hence he must have known me well. Failing this, a proxy must choose what is judged to be in my best interest.

STUDY QUESTIONS

1. Why have so many questions surrounding death and dying all of a sudden (the last twenty years) become so controversial?
2. If I have a moral and a legal right to make my own health care decisions, especially in life-and-death situations, what means are available to me that will assure that my wishes will be respected?
3. Describe how our contemporary American society has influenced the way we think about death and dying.
4. What doctrinal and moral principles lie at the heart of the Roman Catholic Church's approach to the question of death and dying? Suppose you are a volunteer teacher in your church's religious education program; formulate your explanation of this approach in terms that can be understood by a sixth grader.
5. Explain how our examination of the values involved in the issue of death and dying seeks to harmonize conflicting views and competing priorities.
6. How does the "ordinary/extraordinary means" distinction fit into the death and dying doctrine of the Roman Catholic Church—and, to a considerable degree, into contemporary legal doctrine—with respect to this issue?
7. Summarize the controversy over artificial nutrition and hydration. Which side of this controversy do you think has the stronger arguments? Explain.

NOTES

1. 205:6, 85–88. For a more detailed discussion of these neurological criteria, cf. *The Canadian Journal of Neurological Sciences,* 26:1 (February

1999) 64–66. The clinical aspects of several similar but different conditions—of coma and of PVS, for example—are discussed by Ronald E. Cranford, "The Persistent Vegetative State: The Medical Reality (Getting the Facts Straight)," *Hastings Center Report,* February/March 1988, 27–32.

2. The broad acceptance of the brain death standard "among the medical, legal, and religious communities" in New York State is noted by the New York Task Force on Life and the Law in its Draft Report, February 1986. For an opposing view, however, see Paul A. Byrne et al., "Brain Death: An Opposing View," in *JAMA,* November 2, 1979, 113–18, and "Brain Death—the Patient, the Physician, and Society," *Gonzaga Law Review,* 18:3 (1982/1983): 429–516.

3. *Defining Death: Medical, Legal and Ethical Issues in the Determination of Death,* President's Commission for the Study of Ethical Problems in Medicine and Biomedical and Behavioral Research. Washington, D.C.: U.S. Government Printing Office, 1981. The issue of brain death is not definitively settled by any means. At the 2nd International Symposium on Brain Death in 1995, speaker James Hughes predicted that the whole definition of brain death would unravel as 21st century technologies introduce the possibility of repair, replacement, and manipulation of brain tissue. See www.changesurfer.com/Hlth/BD/Brain.html#RTFToC3.

4. American Medical Association, March 16, 1986.

5. *JAMA* 267:165, April 22/29, 1992, 2229–33.

6. Kirk Payne et al., "Physicians' Attitudes about the Care of Patients in the Persistent Vegetative State: A National Survey," *Annals of Internal Medicine,* July 15, 1996, 104–10; cf. also note 1.

7. Nancy S. Jecker, "Knowing When to Stop: The Limits of Medicine," *Hastings Center Report,* May/June 1991, 5–8.

8. Irwin and Pratter, "Making Clinical Decisions for the Critically Ill: A View from Critical Care Physicians," *Journal of Intensive Care Medicine,* 1986, 63–65.

9. Justice Cardozo: "Every human being of adult years and sound mind has a right to determine what shall be done with his own body." *Schloendorff* v. *Society of New York Hospital,* 211 N.Y. 125 (1914); cf. also *In re Brooks Estate,* 32 Ill 2d 361, 205 NE 2d 435 [1965]; *In re Osborne,* 294 A2d 372 [1972].

10. *Bartling* v. *Superior Court,* 163 Cal App 3d 186, 209 Cal Rptr 220 (1984).

11. The New York State Court of Appeals in *O'Connor* ruled that "clear and convincing" evidence was required to establish the wishes of an incompetent patient when her family asserted her wish to forego life-sustaining treatment. *In re Westchester County Medical Center* (O'Connor) 72 N.Y. 2nd 517, 534 N.Y.S. 2nd 886 (1990). Missouri also has a similar requirement. For a

more nuanced view of the question, however, cf. Ira Mark Ellman, "Can Others Exercise an Incapacitated Patient's Right to Die?" *Hastings Center Report*, January/February 1990, 47–50. For a commentary on the New York Task Force document, *When Others Must Choose*, cf. Jonathan A. Morano, "Who's to Choose?" *Hastings Center Report*, January/February 1993, 5–11.

12. For commentaries on the PSDA, cf. Charles P. Sabatino, "Surely the Wizard Will Help Us, Toto?" *Hastings Center Report*, January/February 1993, 12–16; Mathy Mezey and Beth Latimer, "The Patient Self-Determination Act," *Hastings Center Report*, January/February 1993, 16–20; Joanne Lynn and Joan M. Teno, "After the Patient Self-Determination Act," *Hastings Center Report*, January/February 1993, 20–24; Linda Ganzini et al., "Is the Patient Self-Determination Act Appropriate for Elderly Persons Hospitalized for Depression?" *Journal of Clinical Ethics* 4:1, Spring 1993, 46–50.

13. John Paris and Richard McCormick, "Living Will Legislation Reconsidered," *America*, September 5, 1981, 86–89.

14. 52 N.Y. 2d. 363. March 31, 1981, New York Court of Appeals.

15. *Origins*, January 24, 1985, 526–28.

16. Cf. note 13, 87–88.

17. Cf., however, John A. Robertson's "Second Thoughts on Living Wills," *Hastings Center Report*, November/December 1991, 6–9.

18. Alan Meisel, "The Legal Consensus About Forgoing Life-Sustaining Treatment: Its Status and Prospects," *Kennedy Institute of Ethics Journal*, December 1992, 315. For a consideration of the related concept of "medical futility," cf. Ronald Cranford and Lawrence Gostin, "Futility: A Concept in Search of a Definition," and the symposium on the subject in *Law, Medicine and Health Care*, 20:4 (Winter 1992): 307–09.

19. Rebecca Dresser, "The Conscious Incompetent Patient," *Hastings Center Report*, May/June 2002, 9.

20. Leon R. Kass, "Is There a Right to Die?" *Hastings Center Report*, January/February 1993, 34–43.

21. See the following chapter for the outcome of this issue before the U.S. Supreme Court in the summer of 1997.

22. Cf. also Yale Kamisar, "Are Laws Against Assisted Suicide Unconstitutional?" *Hastings Center Report*, May/June 1993, 32–33; Thomas Marzen et al., "Suicide: A Constitutional Right?" *Duquesne Law Review*, 24 (1985): 1–241.

23. For a recent summary of the Roman Catholic position on this question, cf. Michael Panicola, "Catholic Teaching on Prolonging Life: Setting the Record Straight," *Hastings Center Report*, November/December 2001, 14–25.

24. *Origins*, January 24, 1985, 526–28.

25. *Origins,* April 6, 1995, 689, 691–727. See especially Chapter Two, "I Came That They May Have Life," 700–707.

26. For a discussion of the use of analgesics in clinical practice, cf. William C. Wilson et al., "Ordering and Administration of Sedatives and Analgesics During the Withholding and Withdrawing of Life Support from Critically Ill Patients," *JAMA* 267:7, February 19, 1992, 949–53.

27. This question has received considerable attention from the clinical standpoint. It is sometimes alleged that such deliberate "starving of patients" is painful and therefore inhumane. What are the clinical facts? Evidence has been accumulating that such is not the fact. A study by Sullivan and his review of the literature seem to indicate that "prolonged dehydration and starvation induce no pain and only limited discomfort from a dry mouth, which can be controlled. For individuals carrying an intolerable burden of illness and disability, or those who have no hope of ever again enjoying meaningful human interaction, the withdrawal of food and fluid may be considered without concern that it will add to the misery." Robert J. Sullivan, "Accepting Death without Artificial Nutrition or Hydration," *Journal of General Internal Medicine* 8 (April 1993): 220–24. Cf. also Robert A. Pearlman, "Forgoing Medical Nutrition and Hydration," ibid., 225–27.

28. See the statement of Bishop Gelineau of Providence, R.I. (*Origins,* January 21, 1988), approving the removal of artificial nutrition and hydration in connection with a case in his diocese, in contrast to the amicus curiae brief of the N.J. Catholic Conference in the *Nancy Jobbes* case and the statement of the Pennsylvania bishops, "Nutrition and Hydration: Moral Considerations" (*Origins,* January 30, 1992, 541, 543–53), which opposed such an action; for a response to this statement, cf. Richard A. McCormick, "'Moral Considerations' Ill Considered," *America,* March 14, 1992, 210–14.

29. *Ethical and Religious Directives for Catholic Health Care Services, Origins,* December 15, 1994, 458–59. Regarding the legal consensus, cf. Alan Meisel, "A Retrospective on *Cruzan,*" *Law, Medicine and Health Care* 204 (Winter 1992): 345–46.

30. This distinction has been incorporated by the Council on Ethics and Judicial Affairs of the AMA in its statement, "Decisions Near the End of Life," *JAMA* 267:16, April 22/29, 1992, 2230. This choice of terminology is not without its critics, however, because of the confusion that can result when the same terms are used by health care providers to designate altogether different realities. Thus a physician would call any therapy that is readily available, easy to administer, and relatively inexpensive "ordinary," and the opposite "extraordinary." To avoid this potential confusion, it is suggested that terminology be adopted that is based on the principle of proportionality. Thus, if the outcome (benefit) is proportionate to the expenditure (burden)—physical,

psychological, financial—then it is morally obligatory. When it is dispropor-tionate, however, one is not bound to employ it.

31. For a discussion of "medical futility" and its impact on patient autonomy, cf. reference to the Helga Wanglie case in the following chapter; cf. also Martin Smith, "Futile Medical Treatment and Patient Autonomy," *Cleveland Clinic Journal of Medicine*, 60:2 (March/April 1993): 151–54.

11 Euthanasia

THE MEDICAL-SCIENTIFIC DIMENSION

Nature

The previous discussion of death and dying naturally leads to the consideration of another closely related question, euthanasia. What was said in the previous chapter, therefore, must be kept in mind throughout this consideration of euthanasia.

The term "euthanasia" is derived from two Greek words, *eu* and *thanatos,* meaning "good death" or "happy death." In contemporary usage, however, the qualification "good" refers to pain and suffering. Hence this "happy death" is one that releases an individual from pain, a death that ends suffering. For this reason, euthanasia is often used to mean the same as "mercy killing" in much contemporary discussion. Keep in mind that euthanasia differs from suicide in that it always involves "somebody else," an individual other than the one who dies. Thus the spouse who fires the weapon, the doctor who administers the lethal injection—someone else—is always involved.

On the face of it, it would seem that the practice of medicine would find euthanasia inimical to its most fundamental values. If the Hippocratic oath requires the physician to do "at least no harm" to the patient, taking the patient's life would surely seem to be the greatest harm that could be done.

> The regimen I adopt shall be for the benefit of my patients, according to my ability and judgment, and not for their hurt or for any wrong.

Euthanasia

> I will give no deadly drug to any, though it be asked of me,
> nor will I counsel such. (Hippocratic oath)

Certainly the AMA has consistently maintained this position. As recently as 1996, in its guidelines for terminating life-sustaining treatment, the association noted that a physician could never deliberately take the patient's life.[1]

Others, however, might insist that the goal of medicine is to support and promote *human* life. Where the level of pain and suffering no longer permits human functioning, the argument goes, it is not unethical for a physician to end a life when suffering allows no further human participation in life.

Whatever the judgment one finally reaches, some fundamental distinctions need to be understood early in the discussion.

Distinctions

First of all, one must distinguish between deliberately and intentionally *causing* death by killing the suffering patient (euthanasia) and simply *allowing* death to occur by withholding or withdrawing life-sustaining treatment. In the latter case, one does not will or intend the death; one simply chooses not to intervene, or one decides to withdraw treatment and thus allow the dying process to take its course.[2] Although some commentators call this decision "passive euthanasia," this discussion of the question will avoid such terminology in an effort to avoid confusion. In this text, therefore, "euthanasia" describes the deliberate and intentional causing of the patient's death in order to end pain and suffering. It should be said, in passing, that not all commentators acknowledge that there is any significant moral difference between the two, but more about this later.

The second set of distinctions is based on the involvement of the patient in the end-of-life decision. Thus if the individual requests or consents to the dying, the decision is said to be *voluntary*. If not, it is *nonvoluntary*, as in the case of one in an irreversible coma or otherwise incompetent.

If these distinctions are kept in mind, it can be seen that euthanasia is not simply the same as suicide. When it is a case of voluntary euthanasia, of course, suicide is always involved. Euthanasia, however, is not a *solitary* act. Someone else, another person, is always involved; this individual causes the person's death in the case of euthanasia. Similarly, another individual—the physician, a family member—is involved in the decision to forego or cease treatment.

Euthanasia needs to be distinguished also from physician-assisted suicide (PAS), which occurs whenever the physician merely facilitates the death of a patient by providing the necessary means and/or information required to enable that individual to end life. Thus strictly speaking, many of the actions of Dr. Jack Kervorkian are not examples of euthanasia, but rather of physician-assisted suicide.

Euthanasia and the Medical Profession

It is no surprise that the prospect of authorizing physicians to administer euthanasia has occasioned much conflict within the medical profession. While the AMA, through its Council on Ethical and Judicial Affairs, has rejected physician involvement in euthanasia, its reflections on the conflict between the value of patient autonomy and the disvalues inherent in euthanasia for the medical profession in particular and for society at large[3] reveal the urgency of the issue.

Arguments by individual physicians, of course, have not been lacking on either side of the issue. It is safe to assume, therefore, that the medical profession will remain embroiled in this controversy for the foreseeable future.[4]

THE LEGAL DIMENSION

Euthanasia

Euthanasia has never received legal sanction in this country. The direct and deliberate killing of a sick person, even if the patient's condition is terminal and the action is requested, is illegal. Indeed, until very recently, the public record shows a continuing determination to forbid such actions and to prosecute those who violate the law against homicide. It is a matter of record, however, that in the Anglo-American tradition no physician, prior to Dr. Jack Kevorkian, has ever been convicted of murder for having killed a patient to end suffering.

226

(Dr. Kevorkian was convicted in 1998 of second-degree murder and is currently serving ten to twenty-five years.) The same cannot be said, however, when nonprofessionals are involved in the killing of a terminally ill spouse or relative.

This legal situation is the same in all fifty states and has been the constant legal tradition in this country. In the 1940s there was a flurry of legislative effort to legalize euthanasia, but no similar activity has occurred since then, until recently. In May 1988 there was a movement in California to place an initiative allowing euthanasia on the ballot for the following fall. This effort was sponsored by Americans Against Human Suffering (the political arm of the Hemlock Society), among others. As a condition for euthanasia, the proposal required that the individual be suffering from a terminal illness, one that would lead to death in six months or less. It also allowed advance directives that authorized euthanasia. For technical reasons this effort failed, but its supporters indicated the intention to return the issue to the voters in California and in other states.

Not surprisingly, therefore, in 1991 State Senator Frank Roberts of Oregon introduced a bill —Aid-in-Dying— that would legalize euthanasia for any terminally ill individual, whether competent or not, whose condition is judged to cause exceptional physical or psychological pain or suffering. The bill would include all permanently unconscious patients, including those in comatose or vegetative states. A legal proxy ("attorney-in-fact") could authorize the action in the case of incompetent patients. This proposal was not enacted into law.

On November 15, 1991, the voters of Washington State rejected (54 percent to 46 percent) an initiative (Proposition 119) authorizing both euthanasia and physician-assisted suicide (PAS).[5] The proposal, had it been approved, would have made the state of Washington the first jurisdiction in the world to approve these actions. The proposition asked the question, "Shall adult patients who are in a medically terminal condition be permitted to request and receive from a physician aid-in-dying?" The title of the proposal placed before the voters seemed innocent enough. Spelled out in the proposal, this "aid" included "aid in the form of a medical service, provided in person by a physician that will end the life of a conscious and mentally qualified patient in a dignified, painless, and humane manner, when requested voluntarily by the patient through a written directive." This directive would be delivered at the time this "medical service" was to be provided.

Proposition 119 was defeated by the electorate of Washington State in 1991. Much the same outcome occurred on November 3, 1992. It was on this date that the voters of California rejected Proposition 161 by a margin of 54 percent to 46 percent, thus losing the distinction of becoming the first jurisdiction to legalize euthanasia. The close character of the vote, however, made it clear to all that almost half the electorate had indicated their preference for the certainty of death over the uncertainty of excessive treatment in their dying. The message to the medical establishment was not difficult to read. Remedy the causes of this broad public concern—the fear that one's dying will be indefinitely extended by the excessive use of technology and, secondly, the widespread suspicion that health care practitioners lack the knowledge and/or the will to provide effective pain management—or the next election might resolve the issue and take the solution out of the physicians' hands.[6]

It came as no great surprise, then, when one of these efforts proved successful. On election day 1994, the voters of Oregon approved Measure 16 by a vote of 52 percent to 48 percent. The proposal authorized physician-assisted suicide. It specified that the individual must be certified as terminally ill (six months to live) by two physicians. A request for a prescription for a lethal dose of drugs to end unbearable suffering must be made at least three times, the third time in writing. After waiting fifteen days the patient would receive and administer the lethal dose, not the physician. The approved referendum was then temporarily suspended by a preliminary injunction "until a court can decide if it is constitutional."

And the courts were busily at work! In January 1994 in the state of Washington, a group of four physicians and several gravely ill patients filed suit against the state and its attorney general, asserting that the Washington statute prohibiting assisted suicide be declared unconstitutional. The plaintiffs asserted that the liberty interest protected by the Fourteenth Amendment extended to a person the choice of physician-assisted suicide, provided that the individual was a competent, terminally ill adult. The petition relied largely on the *Casey* and *Cruzan* decisions of the Supreme Court. The district court agreed with the petitioners and also noted that the statute violated the equal protection clause of the Constitution. This decision was then reversed by a panel of judges of the Court of Appeals for the Ninth Circuit, only to have this judgment reversed again by the entire court of appeals. Indeed, the court declared that there is in fact a constitutionally recognized "right to die." It did, however, reject the district court's holding regarding "equal protection." In 1996, the case arrived before the Supreme Court for its review and decision.

Meanwhile, across the country in New York, an almost identical process was taking place. Again a group of physicians and patients brought suit against the state and its officials alleging that the New York statute prohibiting assisted suicide was unconstitutional—this time arguing that allowing some terminally ill patients to refuse life-saving medical treatment while making it a crime for others to commit or attempt suicide violated the equal protection clause of the Fourteenth Amendment, since both acts were "essentially the same thing." This time the district court disagreed with the petitioners, only to be reversed by the Court of Appeals for the Second Circuit. This case *(Vacco et al.* v. *Quill et al.)* joined the Washington case *(Washington et al.* v. *Glucksberg et al.)* on the desk of the Supreme Court.

On June 26, 1997, the Court spoke. In the Washington case (96–110), it decided that it did not recognize the asserted right to commit suicide as a fundamental liberty interest protected by the due process clause. Even further, it accepted that the state indeed had legitimate interests in establishing its ban on assisted suicide—citing, for example, the preservation of human life, the threat of suicide for vulnerable groups (e.g., the young and the elderly), the link between suicide and psychiatric illness, and the integrity of the medical profession. In the final paragraph of its decision, the Court noted that American society is engaged in an "earnest and profound" debate about the question of physician-assisted suicide and the Court's decision allows the debate to continue "as it should in a democratic society."

The Court's decision in the *Vacco* case (95–1858v) rejected the argument that the distinction between refusing life-preserving treatment and assisted suicide was "arbitrary" and "irrational." Indeed, the Court found that this distinction was both logical and consistent with contemporary practice. It then listed all the reasons that it had developed in the *Washington* case and affirmed that these were "valid and important public interests" that easily justify the constitutionality of the New York statute.

In October of 1997, following these landmark decisions, the Supreme Court refused to hear an appeal that had kept Oregon's 1994 law from taking effect. The statute then ended up back with the Oregon legislature. The legislators thereupon voted to request another referendum, this time by mail. By a majority vote (3 to 2), Oregonians reaffirmed their intention to authorize physician-assisted suicide. Since that time, the Oregon Health Services Commission voted to let the state pay for the expenses associated with assisted suicide in the case of Oregon's poor. In March 1998 the first suicide permitted under the new law was revealed by the Oregon Compassion-in-Dying group. While sixty-seven prescriptions were written in 2003, only forty-two individuals made use of the lethal doses. This represented an increase over the thirty-eight deaths in 2002. ALS, HIV/AIDS, and cancer were the most frequently cited morbidities.[7]

The Dutch Experience and the Slippery Slope

All of these legal efforts dealing with end-of-life decisions clearly indicate that there is considerable interest and support for legalized euthanasia. Indeed, those opposed to it view much of the public discussion and recent court decisions regarding the termination of life support as a growing sympathy in this country for euthanasia itself. In this context, the Pro-Life Committee's "Guidelines for Legislation on Life-Sustaining Treatment"[8] and the "amicus curiae" brief of the New Jersey Catholic Conference in connection with the Nancy Jobbes case[9] call attention to the "slippery slope" that may be the road to legalized euthanasia. This is, perhaps, no empty fear. For a number of years in Holland, euthanasia has been practiced without outright legalization. Even though the action was a crime in Holland for the past twenty years, carrying a penalty of up to twelve years in prison, it was never prosecuted. The Dutch parliament finally legalized the world's least restrictive euthanasia policy, establishing strict rules that would allow a physician to assist in a suicide or kill a terminally ill patient at the patient's explicit request. The recognized conditions include (1) competence, (2) voluntary request repeated consistently and frequently over a reasonable time, (3) intolerable suffering without hope of relief, and (4) performance of the process by a physician in consultation with a second physician not involved in the medical care of the individual. In every instance, the physician is required to report any participation in either assisted suicide or euthanasia. The usual method of administering euthanasia is to deliver a barbiturate followed by curare. It is not required that the patient be suffering from a terminal illness.

Although these regulations seem quite clear, it has become obvious, as a result of several studies ordered by the Dutch government, that many physicians have not been reporting their participation in these actions. It is even more significant that individuals are being euthanized who are not competent or who are competent but have not requested death. In such cases, the doctors have been justifying their decisions by asking, "What would I want if I were in the patient's place?" The practice of euthanasia has recently been extended to cause the death of a newborn with disabilities and of a severely depressed but physically healthy patient. Certainly, the Dutch experience offers a dramatic insight into what is known as the slippery slope!"[10]

Withholding or Withdrawing Treatment

As already explained in the previous chapter, the various state laws and court decisions regarding the withdrawing or withholding of medical treatment when life support is the issue have established a consensus that affords legal recognition to such a decision. Naturally, the choice must be freely made by the patient or clearly established in the evidence available. As Meisel is careful to point out, however, a consensus is not "a monolithic body of law." There are dissenting voices on the question, but the majority view is clear and firmly in possession at this time.

Also mentioned previously, in January 1988, New York State enacted a DNR (Do Not Resuscitate) statute that permits a patient, whether personally or through a proxy, to request the attending physician to indicate in the medical record that the individual wishes that no resuscitation be attempted in the event of cardiac arrest. An interesting and perplexing situation—in a sense, the reverse of what has just been described—occurred in 1990. Up to the present, most legal activity and ethical reflection have been concerned with the patient's decision to refuse or discontinue medical treatment, especially when that is necessary to sustain life. In the Minnesota case of Helga Wanglie, it was the doctors caring for her who judged—after repeated attempts to wean her from the respirator and in view of her numerous medical problems—that their treatment was futile and Mrs. Wanglie should be taken off the respirator that kept her alive. Mrs. Wanglie's husband and family objected and insisted that all treatments be continued. By the time the hospital placed the issue before the court in May 1991, Mrs. Wanglie's hospital care had cost $800,000. It was the first time a hospital had sought court intervention to name a guardian who might request the discontinuation of life support against the wishes of a patient's family. On July 1, 1991, Judge Patricia Belois ruled against the hospital's petition, thus continuing Oliver Wanglie as guardian. Helga Wanglie died on July 4, 1991.[11]

THE SOCIOCULTURAL DIMENSION

What societal values influence our views on euthanasia?

A pleasure-oriented society. There is no doubt that pleasure holds a high place in contemporary American culture. Unabashed consumerism and widespread affluence promote the "good life." A hedonistic spirit is scarcely below the surface, for example, in the values trumpeted by the advertising industry. And if comfort and pleasure are so highly regarded, must not pain and suffering become more difficult to accept?

Extended life expectancy. In the last one hundred years, our society has doubled its average life expectancy. But what purpose have we found for the aged? What meaning and value do we place in advanced old age? In traditional Asian cultures, for example, the elderly are seen to possess great wisdom and dignity; thus they are treated with respect and reverence. No such attitude characterizes our society, however, and hence many elderly live out their old age in isolation and purposelessness.

Human Dignity. Americans subscribe to the notion of an inherent dignity in the human person. We have yet to harmonize that value, however, with our ability to prolong life through the administration of advanced medical technology. Too often this remarkable development of medical science seems in the view of many rather to strip the patient of dignity even as it struggles to cure illness and extend life.

232

Individualism. The American ethos has always idealized the individual, whether it was the pioneer who pushed the frontier westward or the aviator who braved a solo crossing of the North Atlantic. The American hero in myth and legend is the individual who has braved insuperable odds in pursuit of a heroic vision. In the context of death and dying, this outlook is reflected in the question, "Whose life is it, anyway?" This question, however, leaves unmeasured the impact on society in general—if any—that would flow from the condoning of any direct termination of life.

Personal Autonomy. This logically translates as the right to make one's own health care decisions and even refuse life-sustaining treatment. But it says nothing about the obligation to care for one's health and life. To many, therefore, it absolutizes autonomy at the expense of serious personal and societal values.

ROMAN CATHOLIC CHURCH TEACHING

The teaching of the Catholic Church—which prohibits the direct taking of innocent life, whether one's own or another's—is amply attested to in church documents throughout the centuries. In the early 1960s at the Second Vatican Council, euthanasia was numbered among "the crimes against life" that it condemned.[12]

Because of the technological advances in intensive care medicine and the development of sophisticated life-support systems, however, new questions have arisen that demanded a fresh look at this question. Accordingly, on June 26, 1980, a new statement on the question of euthanasia was issued by the Congregation for the Doctrine of the Faith.[13] The question was revisited once again in 1995 by Pope John Paul II in his encyclical *Evangelium Vitae.*[14]

In his encyclical, the pope reaffirmed the Christian conviction regarding the value of human life and the individual's responsibility to care for it, in the context of modern medicine and other developments within society. With great solemnity the pope wrote:

> ...In harmony with the magisterium of my predecessors and in communion with the bishops of the Catholic Church, I confirm that euthanasia is a grave violation of the law of God, since it is the deliberate and morally unacceptable killing of a human person.

This doctrine is based upon the natural law and upon the written word of God, is transmitted by the church's tradition and taught by the ordinary and universal magisterium.[15]

In addition to reaffirming the church's rejection of euthanasia, John Paul II spoke of the meaning of human suffering and the use of painkillers. Finally, he reaffirmed the traditional teaching regarding the obligation to use ordinary means and the freedom to reject extraordinary means in preserving life.

Euthanasia must be distinguished from the decision to forgo so-called "aggressive medical treatment," in other words, medical procedures which no longer correspond to the real situation of the patient either because they are by now disproportionate to any expected results or because they impose an excessive burden on the patient and his family. In such situations, when death is clearly imminent and inevitable, one can in conscience "refuse forms of treatment that would only secure a precarious and burdensome prolongation of life, so long as the normal care due to the sick person in similar cases is not interrupted."…To forgo extraordinary or disproportionate means is not the equivalent of suicide or euthanasia; it rather expresses acceptance of the human condition in the face of death.[16]

Interestingly, while affirming that a terminally ill person was not required to use treatments that were merely death-prolonging, the pope reasserted the congregation's caution that "all normal care due to the sick person must be continued." While not naming hydration and nutrition explicitly, he may have thrown his weight on the side of those who insist on the continuation of measures providing hydration/nutrition.

Basically, then, the argument against euthanasia—based on religious belief—is rooted in the Judeo-Christian conviction discussed in the previous chapter. This view sees human life as gift and grace—the gift of a God who loves us. Men and women are called on to cherish this gift, to preserve and protect it. We never enjoy absolute dominion over it; rather, we are stewards of the gift of life and therefore responsible and accountable for the care we take of it.

THE MORAL DIMENSION

Moral Values

Euthanasia decisions obviously involve a choice between conflicting values. What moral values are proposed by those who support
and by those who condemn euthanasia?

Elimination of Pain and Suffering

First of all, obviously, there is the intention to eliminate suffering.
Although many observe that pain and suffering are unavoidable in our
human condition, few would propose suffering as a good. When an
individual's physical condition has so deteriorated, when—affirm the
euthanasiasts—that pain constitutes one's entire experience, it is a
morally good thing, a true mercy, to bring that life to an end.

Autonomy

Another moral value proposed in support of euthanasia—at least
in the case of voluntary euthanasia—is the personal freedom and autonomy of the individual. Any competent adult, so the argument goes, has
the right to have others respect that individual's free and rational
choices, even the decision to end life to escape intolerable suffering and
pain. Interestingly, Courtney Campbell suggests that it is precisely society's inability to find meaning in suffering, dying, and death that has
given rise to the assertion of some that it is in fact human autonomy and
self-determination that confer significance and create meaning through
the choice of an authentic manner of dying.[17]

It is important to note in any discussion of "rational suicide" in
connection with euthanasia and physician-assisted suicide that psychiatric studies have indicated that "90 to 100 percent of [suicide] victims die while they have a diagnosable psychiatric illness."[18] In other
words, this self-destructive behavior almost always occurs in cases in
which the individual suffers from a mental illness that is susceptible to
both clinical diagnosis and treatment—which when promptly administered is usually successful. Equally important are two additional

facts—those suffering from such depressive affective disorders are sel-
dom aware of the severity of their illness or of the hopelessness it
begets, and primary care physicians often fail to detect major depression in their patients, especially among the elderly. If these studies are
accurate, then, "rational suicide" may well be an oxymoron, while
those responsible for judging their patients' competence may be ill
equipped to make such a determination.

Control of Medical Technology in One's Dying

It is further affirmed by those supporting the legalization of
euthanasia that the entire population would then never need fear
becoming the prisoners of medical technology. Rather, euthanasia
would always be available as an escape should their condition become
unbearable.

Finally, this view maintains that not only would euthanasia free
a patient from suffering, but this would be done quickly and
humanely—an outcome that could not be claimed by a nontreatment
or a termination of treatment decision.

The Exercise of Freedom in the Service of Life

On the other side of the argument is the view that the choice of
death is the ultimate injury to a person, the final insult to free will,
since it destroys both. While agreeing that pain and suffering may be
mitigated in every way possible—even to the point of allowing the use
of such powerful painkillers that life itself may be indirectly short-
ened—still, in this view, the direct and intentional taking of an innocent life—even one's own—can never be condoned. How justify the
use of freedom, they ask, in freedom's own destruction?

The Value of Human Life

Add to this understanding of the value of life for the individual,
the value of human life to society at large. Should society ever approve
the deliberate destruction of innocent life for any reason whatever, it
is argued, the value of all human life would be reduced. Once the

direct killing of an innocent person is seen to be acceptable in one set of circumstances, it will become increasingly difficult to limit the exception to cases of intractable physical pain. The Dutch experience surely bears this out. This reasoning, the "slippery slope" or "wedge" argument, does not claim that the extension of euthanasia to other circumstances and situations will inevitably follow, but merely that it will become increasingly more difficult to limit the situations in which the killing of innocent individuals would be condoned because of a lack of agreement among people regarding the terms in question. How judge when pain becomes humanly unbearable? When is dependence on others unacceptable? How judge when the level of rational functioning is so minimal, the capacity for human interaction so reduced, that causing death becomes preferable to supporting life? What kind of broad societal agreement might we hope for? Further still, how keep from sliding over from "lives devoid of human dignity" to "lives devoid of human worth, or usefulness, or value to society"?[19]

Euthanasia and Physician-Assisted Suicide—Impact on Public Morality

As society continues to wrestle with these controversial questions, the following points need to be kept in mind:

1. Suicide—the decision to end one's life—has little to do with terminal illness statistically (at most 2–4 percent). Two-thirds of those who end their lives after they have reached sixty (25 percent of all suicides) enjoy reasonably good health.
2. As already pointed out, most suicides (90–100 percent) occur in people suffering from treatable mental illness.
3. In a society that recognizes suicide as a rational, reasonable choice, it is not a long step to conclude that suicide may easily become a choice that is unreasonable not to make. Consider what pressures could be exerted upon the ill and the elderly to choose a swift exit from a life characterized by isolation and dependence, by uselessness in the present and uncertainty and hopelessness in the future.
4. While most legislative initiatives frame the issue in terms of the terminally ill and the dying, no serious reason can be offered for such a limitation. If I find my life to be no longer endurable, then my death becomes a rational choice for me. It is my pain. It is my life. It is my

decision. Ultimately this is what society is being asked to approve—a personal autonomy over life and death that is absolute, subject to no arbitrary limitations. If the values that support the choice of death are autonomy and an escape from pain and suffering, what reasoning could limit this decision to terminal cases?

5. Both euthanasia and physician-assisted suicide place obligations on society to be involved in my causing of my death—either as one who actually makes me dead or as one who aids me to cause my own death. Whom will we deputize to do this? An agent of the state? Then we authorize the state to kill any citizen who requests death competently, repeatedly, passionately. A physician? Then we have forever surrendered the basic trust on which the physician/patient relationship has depended for two thousand years.

6. It will be impossible to limit this practice to those who request death deliberately—with knowledge and freedom. Any such stated limitation will disappear in the essential privacy that characterizes the physician/patient relationship. Neither is there the possibility of policing such a limitation on the part of public authority. The experience of Holland should have made this clear, where it is public knowledge that physicians are administering lethal injections to incompetent individuals, despite the requirement that death must be a personal and individual request. As Kass has observed, "The vast majority of persons who are candidates for assisted death are, and will increasingly be, incapable of choosing and effecting such a course of action for themselves."[20]

The Moral Distinction

Is there a difference—a morally significant difference—between killing a person in pain and letting that person die by withholding or withdrawing treatment? Some commentators say "no." Thus James Rachels insists that how a person dies, whether by lethal injection or by withholding life support, is not morally significant. What makes the difference morally, he asserts, is one's end or motive and the act's consequences. Indeed, he argues, it is more humane, more human, to end the sufferer's pain at once than to allow the individual to experience a protracted, lingering death.[21]

In response, it is argued that Rachels has the right principle but reaches the wrong conclusion. Morality does indeed hinge in part on motive. To will and cause a person's death is morally unacceptable—

whether by firing a shotgun or disconnecting the respirator. In such an instance, as Rachels rightly insists, the means used is morally irrelevant. What Rachels neglects to consider, however, is that in the refusal of life-sustaining treatment one does not will the death at all. What one wills is not to interfere in the dying process when dying can only be delayed. Thus it is a decision not to prolong the dying, but to allow the disease, the injury, the disruption of bodily functioning to take its natural course.[22]

Final Moral Assessment

What moral judgment is offered, then, regarding euthanasia? Euthanasia cannot be justified morally. What value might be suggested in such a situation that would outweigh the value of the human life at stake, even in its reduced and pain-racked condition? This would be true even in cases in which the patient requests death as relief from pain and suffering.[23] Objectively speaking, the value of this life surpasses the value of freedom from pain and suffering, even for this individual. This view in no way denies the reality of that individual's temptation to escape from pain, but neither the appeal to autonomy nor the demand for human dignity seems to justify the deliberate destruction of the very basis for both.

And what of the refusal of life-sustaining treatment? It seems clear that there can be situations in which this is morally defensible. It has already been explained that no one is obliged to use extraordinary or disproportionate means to preserve life—a medication that is more burdensome than beneficial, a surgical intervention that harms more than helps, technological support that produces results that are not proportionate to the cost to the individual. The dying person—note that this situation is only conceivable when the individual is terminally ill—does not choose or will to die. That has already been determined by some disease process or by some accident. The dying person chooses not to make use of what might be medically useful in another set of circumstances. The patient wills to forego what would only forestall the inevitable, and at a disproportionate cost physically, or emotionally, or financially. This is the will-act in which the physician—or the spouse, or the family member, or whoever is the "other person"—concurs. That is a far cry from willing the death of the terminally ill person by employing a lethal injection or providing the patient with the means to kill herself.

STUDY QUESTIONS

1. In considering the question of euthanasia, a number of important distinctions must be kept in mind. Explain the most important ones.
2. What does the law say about euthanasia? About physician-assisted suicide?
3. What aspects of American culture are most influential in shaping the contemporary challenges to our statutes regarding euthanasia?
4. What is the Roman Catholic Church's position regarding the morality of euthanasia? What general theological insights does it base this evaluation on?
5. At the concrete level of individual experience, the euthanasia debate highlights a conflict of values. What are these values and how would you prioritize them? Explain your reasons.

NOTES

1. AMA, E-2.21 Euthanasia. Issued June 1994; updated June 1996.

2. This distinction has been reaffirmed by Pope John Paul II in his 1995 encyclical *Evangelium Vitae*, n. 65. *Origins*, April 6, 1995, 712.

3. "Decisions Near the End of Life," *JAMA* 267:16 (April 22/29, 1992): 2232.

4. M. Angell, "Euthanasia," *New England Journal of Medicine* 319 (1988): 1348–50; S. F. Hunter, "Active Euthanasia Violates Fundamental Principles," *JAMA* 262 (1989): 3074; M. Parker, "Moral Intuition, Good Death and Ordinary Medical Practitioners," *Journal of Medical Ethics* 16 (1990): 28–34; W. Reichel and A. J. Dyck, "Euthanasia, a Contemporary Moral Quandary," *The Lancet* (1989): 1321–23; P. A. Singer and M. Siefer, "Euthanasia—A Critique," *New England Journal of Medicine* 322 (1990): 1881–83; Guy I. Benrubi, "Euthanasia: The Need for Procedural Safeguards," *New England Journal of Medicine* 326:3 (January 16, 1992): 197–98; Franklin G. Miller and John C. Fletcher, "The Case for Legalized Euthanasia," *Perspectives in Biology and Medicine* 36:2 (Winter 1993): 159–76.

5. For a discussion of PAS, cf. Yale Kamisar, "Are Laws Against Assisted Suicide Unconstitutional?" *Hastings Center Report,* May/June 1993, 32–41.

6. Alexander Morgan Capron, "Even in Defeat, Proposition 161 Sounds a Warning," *Hastings Center Report,* January/February 1993, 32–33.

7. See *The Oregonian* at www.oregonlive.com, March 16, 2004.

8. *Origins,* January 24, 1985, 526–28.

9. New Jersey Catholic Conference, "Amicus Curiae in the Jobbes Case," *Origins,* January 22, 1987, 582–84.

10. In 1991 a report was issued by the Remmelink Commission established by the Dutch government on "euthanasia and other medical decisions concerning the end of life." The authors of this report indicate that approximately 2,000 instances of euthanasia occur in the Netherlands annually. Cf. Paul J. Van der Maas et al., "Euthanasia and other medical decisions concerning the end of life," *The Lancet,* September 14, 1991, 673. A challenge, however, to Van der Maas's interpretation of the numbers and his use of terminology is offered by Gerald S. Brungardt and Anne M. Egbert in "Blurring the Distinctions: Euthanasia vs. Withdrawal of Care," *Linacre Quarterly,* February 1994, 72–80. The authors claim that as many as 58 percent of the euthanasia deaths in Holland have been nonvoluntary. Cf. also Johannes Van Delden, "The Remmelink Study: Two Years Later," *Hastings Center Report,* November/December 1993, 24–27.

11. Several articles in *Hastings Center Report,* July/August 1991, 23–35, offer analyses of this case; cf. also Alexander Capron, "*In Re Helga Wanglie,*" *Hastings Center Report,* September/October 1991, 26–28; also Alan Meisel, "The Legal Consensus About Forgoing Life-Sustaining Treatment: Its Status and Its Prospects," *Kennedy Institute of Ethics Journal,* December 1992, 331–32.

12. *Gaudium et Spes* n. 27, *The Documents of Vatican II,* Walter J. Abbott, S.J., ed. New York: Herder and Herder, 1966, 226.

13. *Origins,* August 14, 1980, 154–57.

14. N. 64–67, *Origins,* April 6, 1995, 712–13.

15. N. 65, ibid., 712.

16. N. 65, ibid.

17. Courtney Campbell, "Religious Ethics and Active Euthanasia in a Pluralistic Society," *Kennedy Institute of Ethics Journal,* September 1992, 255.

18. Cf. note 5; cf. also Linda Ganzini, "Is the Patient Self-Determination Act Appropriate for Elderly Persons Hospitalized for Depression?" *Journal of Clinical Ethics* 4:1 (Spring 1993): 46–50.

19. The reality of the "slippery slope" was brought home when the Netherlands's highest court exonerated a Dutch psychiatrist for having provided a severely depressed patient with the means of committing suicide—

contrary to the conditions set by the government. The physician in question, Dr. Boudewijn Chabot, contended that "intolerable psychological suffering is no different from intolerable physical suffering." His lawyer commented that this ruling "recognizes the right of patients experiencing severe psychic pain to choose to die with dignity." *Time,* July 4, 1994, 61.

20. Leon Kass. "Is There a Right to Die?" *Hastings Center Report,* January/February 1993, 42.

21. James Rachels, "Active and Passive Euthanasia," *New England Journal of Medicine* 292 (January 9, 1975): 78–80; Dan Brock, "Voluntary Active Euthanasia," *Hastings Center Report,* March/April 1992, 12–14.

22. For Richard McCormick's response to Rachels's arguments, see *Notes on Moral Theology 1965 Through 1980.* Washington, D.C.: University Press of America, 1981, 607–9. The Supreme Court's 1997 decision clearly establishes in the law the legal distinction between the two actions.

23. For a discussion of the arguments for and against active euthanasia, cf. John J. Paris. "Active Euthanasia," *Theological Studies,* March 1992, 113–26; Daniel Callahan, "When Self-Determination Runs Amok," *Hastings Center Report,* March/April 1992, 52–55; Dan Brock, op.cit., 10–27; Sanford Kadesh, "Letting Patients Die: Legal and Moral Reflections," *California Law Review* 80 (1992): 857–58.

PART FIVE

Questions Concerning Health Care in General

The final section of this book is concerned, as the title suggests, with questions that are not limited to a particular medical-ethical dilemma, such as abortion or newborns with disabilities. These two chapters raise questions that have applicability to health care in general. Chapter Twelve introduces the concept of informed consent, the free, autonomous response of a competent, adult patient to the medical information provided by that individual's physician. It represents the patient's decision to accept the physician's recommended therapy, or it expresses an equally deliberate choice not to participate in the treatment. Whichever it is, it represents the right of a patient to give or withhold consent to the health care recommendations of a physician.

Chapter Thirteen introduces the question of health care reform, and particularly the issue of universal access to health care. The nation has struggled with this problem for almost one hundred years, which attests to its complexity and its inherent difficulties. The chapter reviews some of these questions and then points to the moral conviction of the Roman Catholic community regarding each individual's right to adequate health care. Finally, some suggestions are made regarding the process necessary to fulfill society's obligation to assure access to health care to all those participating in the life of the nation.

12 Informed Consent

THE MEDICAL-SCIENTIFIC DIMENSION

A question that looms large in contemporary medical practice involves the communication of information between physician and patient. What must the doctor tell the patient? Must the doctor tell everything, absolutely all? Or is it sufficient for the patient to be told only some things and, if the latter, which?

Must the doctor always tell the truth when communicating with the patient? Can the physician hold some facts back? Can the patient ever be deliberately told what is not fact, not true?

A second, more specific but related question concerns making decisions about health care. Who really should decide which treatment to choose, which procedure to elect? Who really should make health care choices? Is medicine so technical, so scientific that only a doctor is equipped to make the right decision? Should the decision be left to the physician or is it the patient who has the right to decide?

The first issue is considered under the general rubric of "truth telling in medicine"; [1] the latter is the issue of informed consent.

Nature of Informed Consent

Informed consent can be an issue in two quite different settings. First, it can be a consideration in view of a particular medical treatment or procedure recommended by the individual's physician (therapeutic). Informed consent can also be a consideration in connection with a research project or an experimental treatment in which an individual agrees to participate (research).[2] The former will be the focus of this chapter.

245

There are two aspects to informed consent in a therapeutic setting: disclosure on the part of the physician and consent that is given by the patient. Disclosure involves making available to the patient an understanding of the nature of the treatment (medication, therapy, procedure), the probability of success, the benefits that may be anticipated as well as the burdens that may be experienced, and finally, any alternative treatments that may be available.[3]

Thus a number of factors are involved—a complete presentation of the necessary information by the doctor, patient competency,[4] substantial comprehension of the information by the patient, freedom, and actual decision making. It should be clear, however, that the human realities of the clinical situation introduce significant variables into the matter—the physician's skill in communicating and style of practice, the patient's intelligence, maturity, and ability to cope with the actual choices presented, and finally the interaction between the physician and the patient.[5]

As it has evolved in this country, informed consent has received a considerable impetus from several developments in American society. First of all, consumerism has become an important aspect of the health care delivery system. Consumer rights and consumer protection have invaded the field of medicine and have changed it immensely in a relatively short time. The second factor is a consequence of consumerism—the development of a "malpractice mentality." The public has come to expect that physicians carry out their professional responsibilities with a high degree of expertise. They must be equipped with the most up-to-date information, and they must practice their skills with a considerable degree of competence. Failure to do so, more often than not, is an invitation to be the object of a lawsuit.

As a principle governing medical practice, however, informed consent has not yet fully evolved. Many issues are, even now, not fully elaborated. Thus, how much information a doctor is obliged to give a patient or, conversely, how much information a patient has a "right" to know is still debated. And what of therapeutic privilege in this consumer age? What kind of information may be considered hazardous to a patient's well-being, and what precisely is the hazard that justifies the omission of informed consent?

The "flip side" of this patient right—to give or withhold consent—is the right of society to participate in some way, at least in some health care decisions. Excessive emphasis on patient autonomy can sometimes run up against the health care policies established within a particular society. Can a patient demand care when it is judged medically futile? Or care that conflicts with professionally accepted standards? The Helga Wanglie case in Minnesota,[6] the Elizabeth Bouvier case in California,[7] indeed the current national debate about euthanasia, all are examples where it is not yet clear whose decision will—or should—prevail.

Reasons

The principal reason for insisting on informed consent in the delivery of health care is to permit the patient to make an autonomous choice, to make an independent health care decision. This principle of self-determination is a fundamental conviction of Anglo-American law.

In addition, it is hoped that this exchange of information and consent will lead to an enhanced physician-patient relationship, to greater trust between the two. As in other fiduciary relationships, one party is in a dependent position with respect to the other, from whom he trusts he will receive some sort of benefit. It is a relationship based on trust or reliance between two parties who are unequal because of the physician's superior knowledge and professional expertise. Informed consent enhances their mutual trust and confidence in each other.

Finally, it is believed that through patient participation and cooperation the benefit of the therapy will be increased. When the patient thoroughly understands the therapeutic regimen and personally commits himself to carrying it out faithfully, the chances of success are greatly enhanced.[8]

Manner

Disclosure can be done orally or in writing or through one of the many audiovisual explanations now available to physicians for this purpose. Consent can be given orally or in writing. In the case of disclosure, the physician or a delegate offers the required information, while consent is given by the patient or a proxy.[9]

Timing

Clearly, informed consent should be sought and given prior to treatment. Ideally this should occur long before the patient enters the hospital or is about to begin the treatment in question. It has been found that a patient is much more likely to accept an active role in treatment decisions before entering a health care institution. The sooner the question is raised, therefore, the more likely the patient is to take charge of his own health care management. Typically, however, once a patient enters a hospital, he becomes much more likely to accept health care decisions passively.

Ideally, then, the physician should share all of the pertinent information with a patient and ask him to "sleep on it." After a reasonable period of reflection and consultation with family members or even another physician, a patient can be expected to bring a mature and serious decision to the treatment question.[10]

Certainly, to present a patient with a long, legally precise but often incomprehensible statement at the time of admission to the hospital fails against the spirit, if not the letter, of the law on informed consent.

THE LEGAL DIMENSION

One of the factors that has led to the development of the informed consent doctrine in this country has been the involvement of the courts.[11] Ironically, however, what began as a mechanism for patient protection has evolved into a means of safeguarding the physician legally.

Disclosure

The basic requirement in this connection is that the doctor provide sufficient information to enable the patient to decide whether treatment is in that individual's best interest. The law has made no precise determination regarding which facts or how much information must be communicated. It is generally accepted that the physician should disclose the nature of the treatment, its risks and benefits, and whatever alternative therapies exist. One commentator suggests that the physician should reveal to the patient whatever information he needs to know in order not to be surprised by whatever happens.[12]

Two norms have evolved regarding the adequacy of disclosure. The first is called the "professional standard." Basically, this corresponds to what other physicians in the same situation would reveal to their patient. Another criterion, the "legal standard," transfers the focus to the patient and requires that the doctor disclose all information that a reasonable person in the patient's position would want to consider. Thus, in any suit alleging failure to disclose, the patient must establish that had disclosure been adequate, the treatment would have been refused—in most states by any reasonable person, in some states by the plaintiff. It was only in 1972 that this second norm received any legal standing.[13] At the present time slightly more than half the states adhere to the original, professional standard.

Consent

The patient's agreement to the treatment must be secured before the therapy is begun. This can be given orally or in writing; the latter is often preferable since it may deter litigation and can be offered as proof of consent in the event of a lawsuit. The consent statement should indicate what information was given to the patient as the basis for the decision. Even a signed statement, however, is not certain evidence of consent, since a patient can say that the statement was not read or that no oral explanation of it was given. When contested, therefore, any judgment about the validity and force of a consent is left up to a jury.

Exceptions

Emergency—It is generally accepted that prior consent is never demanded before treatment is given in emergency situations. Often, however, in a hospital setting some representative of the institution will seek consent from a family member or relative if such an individual accompanies the patient.

Incompetence—Whatever the cause of the lack of capacity to consent—unconsciousness, lack of majority, limited intelligence or awareness—incompetence makes the giving of consent impossible, and therefore consent is not required prior to treatment. Concretely, however, in most such situations the consent of a surrogate or proxy will be sought, if one is available.

Waiver of Right by Patient—It is possible at times that the patient will tell the physician to do whatever the doctor thinks best but that the patient does not want to know what is wrong. While not a very responsible approach to health care decisions, such an approach releases the physician from the obligation to secure the patient's consent. Because of the legal risk, however, it might be rash to proceed with treatment in such a situation without some signed statement authorizing treatment.

Therapeutic Privilege—The final exception is known as "therapeutic privilege." This describes the situation in which the physician believes that the patient will suffer immediate grave injury if told about the nature of his condition. In such a case the doctor is excused from the normal requirements of adequate disclosure so long as the danger of injury continues. Thus, for example, if the physician judges that a cardiac patient might have a heart attack if told about the gravity of his or her condition, full disclosure would not be required.

Not all commentators would concede that the presumption favors the doctor as the one best equipped to know what is best for the patient or how much information should be given to a patient. There is no evidence, these observers insist, that doctors are well qualified to evaluate the benefits and burdens of withholding the truth. They have no special training to discern which values should prevail in such a decision; neither do they have special training or expertise in assessing psychological states. Therefore, they have no right, it is asserted, to withhold information and effectively negate patient self-determination.[14]

THE SOCIOCULTURAL DIMENSION

What cultural attitudes, societal values, accepted behaviors, and expectations influence the way Americans regard informed consent?

Developments within Medicine

Modern medicine, especially high-tech medical care, requires considerable sophistication and intelligence to be adequately understood by a patient. Similarly, it requires special efforts on the part of doctors to convey appropriate information to patients. Diagnostic procedures, for example, sometimes provide health care specialists with information long before any symptoms develop that might alert the patient to the onset of medical problems. In such a situation, it is often difficult to convince an individual to seek treatment for an ailment whose effects have yet to manifest themselves.[15]

Furthermore, modern medicine frequently requires the patient to deal with medical specialists and technical experts, often as a team. This complicates the patient's ability to develop a trusting relationship with any one of them. On their side, the health care providers find it difficult to determine accurately the information needed by the patient who is not well known to them.

At the same time, a different trend is accentuating the demand for full and accurate information. As the general population grows in its level of education and sophistication, the aura of omniscience and infallibility that traditionally surrounded medical practitioners has come under more frequent challenge. Moreover, media exposure of abuses by health care providers and medical researchers has further eroded their privileged status. Less and less, therefore, are people willing to accept a passive role in health care decisions.

Finally, the involvement of the courts in narrowly circumscribing therapeutic privilege has challenged the discretionary use of information by medical practitioners that has so long been traditional in the "art" of medicine.

Litigiousness

American society today is a litigious one. Disagreements and misunderstandings are routinely submitted to the judiciary for settlement rather than being settled by the parties involved. The practice of medicine is no stranger to this phenomenon. Malpractice litigation has reached epidemic proportions, swelling the business of the courts and threatening the traditional physician-patient relationship.

As mentioned earlier, the same consumerism that has led the public to seek information about goods and services in order to make an informed decision about a dishwasher or an automobile has spread to the practice of medicine. An intelligent and at times challenging public increasingly demands a full disclosure of information on which to base its health care decisions.

Autonomy

If the autonomous individual has always been an ideal of western civilization, it is only relatively recently that public policy has clearly delineated what is required for the exercise of independent judgment in health care. As the legal doctrine becomes increasingly specific and defined, the paternalism that has historically characterized the practice of medicine grows less acceptable.

The Contemporary Situation

In view of these developments, what can be said of the actual experience of informed consent in the contemporary practice of medicine? In 1982 the President's Commission for the Study of Ethical Problems in Medicine and Biomedical and Behavioral Research commissioned two studies on the question.[16] Previously a number of surveys had been done, but no useful conclusions had been generated due to flawed methodology.

The commission chose the Lou Harris Associates to do a self-report study. Two parallel surveys were conducted among 800 physicians and 1251 adult patients regarding their attitudes and experiences with this question. The patient population reported that they (94 percent) wanted full information, even unfavorable, about their health, (89 percent) wished their right to be protected by law, and (72 percent) elected to make treatment decisions jointly with their physicians. At the same time, physicians (98 percent) said that they routinely discussed their patient's condition and outlook with the individual, (96 percent) always explained the nature and goals of the therapy, (93 percent) notified the patients of potential side effects, and (84 percent) evaluated the benefits and burdens of the treatment with the patient.

At the same time, the commission selected Lidz and Meisel to do an observational study of physician-patient communication in several university-based teaching hospitals. The actual practice of the doctors departed significantly from what had been described in the self-reports. Similarly, the patients' actual behavior was quite different from what they had reported to be their need and desire to participate in their health care decisions. This was particularly true of patients who, when hospitalized, often appeared passive and allowed the decisions to be made by the doctors. It was evident that patient involvement fell dramatically when they were removed from their usual environment and deprived of their routines and their support systems. Only 5 percent of those studied (two hundred) were actively involved in the decision-making process. The investigators concluded that hospitalization, ill health, and a dependent status explain in large measure patient passivity in health care decisions.

The commission concluded that it was not laws that were needed; rather, the conviction among physicians and health care professionals that informed consent was an ethical imperative would have a much more significant impact. To this end, the commission suggested that patients be invited to ask questions and restate information to assure comprehension. Ideally, they should take home consent forms for reflection, it said, prior to signing them. Finally, doctors should use written and verbal reinforcement to increase patient understanding.

ROMAN CATHOLIC CHURCH TEACHING

The *Ethical and Religious Directives for Catholic Health Care Services* contains the following directives:[17]

1. The free and informed consent of the person or the person's surrogate is required for medical treatments and procedures, except in an emergency situation when consent cannot be obtained and there is no indication that the patient would refuse consent to the treatment.
2. Free and informed consent requires that the person or the person's surrogate receive all reasonable information about the essential nature of the proposed treatment and its benefits—its risks, side

effects, consequences, and cost—and any reasonable and morally legitimate alternatives, including no treatment at all.

3. Each person or the person's surrogate should have access to medical and moral information and counseling to be able to form his or her conscience. The free and informed health care decision of the person or the person's surrogate is to be followed so long as it does not contradict Catholic principles.

THE MORAL DIMENSION

Moral Values

What moral values are involved in informed consent? Informed consent is a practical and effective recognition of human dignity. Concretely, it respects autonomy and personal freedom, since it permits the individual to play a primary role in health care choices. Thus, it acknowledges that each competent adult has primary *responsibility* for personal health care decisions. To deny this right to a patient is, at best, to treat an adult as a child, at worst as an object—but certainly not as an autonomous subject.

Informed consent enables the physician to receive the patient's trust; indeed it promotes this trust since it enhances respect for the health care professional.

For society in general, informed consent promotes a responsible citizenry in a democracy and is always more appropriate in such a political setting, since paternalism is never egalitarian. In addition, it supports the goals of public health and has long-term benefit to the medical profession in general.

Obstacles

On the part of the patient, the greatest obstacle is fear—fear of the information to be imparted, of the consequences, of the responsibility that accompanies knowledge. In addition, as mentioned earlier, contemporary medicine can be quite complex and technical. Hence, the patient's level of intelligence and sophistication is vitally connected with the receiving of information and the giving of consent.

254

Lack of attention due to emotional factors or pressure from excessive efforts to persuade also interferes with freedom and hence with informed consent.

From the doctor's perspective, unwillingness or inability to take sufficient time for adequate disclosure is a prime obstacle to proper consent. The paternalistic tradition of the medical profession is another hindrance, as is the arrogance of any health care professional who believes the ordinary layperson incapable of comprehending real health needs. Finally, there is the possibility of a conflict of values between the goals of the doctor and the needs of the patient.

As mentioned above, the tradition of the medical profession runs counter to the modern doctrine of informed consent. The Hippocratic oath itself expresses a benevolent paternalism and permits the physician to conceal or withhold information from the patient. Percival's *Medical Ethics* (1803) and the first AMA Code (1847) also made the physician solely responsible for interpreting the patient's health needs. This tradition, like any other, dies slowly. Thus, the contemporary emphasis on individual autonomy and consumers' rights not infrequently is confronted by practitioners cut in the traditional mold.

Moral Analysis

In a therapeutic situation, the following principles are suggested to protect the moral values involved in informed consent:

1. Every competent adult has the right to decide freely about all matters relating to that individual's own health and about any treatment or procedure proposed for the sake of health.
2. Such a decision requires that full, sufficiently detailed information be provided by the physician regarding the nature of the treatment/procedure, its risks and benefits, and alternative therapies.
3. This right is based on an understanding of health and health care as a basic good of the individual and on a competent adult's primary responsibility for health care.
4. Any failure on the part of the physician, whether deliberate or through negligence, is morally unacceptable and represents a fundamental failure of the physician in her/his responsibility to the patient.

5. In the case of an incompetent patient, the decision should be made by that individual's legitimate guardian, acting for the patient's benefit and, as far as possible, in accordance with the patient's known and reasonable wishes.

STUDY QUESTIONS

1. What do we mean by "informed consent"? What reasons can be offered in support of this doctrine?
2. What does the law require regarding "informed consent"? Does it allow any exceptions? Explain.
3. What developments in American society have been particularly influential in the development of the "informed consent" doctrine? Explain.
4. The Roman Catholic Church's teaching set forth in this chapter offers no reasons for the principles set forth. Based on your knowledge of Roman Catholic theology gained from earlier chapters, what reasons could you suggest?
5. What moral values support the concept of "informed consent"? If this doctrine seems so desirable, why is it frequently not realized in the actual delivery of health care?

NOTES

1. Robert Weir, "Truthtelling in Medicine," *Perspectives in Biology and Medicine,* Autumn 1980, 95–112.

2. J. L. Kaufman, "Protection of Research Subjects," *New England Journal of Medicine* 349 (July 10, 2003): 188–92.

3. On this question, see Dennis Mazur, "What Should Patients Be Told Prior to a Medical Procedure?" *American Journal of Medicine,* December 1986, 1051–54.

4. J. H. T. Karlawish, "Research Involving Cognitively Impaired Adults," *New England Journal of Medicine* 348 (April 3, 2003): 1389–92.

5. Paul P. Hartlaub, et al., "Obtaining Informed Consent: It Is Not Simply Asking 'Do You Understand?'" *Journal of Family Practice* 36:4 (1993): 383–84.

6. Cf. Chapter Eleven on Euthanasia.

7. Francis I. Kane, "Keeping Elizabeth Bouvier Alive for the Public Good," *Hastings Center Report,* December 1985, 5–8.

8. The need for improving this relationship seems evident from a Gallup poll commissioned by the AMA and reported in the *New York Times,* February 20, 1990.

9. M. K. Paasche-Orlow, et al., "Readability Standards for Informed Consent Forms Compared with Actual Readability," *New England Journal of Medicine* 348 (February 20, 2003): 721–26

10. Ann Neale, "Patient-Physician Dialogue Improves Medical Decisions," *Health Progress,* November 1981, 45–47.

11. For an example of an informed consent statute, cf. New York State Public Health Law, Section 2805d.

12. Heather Gert, "Avoiding Surprises. A Model for Informing Patients," *Hastings Center Report,* September/October 2002, 23–32.

13. *Cobbs* v. *Grant,* 502 P. 2d 1 (October 27, 1972).

14. Cf. note 1.

15. M. J. Khoury, et al., "Genomic Medicine: Population Screening in the Age of Genomic Medicine," *New England Journal of Medicine* 348 (January 2, 2003): 50–58.

16. *Making Health Care Decisions—The Ethical and Legal Implications of Informed Consent in the Patient-Practitioner Relationship,* vol. 2. President's Commission for the Study of Ethical Problems in Medicine and Biomedical and Behavioral Research. Washington, D.C.: U.S. Government Printing Office, 1982.

17. N. 26–28, National Conference of Catholic Bishops. Washington, D.C.: 1994. *Origins,* December 15, 1994, 455–56.

13 Health Care Reform

The final chapter of this book will address the contemporary issue of health care reform. If this had been written shortly after the election of 1992, it would surely have conveyed a sense of optimism, a conviction that the nation was at last prepared to wrestle with this most complicated and vexing question. Three years later, however, after the efforts of the Clinton administration came apart without any results to show for all the sound and fury, it became more difficult to consider this question with any assurance that some resolution was possible any time soon. Now, more than a decade later, it seems clear that the question is far from enjoying any priority whatsoever on the agenda of the administration or the Congress. Whatever the political realities, some consideration of the issues is desirable, for this is surely a medical-ethical dilemma!

In an effort to highlight some of the central values involved, this study will review the question from various standpoints, much as was done in earlier chapters—the medical, legal, and sociocultural dimensions, the teaching of the Roman Catholic Church, and finally, some moral assessment of the issues. The matter is far too complex and too technical to suggest any final resolution of the question. At the same time, health care reform is too important not to encourage some reflection and dialogue that are so essential to the nation's successful resolution of this challenge.

THE MEDICAL DIMENSION—
THE STATE OF THE QUESTION

Even though the question of access to health care will be the primary focus of this ethical analysis, it would be a mistake to think that

this is a single-issue question. Additional problems emerge at once—
quality of care, unevenness of care, and the costliness of the delivery
of health care at this time in the nation's history.

Quality of Care

It has been suggested[1] that pressures to exert more effective cost
control at the same time that access is increased will almost certainly
have adverse consequences on the quality of care available. The effort
to reduce costs will confront reformers with the issue of rationing,
surely one of the primary ways to control costs. Rationing will bring
with it exclusions—of populations and of services. It may also reduce
the availability of health care providers and require staff reductions in
health care facilities. There can be no doubt that such cost containment
efforts have the potential for reducing the quality of care provided. Add
to this the effort to increase access to health care—indeed, to assure
universal access—and it is safe to say that the introduction of new populations will place considerable new stresses on health care delivery and
costs. These three factors are so interdependent, therefore, that any
program of reform must keep all three "juggled" at the same time. Any
solution that promises access for all but with noticeable loss of quality
will surely be unacceptable to the American people.

Unevenness of Care

It is well known that one of the nagging problems in the delivery of health care is the uneven distribution of health care providers
and facilities. It is not only our inner cities that go begging for adequate facilities. As Chelimsky has noted:

> In El Paso, for example, only 30 of the city's 800 physicians (4
> percent) maintained practices in the poorer part of the city. Yet
> this area houses 170,000 people, or one-third of El Paso's popu-
> lation.[2]

This problem is widespread, particularly in many rural sections
of the country as well as in economically depressed inner cities. Philip
Keane cites studies that indicate that fifty-one of Mississippi's eighty-

two counties have no obstetrician, while fifty counties are without a pediatrician. It is difficult to imagine how to woo health care providers into these underserved areas of the country; yet any health care reform that promises universal access but fails to address this problem will end up by compounding it.[3]

Costliness of Health Care

One of the factors that make it difficult to extend access to health care is its costliness. Earlier attempts to contain costs have had decidedly negative effects on the delivery of health care. Thus, when the prospective payment system and the diagnosis-related groups were introduced in 1984 to reduce Medicare costs, the end result was to reduce access to health care for the elderly and to lower the quality of the care provided. Driving the seemingly inexorable spiral of health care costs are such factors as the continuing expansion of advanced medical technologies and the persistent preference for the practice of medical specialties. Equally significant is the practice of "defensive medicine" on the part of physicians and the psychological attitude on the part of patients covered by insurance that "everything is paid for."

Lack of Access

It is frequently estimated that as many as forty-four million Americans have no health insurance whatever. Many more millions lack health insurance some time during each year.[4] Finally, there are those who are judged to be "underinsured," that is, their coverage is not adequate to meet their health care needs. These problems are particularly noticeable among young adults and children and are of special concern among the elderly, who typically experience more serious health problems than other age groups. Not surprisingly, lack of access to health care is particularly evident among Hispanics and African Americans. Since most health insurance is linked to employment, there is a correlation between lack of access to health care and educational and economic level.

These, then, are some of the factors that must be juggled as the nation faces the imposing task of fashioning a more equitable health care delivery system.

THE LEGAL DIMENSION—
A BRIEF HISTORY OF HEALTH CARE REFORM

The twentieth century witnessed innumerable attempts to secure some sort of guaranteed access to health care for all citizens. In the first two decades of this century the American Association of Labor Legislation lobbied for "sickness insurance" as an integral part of its overall program of comprehensive social insurance. It would be the logical successor to industrial accident insurance that businesses were required to fund on behalf of their laborers. To be funded jointly by employers, wage earners, and government, this benefit was conceived as protection against poverty on the part of the workers. To the dismay of the AALL, the plan met strong resistance from the National Association of Manufacturers because of the added taxes that would be levied. The American Medical Association also actively opposed the move out of fear of governmental intrusion and regulation of the practice of medicine. Even some labor leaders failed to rise to the support of the program, reckoning it an intrusion into union autonomy. What had seemed inevitable during the first decade was broadly defeated during the second, and by 1920 the movement was dead.

The concept of national health insurance was resurrected in the 1930s and 1940s during the New Deal administration of Franklin Roosevelt and the presidency of Harry Truman. It was assumed that it would be a natural follow-up to the Social Security legislation of 1935, but it was never enacted—once again due in part to the opposition of the AMA. Truman made universal health insurance a plank in his bid for reelection but after his come-from-behind victory, the inevitable once again became the unthinkable. It was during World War II and immediately after it that major industrial employers adopted the notion of health insurance as a "fringe benefit" for the working middle class in return for tax write-offs, and they joined the AMA in opposition to national health insurance.

For more than three decades after that most recent effort, the system remained largely unchanged. In 1968, with the enactment of Medicare and Medicaid legislation, the nation acknowledged the need to provide an added "safety net" for the elderly and for poor women and their dependent children. No national sense of concern for the uninsured developed, however, until the beginning of the final decade of the twentieth century. A convergence of circumstances—spiraling health care costs, pressures to reduce employer coverage, increasing demands for co-payments and larger deductibles, and especially economic recession and increased unemployment—made the issue one of concern for the middle class. The question burst into public view in 1991 in Pennsylvania when underdog Harris Wofford won a special election to the Senate largely by his trumpeting of a call for national health insurance.[5]

Although the Washington establishment was taken by surprise by the force of public sentiment, it did not take the politicians long to catch on. Bill Clinton made health care reform a major plank in presenting his candidacy to the American people, and his victory over George Bush guaranteed that reform legislation would be presented to the Congress early in his administration. He was not alone, of course, in sensing the need to address this problem. Indeed, since the mid-1980s a number of members of Congress had attempted unsuccessfully to gain support for health care reform. The election of 1992 changed all that, and once again the stage was set to witness the "inevitable" reform of the American health care delivery system. Ironically, the events of 1994 once again called into question whether there truly was a genuine "window of opportunity" for universal access to health care at that time. The failure of the Congress to unite behind the Clinton plan or any other, the intense lobbying of special interest groups, and the retreat of the middle class from the specter of higher taxes all conspired to defeat what had appeared to be a "done deal."

Another decade has now passed. Is there no hope, then, that this country might devise a way to provide some minimum but adequate health care for all Americans? One commentator has not given up. The problem is political, he insists, not ethical or economic. A system must be crafted that will be acceptable to all—or most—constituencies: the government, employers, the private health insurance industry, health care providers, and most importantly, ordinary Americans. Ezekiel Emanuel proposes a universal health care voucher system provided by either the government or by employers. These vouchers would permit individuals and families to purchase health insurance from a private managed care or insurance system. Their value would be set at a level that would ensure a decent basic package of services for all, while allowing wealthier Americans to purchase additional coverage. He allows that a huge number of details remain to be worked out but some such system would be better, he insists, than what we have now.[6]

THE SOCIOCULTURAL DIMENSION

What are the aspects of the American character that might enter into this great national debate regarding health care reform? A number of characteristics come to mind.

Pluralism

One of the strengths of the national character has been the ability to bring together a great diversity of ethnic, racial, religious, and socioeconomic groups, thereby enriching the whole through the particular strengths of each part. At the same time, this is also a source of difficulty in establishing a sense of community in the population. Because these subgroups retain a strong sense of identity, of difference, it is difficult to engender a strong appreciation for interconnectedness for the common good. So long as health care is conceived primarily as an economic issue, it will not be a problem of the community caring for its own members.[7]

Individualism

The awareness of individual rights, of personal autonomy, has never been stronger in the American experience. This is just as true with respect to health care as it is in other areas of self-determination. The conflict between community values and personal autonomy is clearly evidenced in the great national debate over abortion, and it certainly appears to be framing the arguments taking shape around the issues of euthanasia and physician-assisted suicide. Again, the strength of the national commitment to individualism generates an energy that makes a communal concern for basic health care difficult to engender.

263

Commercialization of Health Care

Is the practice of medicine and the provision of health care the expression of a professional commitment to the common good of society, or is it rather a business, an industry, an undertaking where the "bottom line" controls the decision-making machinery? If the question had been asked in the middle decades of the past century, there is no doubt what the answer would be. Asked today, the question would elicit a broad range of responses. The evolution of a for-profit health care industry is but one indicator that the direction taken in the contemporary practice of medicine is clearly related to financial return. If this is, in fact, the contemporary medical ethos, then cost containment and universal access will be more difficult to achieve.

Equality

Not all aspects of the American character are inimical to a sense of caring, an appreciation of responsibility for the vulnerable, the marginalized of society. There is in the nation a profound and abiding commitment to the concept of equality. It is not something that Americans live out fully or perfectly, but it surely is an ideal that powerfully influences society. Concern for individuals with disabilities is but one recent expression of this ideal. The question is, of course, whether this commitment is strong enough to overcome the forces that draw Americans to seek financial gain over compassion for the needy, to insist on individual responsibility and accountability rather than communal caring and concern.

ROMAN CATHOLIC CHURCH TEACHING

It should not be surprising that the Catholic Church, with its long tradition of concern about medical-ethical questions, should include access to health care within its body of teaching in this field. This section will, therefore, first set forth several examples of the church's formal and authoritative teaching on the question. Then it will seek to analyze the most prominent beliefs and values of the Catholic faith community relative to this issue.

Health Care Reform

Pope John XXIII—*Pacem in Terris* (April 1963)

> 11. But first we must speak of men's rights. Man has the right to live. He has the right to bodily integrity and to the means necessary for the proper development of life, particularly food, clothing, shelter, medical care, rest, and, finally, the necessary social services. In consequence, he has the right to be looked after in the event of ill health, disability stemming from his work, widowhood, old age, enforced unemployment, or whenever through no fault of his own he is deprived of the means of livelihood.[8]

United States Catholic Bishops—Pastoral Letter on Health and Health Care (November 1981)

> It is appropriate...to call attention to the significant impact that public policy has on health care in our society. The government, working for the common good, has an essential role to play in assuring the right of all people to adequate health care is protected. The function of government reaches beyond the limited resources of individuals and private groups. Private agencies and institutions alone are unable to develop a comprehensive national health policy, or to ensure that all Americans have adequate health insurance, or to command the vast resources necessary to implement an effective national health policy. These functions are in large part the responsibility of government. However, in accord with the traditional Catholic principle of subsidiarity, we believe voluntary institutions must continue to play an essential role in our society.
>
> Christian people have a responsibility to actively participate in the shaping and executing of public policy that relates to health care. On this issue, as on all issues of basic human rights, the Church has an important role to play in bringing Gospel values to the social and political order.[9]

United States Catholic Conference— Statement on National Health Insurance (July 2, 1974)

> ...As representatives of the Catholic Church's concern for adequate health care in America, our basic approach to the issue of national health insurance is rooted in the fundamental tenet that every person has the right to life, to bodily integrity, and the means

which are necessary and suitable for the development of life. The right to life clearly implies the right to health care; indeed, the two are philosophically and practically inseparable. The right of persons to health care further implies that such health care will be available, and that the route of access to necessary and comprehensive care will not be strewn with impediments.

In spite of the enormous dimension of the national commitment to health, we recognize the inadequacies of the health system. There exist presently widespread disparities throughout the country in the availability of treatment, facilities, and personnel. And in a significant number of rural areas, inner cities, ghettos, and barrios, there are few medical facilities and, in some cases, no physicians or nurses, contributing to haphazard and generally poor standards of health for millions of people. Health care costs have risen to the point where many will not or cannot seek necessary treatment because of severe or ruinous financial demands.

...With such facts and statistics in mind, we strongly endorse the prospect of a national health care insurance program. We believe it is only through a well-planned national approach that the United States can begin to strike the balance between the actual delivery of health care to all persons living within our borders and our undisputed excellence in the areas of health research and technology. We believe that there can be no further delay in recognizing the moral necessity of developing a national health care insurance program within which all participate. The question, in other words, is not whether we should have a national program; it is how such a program should be developed and implemented.[10]

ROMAN CATHOLIC BELIEFS AND VALUES RELATED TO HEALTH CARE ACCESS

The Dignity of the Human Person

In an earlier chapter, a fully developed anthropology of the human person was set forth. There an appreciation was developed of the human person "integrally and adequately conceived." A further theological understanding was then elaborated—we are created by God in God's own image and likeness, so loved by the Father that the Second Person of the Trinity became man in order to save the human race and thus lead it to its final destiny in union with its God. Small wonder that such a concept of the human person would play a central role in the church's understanding of health care and the many medical-ethical questions that have arisen in the contemporary practice of medicine. It is this lofty appreciation of the human person that leads the church to call so firmly for access to adequate health care for all women and men—not only in this country but in all nations. As the great debate moves forward, then, the Roman Catholic Church insists that the great dignity of the human person demands health care as a right.

Community and Human Relationships

Flowing from both the natural and the theological understanding of the nature of the human person, as was pointed out earlier, human beings are destined for community. Relatability is an essential characteristic of each individual, therefore, and human living calls all human persons to achieve human fullness and perfection in the multiple relationships that each life makes possible. From a religious viewpoint, the Roman Catholic faith community understands itself as the people of God, that is, a people joined in faith and commitment to each other and to the God who calls them. Health care, in such a community, is the practical consequence of caring, of compassion for one's own. It can never be simply a matter of an individual's economic capability or the proximity of health care facilities and personnel.

Human Sickness and Suffering

Closely related to ideas concerning human mortality and the meaning of death are the experience and understanding of human sickness and suffering. It was pointed out in an earlier chapter that suffering—although surely a disvalue in itself, a physical evil—can have special meaning for the Christian. It was through suffering and death that Jesus reestablished the bond between sinful humanity and its God. In imitation of Jesus, therefore, his suffering disciples join their pains to his in loving submission to the Father. But human sickness and suffering have another meaning, whether one is a follower of Jesus or

267

not. More than any other human experience, serious illness calls people to an awareness of the reality of death. As Philip Keane has noted so well:[11]

> At the time of serious sickness, a person's awareness of death causes the person to ask some very basic questions. What is life about? Is my life in good order? Am I in need of reconciliation with God or with my fellow human beings? Am I willing to accept my own death, once it becomes clear that it can no longer be prevented? Have I done everything I can to provide for the needs of my family and loved ones? If I am able to live for a while longer, are there any aspects of my lifestyle which I need to change? These kinds of questions make serious illness a very special time, a time for those around the sick person to have a special respect and reverence. In the end, sickness reminds us not only of the mortality of the human person; it reminds us as well of the dignity and worth of human life and human freedom.

A truly human response to sickness and suffering, therefore, must appreciate the human person's origin and destiny, the patient's dignity and worth. Anything short of this runs the risk of being merely a mechanical response to human breakdown, a technical attempt to repair the human "engine." Wonderful as modern medical technology is, there comes a time in every life when all therapies must be called off and the individual must be allowed to deal with life's final event.

THE MORAL DIMENSION—
SOME TENTATIVE REFLECTIONS

In order to achieve a morally acceptable reformation of the American health care system, therefore, what might be some of the fundamental convictions to be kept in sight?

1. Universal access to health care must be based on the right of every woman and man to life and the means necessary for life arising from the fundamental value and dignity of the human person.
2. The level of health care must be adequate to permit a reasonable and dignified human functioning.

3. The delivery of health care in this country must, therefore, be reformed in such a way as to assure the universal access.
4. The guaranteed basic health care "package" must be the same for all, even though it will probably be possible for those who wish additional health care coverage to purchase this—provided, of course, that this does not dislocate the systematic availability of the basic health care coverage for all.
5. The details of a basic health care package and its delivery system need to be determined through some sort of national dialogue, as was developed in Oregon for that state's health care reform program.
6. It may be necessary to accept as a first step an improved—but still imperfect—program of reform. This would be morally acceptable, provided the ultimate goals of reform can be finally achieved.

STUDY QUESTIONS

1. The reform of the United States health care system has been called for since early in the twentieth century. Why has this goal so long eluded the nation?
2. What complexities within the delivery of health care itself make this reform difficult?
3. The American character brings together attitudes and values that both challenge and promote the concept of universal access to health care. Do you agree? Explain.
4. What theological understandings within the Roman Catholic faith community undergird the church's call for universal access to health care? Are the values of this faith community in harmony with those of the larger society or at odds with them? Explain.
5. If there is to be universal access to health care, what agreements must be reached with respect both to substance and to process regarding this question? Explain fully.

NOTES

1. Eleanor Chelinsky, "The Political Debate About Health Care: Are We Losing Sight of Quality?" *Science,* 262 (October 22, 1993): 525–28.
2. Ibid., 526.
3. Philip S. Keane, *Health Care Reform: A Catholic View,* Mahwah, N.J.: Paulist Press, 1993, 12.

4. See the Congressional Black Caucus Foundation at www. cbcfhealth.org/content/contented/1555.

5. Wofford's TV commercial was particularly effective—"If every criminal in America has the right to a lawyer, then I think every working person should have the right to see a doctor when they're [sic] ill."

6. Ezekiel Emanuel, "Health Care Reform: Still Possible," *Hastings Center Report,* March/April 2002, 32–34.

7. Charlene Galarneau, "Health Care as a Community Good," *Hastings Center Report,* September/October 2002, 33–40.

8. Kevin D. O'Rourke, O.P., and Philip Boyle, O.P., *Medical Ethics: Sources of Catholic Teachings.* St. Louis: Catholic Health Association, 1989, 149.

9. Ibid., 265.

10. Ibid., 189. Issued in conjunction with the Catholic Hospital Association and the National Conference of Catholic Charities.

11. Cf. note 3, 65.

green press
INITIATIVE

Paulist Press is committed to preserving ancient forests and natural resources. We elected to print this title on 30% post consumer recycled paper, processed chlorine free. As a result, for this printing, we have saved:

9 Trees (40' tall and 6-8" diameter)
3 Million BTUs of Total Energy
849 Pounds of Greenhouse Gases
4,087 Gallons of Wastewater
248 Pounds of Solid Waste

Paulist Press made this paper choice because our printer, Thomson-Shore, Inc., is a member of Green Press Initiative, a nonprofit program dedicated to supporting authors, publishers, and suppliers in their efforts to reduce their use of fiber obtained from endangered forests.

For more information, visit www.greenpressinitiative.org

Environmental impact estimates were made using the Environmental Defense Paper Calculator. For more information visit: www.papercalculator.org.